CW00736035

BEYOND LIMITS

STE
MAC

BEYOND LIMITS

A LIFE THROUGH CLIMBING

STEVE McCLURE

VERTEBRATE PUBLISHING

Vertebrate Publishing, Sheffield
www.v-publishing.co.uk

Beyond Limits
Steve McClure

First published in 2014 by Vertebrate Publishing.

 Vertebrate Publishing
Crescent House, 228 Psalter Lane, Sheffield S11 8UT.
www.v-publishing.co.uk

Copyright © Steve McClure 2014.

Photography copyright © McClure Collection unless otherwise credited.

Steve McClure has asserted his rights under the Copyright, Designs
and Patents Act 1988 to be identified as author of this work.

This book is a work of non-fiction based on the life of Steve McClure.
The author has stated to the publishers that, except in such minor respects not
affecting the substantial accuracy of the work, the contents of the book are true.

A CIP catalogue record for this book is available from the British Library.

ISBN: 978-1-910240-19-9 (Hardback)
ISBN: 978-1-910240-20-5 (eBook)

All rights reserved. No part of this work covered by the copyright hereon may be reproduced
or used in any form or by any means – graphic, electronic, or mechanised, including photocopying,
recording, taping or information storage and retrieval systems – without the written permission
of the publisher.

Every effort has been made to obtain the necessary permissions with reference to copyright material,
both illustrative and quoted. We apologise for any omissions in this respect and will be pleased
to make the appropriate acknowledgements in any future edition.

Design and production by Jane Beagley. Cover design by Nathan Ryder.

 Vertebrate Graphics Ltd.
www.v-graphics.co.uk

Printed and bound in the UK by T. J. International Ltd, Padstow, Cornwall.

CONTENTS

ACKNOWLEDGEMENTS

So why write this book? Now there is a question. It began as a magazine article that drifted from its subject, expanding into areas requiring deeper thought. Memories of younger days began to shine and I felt the need to order them before they faded, like carefully sticking old photos in a scrapbook. As I travelled along my journey though life I began to see something of a path I'd trodden, rather than just living in the moment. I made some sense of where I've ended up and all the people along the way who have helped me to get here.

A long list of thanks is not required here; it would be too big. To my many friends, those that held my ropes, shared a belay, danced until 6 a.m. or simply shared a view, you know who you are and I owe you big time.

But some special thanks need to be made. First, to those behind the lens: Keith Sharples, Tim Glasby and Simon Carter for the stills, and Rich Heap, Ben Pritchard and Alastair Lee for the films; my relationship with these guys runs deeper than professional. Thanks also to the companies behind me; Petzl, Marmot and 5.10, which have not only provided the best gear in the world, giving me the edge, but have offered me the chance to lead the life I'd always dreamed of. And to Ian Parnell, mountaineer extraordinaire, who took on the job of editing my work, giving me the confidence to push it on into print. Without him it would have probably remained on my hard drive for ever.

But the biggest thanks goes to my parents, my partner Vic and my kids Amelie and Harry. They have made me who I am and taken me to a place beyond limits.

Steve McClure
October 2014

1 PARADISE FOUND

Thailand 1993

I was in open water now, far away from port. Sitting back in the sun I tried to relax aboard the wooden long-tail boat as it pitched and yawed through the choppy waves of the warm Andaman Sea off the west coast of Thailand. Shading my eyes I tried to judge the distance to my destination: a distant strip of shimmering white limestone hovering above the sea. The connection between water and land blurred in the humid air, making it look closer than it really was – or maybe further; hard to tell. One thing was for sure, it was a fair way off, a kilometre at least. As the swell increased, my mind wandered. I figured I could probably swim it if I really had to; optimistic as usual about my physical abilities, I wouldn't, to be fair, have stood a chance. Suddenly the guidebook description of a simple journey out to the resort of Railay Beach appeared to have been somewhat under-estimated, but with the promise of climbing heaven, any journey would have been worth the risk.

Obviously the battered, floating wreck wasn't going to sink, but there was no harm in making a plan, just in case. I glanced over at my bloated POD rucksack; there'd be no rescue for this monster. Filled with essential stuff that apparently no one else needed, it looked out of place, the other cool rucksacks barely big enough to hold my lunch. They belonged to the other people on board – hardened travellers with well-established tans. I should have felt at home, being five months into my big 'Asia experience', but I still felt like a bumbly.

Boarding the boat in the sun at the port of Krabi I'd tried to look like I'd been travelling forever, dumping my bag in the back and taking a seat up front, sandals off, feet bare to the rotting wood and salty puddles in the ever-leaking hull. Others took their places further back, no doubt not needing a prime view, having seen it all before. In reality, they knew that as we left port and the wind picked up and the chop grew bigger, the boat would be tossed around like a matchstick, soaking the front with spray. Attempting to look like it was no big deal I slid towards the rear as the waves grew, resisting the urge to ask if it was always like this; the boat seemingly wholly inadequate for the current conditions. No one appeared fazed, particularly not the driver who, between cigarettes, casually bailed water from the boat as if he'd been doing it all his life. I glanced at my bag again, my whole world packed inside. Mentally I scanned the contents: clothes, sleeping bag, trainers, torch, general junk – stuff that I could replace for peanuts, if I had any peanuts. The passport and minimal amount of cash would be trickier, though do-able, but my beloved diary was invaluable; my friend out here in my new life, it was tethered to me like a toddler's blanket. I needed it to talk to, to pour my feelings into when no one else would listen. If this boat sank, I was going down with the book. Without the book I'd really have nothing. There used to be a lot more to my world, a lot more than I could fit in a bag or on the pages of a green-lined scrapbook, but I'd left it all behind what seemed like a very long time ago. So long ago that there seemed no life before this, nothing I could relate to. That had crumbled away to leave a shell of what I assumed I once was. There had been a plan giving focus and direction, but it was now long forgotten and as distant as a dream; disconnected and random.

I found my thoughts drifting off despite the salt water stinging my eyes and the ever-present danger of simply tipping over and instantly drowning. It was easy to do these days, drift aside, and there was a lot of stuff going on between the ears that needed untangling. I had to wonder why I'd left my home in Sheffield. Apparently I was on the travelling trip of a lifetime, supposedly the best time of my life, but perhaps I was just on the conveyer belt of student kids taking the easy path, following what the others did because I couldn't think of anything else to do. School, college, university, the classic 'gap year' ... all part of the easy path; the path of least resistance. It seemed that way, my own journey; un-thought out and ill-considered. Most people use their travel time as a last big break before embarking on a well-scripted and willingly accepted life: employment, house, kids, pension. It's what most people do. For me it was different, the road I'd been following had reached the edge of the map and now I was plugging an opening void. I was free-styling, making it up as I went along as previous direction fizzled out to nothing.

As my ponderings tumbled and clashed I drifted back into reality, afraid of the volume of unanswerable questions. For once, it seemed a step in the right direction as today, on this boat journey, I was chasing a rare spark of hope: the promise of fantastic rock climbing in a paradise-like setting. Though climbing seemed a distant memory, like vaguely remembered tales from another person's life, the thought of moving over stone stirred some kind of subconscious and uncontrollable excitement. Deep down, through and through, I was a rock climber. I'd been doing it all my life from my earliest beginnings with my parents. Climbing defined me and motivated me and I leaned on it for purpose and direction, but somehow I'd let it drift from my life. It hadn't seemed such a loss, at least at first …

I became aware of my surroundings once more. We'd covered a lot of distance. For once my depressive headspace had been a welcome escape from the uncomfortable and worrying journey. Suddenly, as we rounded a rocky corner, the waves dropped like we'd passed into a different world. The landscape took a sudden turn for the better – not that it had been bad before – but now there was rockiness everywhere, demanding my attention, huge lumps of towering limestone mushrooming out of the sea. For sure this was a set from a James Bond film. Short-cutting under an enormous low roof, the deafening clatter of the two-stroke petrol engine changed pitch, the sound bouncing from stalactite-strewn ceilings only metres above us. Turning again, the cliffs soared upwards to colossal heights, impossible to put a scale to. Walls and faces in all directions, striped orange and blue, with curtains of stalactites and tufas. The hair on the back of my neck was prickling, my heart racing. The climber in me was remembering; the long-lost but deep-rooted passion was coming to the surface.

I was filled with the child-like excitement that climbers get when they see the cliff – their play park. This was on a whole new level. Overwhelmed and wide-eyed I scanned the other travellers for a similar state of awe, hoping we could share something of the majesty, but they'd seen it all before, or weren't interested, the incredible cliffs merely a backdrop and convenient windbreak to the paradise beach that was the reason they were here.

Bumping violently onto the sand of Railay Beach, the boat quickly ground to a halt and emptied just as fast, each passenger paying the boatman the 50 Baht without asking the price. Following suit I awkwardly hauled on my pack and staggered over the side, almost toppling backwards into the sea, a sea so clear it barely looked like it was there at all. The passengers soon dispersed, knowing where they were going and what they were doing, as I stood rooted to the boiling sand feeling like I'd got off a train at the wrong station. I turned on my climbers' auto pilot: if in doubt, head for rocks and away from normal people. Luckily, I did have a vague idea of where I was going and the scrap of dubious knowledge I'd gained from a stoned waster after a party led me along the beach to where it ended abruptly by a tumbling hillside and dense jungle jutting into the sparkling sea. Trusting my info I pushed on through into the jungle, totally missing the path and battering myself against all things spiky. Untangling myself from cobwebs and gripped by my lack of wildlife knowledge I was losing faith in my source and moving rapidly towards a decision to retreat. It would have been just typical of me to have followed some bullshit story out into the middle of nowhere, but this time my own judgement drove me on. The rocky terrain was too promising; there had to be climbing – there was just so much rock. Ahead the vegetation seemed to thin, so I pushed through, beams of sunlight streaming through the canopy above, until a glimpse of sand confirmed my faith that I was about to arrive and I suddenly tumbled out into heaven.

Standing motionless I took in the vista, rooted to the spot. Here the cliffs towered even higher, blasting straight up from pure white sand and baking in the sunlight. With the waves gently lapping at my feet I made my way along the beach, feeling as though I had walked into the lost climber's world. Ahead of me was a vast expanse of smooth grey limestone, curving over like a tidal wave. It looked impossible to climb, but, surprisingly, a figure swung into view high on the cliff. A heavily muscled and tanned dude was climbing something steep and hard looking; white patches on dark rock marked the way. He clipped his skinny single rope into a bolt anchor and lowered down, fairly close to me and miles away from his belayer. Untying, he sat in the pure white sand and peeled off his shoes. 'Hi' I ventured, feeling insecure, hoping that just because I had climbed some rocks in the distant past he would somehow want to talk to me, that my identity as a rock-climber stood proud forming an involuntary bond between us.

'Howdy' was the reply; American. He glanced at me, and then my pack. 'You here for the climbing?' I smiled, 'Yeah … yes, that's right. I'm here to climb.' I thought back to Waster and our conversation on the beach just a few days earlier, and thanked him for his enthusiasm, I knew I was home.

Waster breathed out a long stream of blue smoke into the black sky. Passing me the joint he continued. 'Man, you just got to go there. It sounds perfect for you. It will blow your mind. That place is just like – off the scale. Tonsai Bay it's called, an easy hike over from Railay Beach. I saw some dudes climbing there and it looked rad. If you climb stuff then you have to go.'

I passed on the joint, already wrecked, and normally I'd have been happy to slip even further into a state of disrepair, blocking out the surrounding reality of my current life, but for once somebody was saying something interesting and I wanted to remember. Most conversations were all bollocks, empty traveller waffle about where you've been, where you're going, where the best hotel could be found, the best restaurant, the best weed. I was sick of it now, happier to read a book or fill endless pages of my diary.

But Waster had got me listening. Somehow we'd strayed onto rock climbing and he was describing somewhere I had to go.

'It's close man, like just a day from here, a boat and a bus, another boat; then you are there. Just get to the beach and head left to another hidden beach, it should be obvious, that's where the climbers hang. It's paradise, way better than here, and if you climb that stuff it's perfect.'

Stretching out over the cool sand I pondered the situation. Right here on the island of Ko Pha Ngan was good, for sure, sun and sand and the full-moon parties, infamous on the traveller circuit, all-night dance parties on the beach with waves lapping at your toes. Last night was a double whammy with a full moon and New Year party combined. It had been awesome. At least that's what I told myself, forcing a rhythm at two in the morning, feet heavy and movement out of time. The throng around were immersed, faces as bright as their luminous body paint, glowing brightly in the UV tubes. I'd hidden mine, feeling tired, trying not to catch eyes and avoiding lovey hugs with skeleton-thin beauties. Maybe it was the drugs, or the lack of the right drugs, beer not exactly known for its energising quality. Now I was amongst the aftermath, the night after, small groups scattered along the endless beaches, slumped around crackling fires. Another big party was coming up in a week or so. I didn't need to go to it, didn't want to go, but probably would if I was still here stuck on the island. I was only here because I had nowhere else to be. I was being dragged around by a tenuous bunch of friends, following their every move simply because I had no moves of my own.

Independently, a whole team of my university friends had organised travel itineraries; similar personalities homing in on the same countries and the same desired experiences. Overlapping plans added the comfort of knowing there'd be a familiar face should the shit hit the fan in a faraway land, but time had changed us, each in differing amounts as personalities diverged into the travelling culture. Our friendships, once strong as iron, were now barely noticeable and even less convincing than the one I was currently making with Waster – who I really didn't mind if I never saw again. I needed the tenuous link with past friends as, without it, I was nothing and had nowhere meaningful to go. More shattering was the crumbled relationship with my girlfriend. Solid before we left England, we'd travelled together but our bond had followed the same path as with my other friends. Once robust, we didn't seem to fit together anymore. Asia had changed us all, the whole experience exposing us to uncharted terrain and drawing forward unknown elements of our personalities. It had changed me the most, and as the others thrived I lost track of who I was and what

I was doing there at all. I pored over the situation, trying to decipher a direction amongst the wreckage, filling page after page of my diaries in the hope that by putting ideas on paper they would become legitimate. It helped me escape, but did nothing to solve the problem that, deep down, I knew couldn't be fixed. Basically I was in the wrong place at the wrong time, following the pack into Asia in an attempt to escape an uncharted future back home in Britain. Now I needed a lifeline, something to cling onto, something familiar to bring me back into myself, but there had been no options … until now.

A nudge on my shoulder brought me back to reality. Now too wrecked to string a sentence together, a coughing and spluttering Waster passed me the bong without speaking. I took it this time. I had enough information on his amazing climbing destination and reckoned I could remember it even after another toke, so I settled down to stare as the embers wafted up into the night sky above me. At last I knew where I was going.

Dropping my oversized bag in the perfect sand of Tonsai Bay I stared around at where I'd ended up. I didn't know it yet, but I'd just walked into paradise. Even at that moment, before I got to know all the beauties and subtleties of the surroundings, it was spectacularly far ahead of just about anywhere I'd ever been. Time seemed to shift and change pace and with my sack I dropped an even heavier load of baggage, one that I'd been carrying for a long time. I could be here, I could do this. This was a place I could be myself. I could feel the pressure release and a blanket of depression lifted to reveal colour in the landscape where I usually saw grey. The few wooden shacks nestled under the wave of rock were the only visible buildings, roughly made from coconut trunks and bamboo. A few people, who were obviously climbers, sat outside – not that there was any real 'inside'. I made my way over and was welcomed into what was to be one of the most precious times of my life.

It's not often that the paths of our lives reach forks or encounter cross-roads where a choice of direction will lead to a radically different place. I generally believe most of the stuff we do is built into our personalities, shaped through our youth to a point where we'll end up at the same place if we go as the crow flies or round the houses. Who I am now and what I'm currently doing, roughly speaking, was probably determined right from the start. But, looking back on my life, very occasionally all roads converged on a single point and from that point all roads spread out, all opportunities and possibilities branching out from a single decision. I see my choice of university as one of these, choosing Sheffield led to my qualification, my job, my friends, my partner, my kids, my house, my everything. To be honest, if I'd gone to Leeds instead of Sheffield I'd probably still be 'me' in most ways, just a bit poorer, or maybe richer. Impossible to tell. I'd like to think I made the best choice. Swapping the parties and friendships on Ko Pha Ngan for the climbing at Krabi was a tough call, but was also one of those life decisions. It may have been on a smaller scale, but I was left with a memory that would shape my climbing, and from it my whole life.

Apart from the restaurant shack there were maybe six wooden huts set way back in the jungle and a slightly fenced-off area near a puddle that was the 'shower block'. Inside the shower block were a few plastic bottles with the tops chopped off serving as the shower heads. You filled the bottles from the puddle and poured the dirty, but at least not salty, water over your head. All the huts were full but the owner let me rent his tent at about 50 pence per night. I pitched this along the beach, creating possibly the most serene campsite of my life. Barely steps away from the shack there was utterly no sign of life, the jungle, thick and totally impenetrable, growing out across the sand and above the lapping waves. I made camp a long way down the beach and at high tide I'd dodge in and out of the jungle, passing vines and bushes hanging down over the sea, and leaving glowing footprints in the sand from luminous plankton. This was my home, utterly isolated from all humans and completely amongst nature. The sounds of the forest were sometimes deafening. I could have been at any point in time; it was probably the same 1,000 years ago, maybe 100,000 years ago. I didn't realise it but in terms of the human development of the area I was right at the start; no one could have foreseen what would happen to the place. Fifteen years from that moment and the very spot where I slept would become a banging nightclub, the entire beach a strip of restaurants, clubs, tacky shops and guide centres. The whole jungle would be chopped back for accommodation with roads and motorbikes and noise and bustle; a million years of nature destroyed in the blink of an eye. It makes me sad, though I guess in a tiny way it was my fault. At least I got to see it at its best.

I quickly made friends with everyone on the beach. Every day, first thing in the morning, we'd set out to climb; a new venue each time. There was rock all over the place, with small faces of perfect orange limestone dotted amongst the steep madness. Slowly the climber in me returned. I felt stronger and more complete with every day, and surprised I'd let my passion go for so long. I was twenty-three years old, I'd been climbing a good while and I was half-decent, maybe even pretty good. Not that I'd admit it. I could hold my own and knew what I was doing. Or at least that's what I thought.

Out there in the unfamiliar paradise my engrained rules of climbing had been shredded and tossed onto the sand. It was a new type of climbing with a new title: *'sport climbing'*. I'd always assumed rock climbing was one all-encompassing game: getting up, using your hands and your feet with ropes for safety if you fell. The 'leader' attempts to safeguard a fall by placing equipment in cracks and holes in the rock and clipping his rope into this 'protection'. The 'second', the guy on the ground, holds the rope to stop the leader should he fall. This is traditional climbing and the leader takes what he can for protection: wires and cams in cracks, slings around trees, *in situ* pegs; anything that is offered. In Thailand it was all about sport climbing, a different type of climbing with its own badge that, although basically the same in terms of moving over stone, seemed so vastly different.

Sport climbing is protected by pre-placed anchors, stainless steel bolts drilled into the rock. These don't come out, and last for years, to be used by everyone. Placed every few metres, they allow the leader to clip in his rope at regular intervals, meaning that even big falls would result in just a few metres' drop onto the rope. But it wasn't just these fixed bolts in the rock or the fancy equipment that was different. It was the mentality they allowed – climb to the limit, immerse yourself in the movement, push on upwards with no thought of retreat. I could see the logic that a fall should be 'safe' but struggled to grasp it. My years of traditional climbing with insecure and untrustworthy protection forcing trepidation and scoring a definite line around my comfort zone over which I dared not cross.

The boys there had it wired. Surging upwards into impossible-looking moves, they'd be giving 100 per cent in the hope they'd fluke their way up. Often they did, the prize being a battle to the end, a big grade, and the extra-special feeling that they'd given everything and still won out. Sometimes routes were 'worked', practised with rests on each bolt and climbed in short individual sections with the aim of eventually climbing the whole route clean in one push from ground to top. This was called a 'redpoint' and seemed for specialists only.

High grade 6s were my domain, like a solid E3, never hard but always a challenge. I stepped into the game exactly the same as I'd stepped out a few years ago: a traditional climber cautiously hunting for measured success. Gradually confidence increased, inspired by new friends who, technically not as good, could push so much harder than I could and hit the bigger numbers. Then, while relaxing in the sand, flushed with success from a well-executed on-sight effort on a brilliant 6c, I was to experience a moment of complete inspiration ...

Looking across an expanse of marbled limestone I watched transfixed as a tanned and honed athlete danced his way over the rock. On redpoint, his moves were flawless, each move wired like a gymnastic floor routine. It looked both desperate and effortless at the same time. It was the most beautiful thing that I'd ever seen – my life's biggest passion taken to a new dimension, displayed in a whole new light and redefining my aspirations. The route, *Knights in White Satin*, graded 7b, was a mile away from me in terms of difficulty and I watched in awe, connected, but at the same time a world apart. It was like a casual runner watching someone run the 100 metres in the Olympics. They'd like to run that fast, of course, definitely, but they won't, not ever. Not something to be sad about, just a nice thought. That was how I felt at that moment. Climbing was my passion and I was doing it only for me. I didn't need to be good at it. But at the same time it was a moment of utter inspiration: being good looked amazing.

This experience had such an effect, like I'd seen the light. Suddenly climbing opened up; there seemed another level and though I knew my place, a relative bumbly amongst the big numbers, another side of me was drawn forwards with a new level of understanding. Of course I knew about sport climbing, I'd seen it in magazines, but I'd never *really* seen it, I couldn't comprehend it or appreciate it, until now. Perhaps I'd made it that way, standing firmly behind the wall of a traditional climber, the sport style had remained hidden, but in a moment of clarity I'd glimpsed a kind of climbing that somehow really appealed. I could picture myself, there, on the blank faces with the tiny holds. Maybe I could do that, be that type of climber. As the days passed I began to explore, tentatively pushing at irrational fears and ingrained techniques, and as my comfort zone fell away my boundaries suddenly moved so far out of view I dared not try and find them.

Most of the guys staying on the beach were just in it for the fun with no need to push the envelope. Though I'd tasted the world of performance climbing, the relaxed attitude of our little team was exactly what I needed and we cruised around all day like kids in the world's best theme park before eventually scrambling home to beer and spliffs and stories of epics on and off the rocks.

I was feeling more and more myself with every day that passed, my spirits lifting from the muddled fog in which they'd been trapped since leaving the UK many months ago. I was still troubled and each night I'd slope away early to retrieve my thoughts, almost feeling guilty I'd hidden them for a while, worried that maybe I might lose my place and have to figure it all out again. I'd stare into the stars for hours while trying to rearrange them into the right order.

Though I'd dropped myself into a right mess on this travelling epic, it had been worth it. I could see I was not a born traveller, complete freedom may give a life of opportunities but, to me at least, it seemed an empty place to be. I needed more, a home, relationships, family and friends – all perhaps previously undervalued in my estimation of life's essential components. My balance had been way off as I'd bumbled through without giving much thought to where I was going. Arriving in Tonsai had cleared my head, turning my half-empty glass into a half-full one and inspiring me to reorganise my direction. But I still needed something to tie life together and make it feel special. Climbing had always been that bond, always there for me, sometimes loosening its grip and at times binding tightly to give complete focus and meaning to everything. I felt alive when I climbed, it felt natural to me; it was what I did and what I'd always done. It defined me just as all people have their own little badges of identity.

It was more than just the movement. It was the environment, the mountains, the cliffs, the fresh air – the whole package of climbing that I needed. For a while it had taken a back seat and I'd stepped into other areas. Now I welcomed it back, surprised at how I'd let it go for so long. There, on the magnificent cliffs of Thailand, I'd tasted a side of climbing I'd all but dreamt of: the movement, a pure enjoyment of moving over stone with all the trimmings of climbing as a beautiful backdrop. Now, energised with a new outlook, I knew that as I moved forward everything would all fall into place.

2 BALANCE POINT

Fifteen years old and invincible. Bounding up the easy starting moves there was no thought of failure, potential to reverse was an option, but I'd climbed this route before, a few times, and never fallen. So I was going up. The protection was poor, so this time I'd dumped the rope and harness, the freedom of soloing without any equipment was so appropriate for the style of climbing on the North York Moors; short and technical. Stopping briefly to chalk my fingers I relaxed on good holds and soaked up the panoramic view from my lofty position high on the Wainstones. Hills and countryside extended before me in a 180-degree spread, gentle rolling moors shimmering in the midday summer sun, the smell of the heather and bracken and warm sandstone adding to the sense of presence. To one side the rugged landscape disappeared off into rarely explored moorland, to the other, softening gradients gradually flattened into farmland, eventually stretching to the North Sea. In the distance chimneys and towers punctured the horizon; an orange flare from one, steam and smoke from others. The huge chemical works of ICI were visible, but too distant to cause offence. In a way they added comfort: my dad was there, at work in the vast factory as he was every week day and as he had been for thirty years. Just out of view was the small town in which we lived. My mum would be at home, passing time with my younger brother in the school holidays, reading, or maybe making something. They'd be wondering what I was up to, having set off first thing that morning on my mountain bike with a huge rucksack full of junk, my vague plan being to spend a day or two out climbing and sleeping on the moors, alone.

The Wainstones is a cliff typical of rock climbing on the North York Moors, good quality sandstone with smooth ironstone intrusions that reward us with sharp incut finger edges. At 10 metres high I'd be up and down this route in minutes and on to the next. I could tick the whole crag in a few hours and that was my aim, except for a few desperates, to cover a lot of ground, to climb a load of routes. In the last year climbing had taken over my life. Before then, when I was really just a kid, I had dabbled with it, playing with climbing like a toy when interest arose, until suddenly all my other toys had fallen aside. What was left was a desire, bordering on a need. I climbed a lot, often alone, usually traversing low to the ground at the base of the cliff or on the scattered boulders, but sometimes higher, challenging myself mentally as well as physically on longer routes where failure was not an option. But I understood about risk. I understood it as a teenager does, which basically means I didn't have a clue.

Bringing my attention back to the rock I swung into steep terrain, the rocky ground below suddenly making its presence felt. Moving carefully now as the climbing difficulty increased, I slowed my pace, concentrating on precision – but as with every other day I felt invincible; I was in control. Setting up for the crux reach, the distance between the holds felt longer than usual and there was a slight creep of my fingers on the tiny edges. For sure this was a big move, way out of character for HVS (now upgraded to E3) but it just required balance, exact positioning of the body using specific holds carefully chosen from the multitude of options. At my height, foot placements on the big ledges had to be avoided, as they were all in the wrong place. Instead each toe was carefully and accurately placed on poor holds, sloping and barely bigger than a postage stamp. This required confidence in friction, with feet as far out from the rock face as possible and a big drop underneath my heels, but in this position the centre of gravity was in a friendlier orientation. Push down on the toes now, but not too hard. Hips turned in and chin to the wall and then an ever so slight 'udge' for the huge pocket handhold that is mockingly just out of reach. For a taller climber this should be easy, and even for the short it's no problem, so long as you commit, because once you go for it there is no going back, make the move and grab the hold or peel off backwards into the void below. The lack of rope insisted that I pulled harder and stretched further, looking for a 'static' method, but there was none to be found, not at 169 centimetres tall, and as I approached my target and my fingers crept up the wall, I felt the balance point begin to tip. Eyeing the handhold with 100 per cent focus I chose my moment, committed to the movement and sprung the mere 10 centimetres upwards to bury my hand in the mother of all jugs. All four fingers positioned perfectly on the incut ironstone pocket handhold, but, with absolutely no warning, my hand shot outwards only to stop right on the lip, only the very tip of my middle finger remaining in contact. Battling to stay on, I pivoted wildly to end up facing outwards with my right arm high above my head, my lone fingertip preventing me from the 8-metre drop into which I now stared. Facing out I prepared for the drop as if I'd already fallen, but somehow my arms and finger operated independently from my brain, hanging on without direction, following their own sense of self preservation. Movement ceased and, without breathing, I slowly extricated myself, carefully unfolding my position to avoid awkward loading. What happened? The pocket was full of water, warmed by the sun so I couldn't even feel it, but rendering the ironstone as slippery as ice. Topping out I was shaken, but not stirred, as any aspiring action star would like to quote. It was almost a buzz, to have been that close, but close to what? I didn't know, not yet, my boundaries still undefined through blissful ignorance.

Things had been closer before, in a way. Closer in that I actually fell off. My first leader fall was from an E2. I was twelve years old and my younger brother Chris was eight. It would have been my first Extreme grade route. I set off upwards with a rack of two rigid stem cams and Chris holding the rope with one hand and no belay device. Peeling off the rounded arête with a single cam a metre below my feet I plummeted straight into the rocky ground from 6 metres, possibly saved slightly by the rope, though the only evidence of any fall arrest was the monumental rope burn on Chris's hand. I got away with that one, the worst part being the massive bollocking that my mum gave me for being such an idiot.

My second leader fall at least employed a suitable belayer, in the form of my dad. This time I had a waist belay, with my end of the rope tied around my skinny waist with a bowline knot. I'd probably top-roped this E3 (now E4) before, but on the lead I tipped backwards off *Lemming Slab* to be caught by a single and incredibly marginal piece of protection, with most of the metal wedge sticking out from the crack. Apart from the rope burns on my ribs I didn't suffer at all, though looking back, from a parent's perspective, my dad almost certainly did.

It's interesting how it's usually the young who are the bravest and craziest, with dangerous rock climbing generally being a young person's game. You'd think it would be the old-timers, with way less to lose in terms of remaining life, who would risk a smash into a jumble of boulders? They are already running out of time and their bodies are shagged anyway. Mostly though, the older you get the more it hurts when you hit the ground and so, peering down between your legs hunting for a comfortable landing zone whilst considering your bad ankle or dodgy hip tends to overwhelm any kind of pleasurable experience. Younger climbers don't even consider falling off, so hitting the ground doesn't matter because it isn't going to happen. Perhaps youngsters simply can't compute the risks, or haven't collected enough stuff yet – they have nothing to lose.

Pushing to physical and mental limits in a dangerous situation can be exciting. I've been there a few times, but I generally choose my moments carefully, or stray there by accident. In general terms, rock climbing used to be all about risk; that was the perception and that's how it was portrayed in the climbing press. Climbing and danger were inextricably linked and 'real' climbers were only validated if they embraced danger. The further they pushed it, the more distinction they achieved. That wasn't my game. I took on a level of risk because that's what I was supposed to do as a climber, but I was never bold, not really. I knew right from the start it was the movement I enjoyed, that's what gave me the buzz. I'd thrive on the challenge of a difficult section of rock, solving its puzzle either against the clock as my arms burned with lactic, or with repeated attempts over hours or even days. I revelled in the deciphering, analysing what was on offer for hands and feet and piecing together a string of movement over the stone. I guess I was in love with the rock – you have to be really, to enjoy the feel of it under your fingers, the bite of coarse sand against skin and the way a hold asks to be used. I'd solve each puzzle from an analytical point of view: if I pull that way I need to push from the other; for every action there is an equal and opposite reaction. The more complex the puzzle, the better it was, with unlikely sequences and the use of non-holds often unlocking a baffling problem. Balancing delicate body positioning and precise foot-work against physical force and hard pulling forms an intoxicating mix, a captivating combination of mind and body working together, taking something from impossible to possible in the most rewarding way. Close to the ground or from the safety of a rope it was easy to become absorbed; it was all fun, an adult's playtime.

Mixed with danger and risk the art of rock climbing forms a unique and compelling challenge. High above the ground and facing a fall, the skill is in holding control and being aware of ability – with going right to the limit giving the biggest rewards. Deep down I struggled with the concept. The prize of a route was never worth the penalty of injury. Despite some close calls, playing with death was a game that I tried to avoid; it seemed unjustifiable. I was never reckless on those early climbs, I just didn't yet know my boundaries and would step over them slightly on occasion, to be let off with a lucky warning. I absorbed my near misses, subconsciously filing alternative outcomes to form a database of acceptability that I could call upon when climbing. On a route the game was about reducing danger and continual assessment. It was about rational and irrational fear and differentiating between the two. With each route I'd think carefully and weigh up the balance between risk and reward and, gradually, I uncovered what I wanted from climbing and who I was as a climber.

3 OUT OF THE BLOCS

I was climbing before I could walk, as they say. There was no escape – not that I wanted any – as both my parents were keen climbers, along with all their friends. But I was never forced. There were no pushy parents and the learning curve was different to now. No indoor walls, no competitions, no training, no sport climbing. Not even bouldering really, not like it is today. We 'bouldered' I guess, but this just involved climbing the start of routes as high as we dared before jumping off onto a half-metre square piece of carpet picked out of a skip. It was all traditional climbing so parents couldn't push, not really – it was probably more about restraint. I was left to my own devices, to dip in and out of climbing as I fancied. But I had been given the perfect grounding.

We lived in Brotton, a small town near the sea on the edge of the North York Moors, pretty close to the major town of Middlesbrough in the north-east of England. Our house, number 20 out of 20 in a 1950s-style avenue of semi-detacheds, was at the end of the road and opened straight onto fields and countryside. As kids we were always outside: rain, sun, hot or cold, even dark, we'd be out straight after school, kicking a ball around or climbing trees. And at least one day in the weekend, and every Tuesday evening from Easter to October, we'd be out climbing on the moors. This was where we spent much of our quality family time, me and Chris and my parents, free from the constraints of work and school and the distraction of toys.

My parents were pretty good climbers really, both managing around E2, which back in the seventies was a pretty solid effort. Their passion for climbing and the outdoors was obvious, even to a child of six or seven years old, and my growing and genuine interest formed a solid bond between us. Like any child I wanted to please them, to make them proud. I mainly climbed with my dad and he'd be ready to help, patiently dealing with my fluctuating interest. He never pushed or made me feel like I'd let him down, but always encouraged me. Though E2 is a fine effort, even today, performance wasn't their main goal, it was all about the package, getting out and enjoying climbing. It wasn't all about them and ticking their routes, and so, if I wanted to get involved, their plans would be dropped or steered around us as a family without a second's thought.

Selfless is the word and their untiring, caring approach often makes me feel guilty today, my own drive and determination clouding my ability as a parent.

On and off the rocks, family life was great. My parents did a good job: they brought me up well, and I think I've turned out just as I would have liked to have turned out. There was never loads of money, but we didn't ever seem to be lacking. Later, as a climber spinning out my dole money and then after, in self-employment, I would reflect on what a good early lesson it was in how being careful can make things go a long way. Luxuries came when they were necessities; I can remember the first TV, first phone and first family car, a Saab 99 UBR 3V. My parents were loving and the family bond strong and I owe them big time. Most kids owe their parents big time, but you never really know until you have your own kids.

And I could feel the bond strengthening as I followed my parents' outdoor passion and took it in my own direction. There had been football and youth club and cycling, even fishing and snooker; all had been tested and had run their course. I even played badminton for the county, but when climbing and the outdoors pushed everything aside I could sense their pride. I was becoming my own person and taking control of my climbing.

The cliffs on the Moors may be small, but the gently sloping bracken-covered hillsides below are scattered with boulders that are ideal for kids, perfect for scrambling over, crawling under and building into dens. I knew the craggy outcrops like the rooms of our house and each cliff had its own character: Scugdale; the Wainstones; Raven's Scar; Park Nab. Scrambling around on the blocks was the perfect introduction to learning the subtleties of balance, the flow of movement and the intricacies of friction, and to gaining strength in the fingers and arms – but at a steady rate, not like today where it's all about performance and physical strengths are pushed to the max at the risk of destruction. Don't they realise climbing is all about movement? Miss that bit as a kid and there's no getting it back.

This was my head start, though I'd never have known it, and looking back you'd not fancy a bet I'd ever make any kind of climber considering the efforts kids and their coaches now put into reaching the stars. People talk of genetic talent, and it could account for something in some people, but climbing performance is a combination of so many elements. Most importantly, in terms of movement, I think it's down to time on the rock, but critically, within the comfort zone. Step out of this and learning plummets, especially for a youngster. Throw in some fear and some expectations, or even just physical effort, and movement reverts instantly to its default and most ingrained. Huge cliffs are no use to the five-year-old, or even ten-year-old, but the sandstone outcrops of the North York Moors and the scattered blocks strewn over the hillside were the perfect school. It was all play and playing is the best way to learn.

But what makes a youngster really want to climb a lump of rock? My exact motivations are hard to pin down. I felt at home in the outdoors, but in other areas of childhood I didn't fit so well. At school I was pretty square and a total outsider to the local town gangs. Brought up Catholic, I went to a different school to most local kids and so immediately became an enemy, ripe for potential beatings. Still, I never lost a fight, size being on my side for once and looking younger than my age worked in my favour. As a child I needed an identity, a place where I could express myself and in the outdoors I felt comfortable and on home ground. I understood the environment and knew how it worked. Occasional trips to the hills with high-pecking-order schoolmates showed them who was boss, taking them out of their comfort zone, and I revelled in the once-in-a-blue-moon opportunity to show that I wasn't totally insignificant. Mostly I climbed with adults as all the adults around me climbed and I felt the need to show what I could do, validating myself to their scene. The top climbers in the area were held with esteem and I wanted in on the action. I'd know when they were watching and there was nothing better than burning them off – although I'd often overestimate my ability. *Stratagem*, a tough E4 at Raven's Scar was way too tough for me in front of Nick Dixon and Ian Dunn and, secretly, I cried at my failure.

Even from a really young age I could sense a connection with climbing, not a skill as such, more of a desire. It was more than showing off or patching over a lack of confidence in other areas of life; I wanted to climb simply for myself. I was drawn to it, I liked it and kind of knew I was pretty good at it, at least for my age and height. I soaked up the praise, setting up the early stages of a deep-set feedback loop where feeling good about myself was inseparably linked with climbing well. Rock climbing was already becoming part of my entire personality.

My first real lead, at about ten years old, was graded 'Diff', and for a day or two I must have been keen and dad-indulged, before I lost interest again to stone-collecting or stream-damming. I didn't lead much at that age – it felt like a job with all the equipment and ropework; too complicated. Top-roping was fun and I trusted the system completely. I understood how it worked and there was never any fear. It felt natural to become absorbed in the movement, playing with moves, sitting back on the rope for a rest if needed, but battling to the bitter end and giving my all. Some routes held my attention and drew me in – like my first 'project', the E3 solo

Shere Khan at Park Nab. It wasn't a proper project, merely a toy that I loved to play with. The starting moves were the crux, stretching across a void into a 'mono' and then pulling hard on this one-finger hold to reach another similar one. Just two tiny, round holds on a totally blank face of rock, conveniently positioned by the aid climbers before us. From the second mono, a long pull reached an edge and some balancey moves up the arête to the top. The hard boys would cruise it as their party piece on the Tuesday night meets where the whole of the Cleveland Mountaineering Club would gather for sun-kissed evenings. They made it look easy. I wanted to be as talented as they were, to be as cool as they were, for people to see I was good at something. I tried again and again, on top rope of course, at first being lifted to the mono, which there was no way I could hang. I probably tried it more than forty times over many months and even years, until the higher moves began to come together and I could, eventually, pull on the monos with a little help at the start. Then suddenly I was tall enough to make the starting reach across the void and I set off on my first 'headpoint project'. At thirteen years old it was my first E3 and my first Extreme grade route, and probably the longest project of my life. Some years later the whole route fell down, huge boulders tumbling into the fields below. Gutted. Not a classic maybe, but one of my finest trophies.

We weren't constrained to the Moors. We travelled a lot, camping in the Lake District almost every month during the summer and making longer trips to Scotland, Wales and Cornwall, as well as Europe in the summer holidays. With climbing as the focus we visited some amazing places, in fact, I see now that the beauty of climbing is the places it takes you. Why else would you find yourself in the striking Glen Etive, standing atop the miles of limestone cliffs at Pembroke or staring over the belvedere railings at the edge of the Verdon Gorge? As members of the Cleveland Mountaineering Club we took advantage of club meets, where many families would gather and parents would share childcare and fit in long multi-pitch routes around playing in streams, building sand castles and beach volleyball. In these exciting places climbing was relatively unappealing for the youngster. I'd dabbled on *Little Chamonix*, scared myself at Three Cliffs Bay and was disappointed that you couldn't simply walk up Etive Slabs, but in comparison to kid games, going climbing seemed like a bit of a job and I was rarely drawn to it. To be fair, the big stuff on the sea cliffs and in the mountains was probably out of my league.

As a pre-teenager the Moors were my only real climbing arena. Here it felt natural, better than playing, it was another level. In terms of mates, I was alone in my climbing at this point – no other kids would 'play' – but there were loads of kids around and the crags were an adventure playground. The boulders and caves would be alive as keen parents tackled familiar Severes while keeping a watchful eye over one shoulder. For the gang of kids that would be dragged out come rain or shine this was the best fun of our lives. I revelled in it and felt totally at home. With the gang I was king, one of the oldest and up for it all. Being outside was shaping who I wanted to be. I felt unconstrained, free to explore my personality in every direction, whether it be climbing with the adults, hanging with the kids or just walking alone on the moors. When I was old enough to be allowed, I'd cycle the 15 miles by myself to the local cliffs and edges and bivvy out under a rock, just to be there.

Without other similar aged partners I looked to my dad as my interest expanded and together we shared some great adventures, strengthening the already solid bond between us. In my eyes he was a climbing hero, bold and technical; he'd been everywhere and done it all. He knew everything there was to know about climbing and I'd hoover knowledge from him at every opportunity. He'd teach me knots, how to abseil, to set up belays and place protection. Inevitably I had that strange moment when my ability passed his; no competition, mostly confusion. 'Why can't he do these moves when I can?' Beyond this point I became the leader and was driving the adventures, choosing the routes and eventually pushing Dad to the limit on top rope. Even away from the Moors climbing became the main event. One of the earliest times I can remember being a 'better' climber was on a route called *The Pinch* on Etive Slabs in Scotland. 'Better' maybe, but only in technique and strength, as his experience far surpassed mine. Just because I climbed first didn't make me the leader. Dad carefully paid out the rope as I teetered up the vast slabs at a snail's pace, trying to force Stone-Age oversized wires into cracks that were far too narrow. Every move was a mental challenge, stepping up further and further above the psychological protection that would surely come undone should I slip. The angle of the slab is not steep; it really is very slabby. You can almost take your hands off at any point, but the rock is barely featured and each footstep must be carefully considered, searching out any slight rugosity or angle change that might give just a little extra friction. I'd pushed the envelope a little too far really and knew I was on my limit, only continuing because Dad was belaying. 'If I get in a real mess Dad will sort it out.'

The last section of the slab is run-out, no worthwhile gear for a long time, but the moves were easing and the belay ledge was not far, I just had to keep it together. Looking down Dad was totally with me, belaying as carefully as probably only a dad could. Just a few more metres and I'd reach safety. Then he shouted up, 'out of rope, son.'

Our 45-metre-long rope was not enough. We'd not even checked the route length, or at least I hadn't, insisting it would be fine and sprinting into the lead before even giving him the chance to read the route description. So I stood and waited, repeatedly repositioning my feet as they gradually crept down while Dad prepared to climb, then we both moved together, and as my moves got easier I tried not to think about Dad teetering into the crux at the start of the pitch, right at his climbing limit and in a pair of zero-friction old EBs and my pathetic last wire some 10 metres below me … but I knew he wouldn't fall. Of course he wouldn't, he was my dad and he'd get me out of this mess.

A big E2 in the Wye Valley a few months later ended in a bit of a near miss after which I adopted a more cautious approach to dragging Dad up every route I fancied. Running two pitches together to the top of the crag I cruised the last half, barely placing any protection as it was so easy. Dad followed, sweating but exhilarated as he appeared a few metres below me. I pointed to a massive jug embedded in the earth that I'd pulled on, wanting to end his efforts and share some of my experience of finding this fantastic hold amongst the leaves before stepping over into easy ground. Pulling hard on it, and thank God I didn't pull that hard, it ripped straight out of the ground, a massive flake of rock some half a metre square and the same thickness. It toppled backwards taking a ton of rubble with it, broke into bits and rained down on the base of the cliff miraculously missing everyone below (including my mum). Totally mesmerised by the unfolding disaster and sounds and smell of smashing rocks I hadn't even noticed Dad slumped motionless on the rope, the block having slammed into his face knocking him straight out. I became aware that I was holding him on the rope and that there was no way I was going to be hauling him up, a good advert for SPA skills. Fortunately Dad saved the day, as dads tend to do. Coming round after a short while he struggled up the final section and we walked off before he somehow drove to the hospital to get his head fixed along with the massive slice in his hand that needed fourteen stitches. What a hero!

4   IN ANOTHER LIFE

Home life was stable and easy and comfortable, and out in the hills adventures came thick and fast. As a family we made a great team as my performance and interest met with my parents' and even Chris was keen when he wasn't immersed in *The Hobbit* or *The Lord of the Rings*. Moving into my teenage years everything seemed to be heading in the right direction, I couldn't have asked for more in my home life, couldn't have been any happier. School life was different; the other part of my life, my existence seemingly split down the middle into completely contrasting halves. Each day began the same. An order from Rich: 'Right, "bush-head", you can get out now.'

'Can I sit somewhere else, there is a free seat today?'

'No! Sit on the floor little shit. You are supposed to be our friend. What friend would want to sit somewhere else. So don't move.'

I got on the school bus at an early stop, my orders to keep a seat for Rich and Kev who boarded at the last stop in Skelton, still fifteen minutes from Sacred Heart School in Redcar. They'd get on and kick me out, usually with a dead leg or punch in the back, but being mates there was no option of a different seat, so I'd sit in the aisle. At break time I'd provide the ball, maybe a birthday present or something I'd bought with pocket money, but be shoved to the side and not allowed to play, only to see the ball deliberately hoofed onto the roof as the bell was rung. Rich used me as a punch bag. I guess his older brother bullied him and so he needed to pass it down. We'd been mates at junior school, building aerial runways in the woods and making dens out of grass and pallets, but big school needed a pecking order and I was an easy target. I took it on the chin, literally, not really seeing a way out. Others joined in too, using me to elevate their 'hardness' status. I cried every morning for three years. I hated school. It can be a tough place. I've no doubt that some had it harder, Findlay just seemed destined to be bullied and Yifter, the chubby lad, was stuffed from the start. I guess I was pretty square and I was skinny and small, nondescript and far from cool. School has lots of kids like this, we just get through it.

Break times were the worst. At least in lessons there were teachers looking on, but out in the playground there was nowhere to hide. It was about keeping out of trouble. The back of the X-Block was where the hard lads would scrap and under the corridor I watched Lasby pluck a blue tit from a nest and bite its head off. I'd roam the blank spaces, hugging the walls.

If it was safe I might even climb them. School had a lot of interesting boulder problems. The X-Block had a tough layback where a steel upright separated the brickwork to form a six-inch wide and one-inch deep crack. Using the gaps in the mortar for one hand and burly laybacking with the other it was possible to thrutch up, but it was powerful and continuous. I never managed this one. The block was two storeys high. I got within a few feet, but to be honest I don't think there was another way down so it's a good job I never topped out. Another good route was on to the roof by the corridor. Starting with a high mantel onto a concrete sill at about four-feet high, it involved a stretch past the glass window to the top of the frame where a small incut meant I could build right up and, smearing my feet on each side of the window on the rough red brick, reach the rooftop. Being that kind of felt flat roof stuff it had good friction and topping out was easy. Not a hard problem this one, but my most used – to retrieve the ball. Possibly I gained some cred for this, though it didn't show. But it was the traverse that was my favourite, the blank, red-brick wall where we'd queue for lunch or huddle against the pouring rain. The grout was set in between the bricks by about a centimetre, giving endless holds everywhere, but the brickwork was not exactly perfect and the gaps varied in height, just by a little, maybe a couple of millimetres, enough to squeeze in thin fingers if I could spot the builder's error. School shoes made this desperate, but I'd bet it would still be hard even in a new pair of 5.10s. An intense crimping exercise, the full traverse must have been at least 7c, maybe my hardest effort at the time, but I could only manage it wearing a stiff pair of leather shoes that had a sticking out sole that could edge onto the bricks.

At the start of the third year I made a bold start and sat at the front of the bus with another relative spod, Mike, who I'd noted as a potential friend who matched my status. Sweat poured off me as Rich and Kev boarded, and later the bruises showed my penalty, but I stuck with it and eventually it paid off. I wasn't that interesting anymore and slid into nobody land where at least nothing happened. Then slowly I managed to let some of my personality out. Being a 'prefect' (I was head boy in junior school) was handy as I was forced, or rather, the 'cool' people were forced, to hang out with me. I wasn't such a punch-bag after all and, without their surrounding mates to impress, most people were actually pretty nice. This was an early lesson in the behaviour of groups and the influence even one person could have on a whole crowd, turning everyone into complete idiots against their natural personality. Most people seemed so impressionable. I knew

I wasn't of that type. Somehow I already knew where I was going, or at least that I wasn't on the same path as the other school kids. Things picked up and by the final year I was in a midway position on the grand scheme of cool and rising steadily. It seemed about the right place to be, I'd never make top dude and didn't want to be anywhere near it. I was a midfield player, content to be the underdog without expectations. With the right people I could be myself and I imported my outdoor personality into school life. At last I began to settle into the person I knew I was. Then, just as everything fell into place … disaster of the highest order.

We skied in the winter. Not abroad, but locally, and we didn't live in Scotland. It seems bizarre now, but plenty of weekends, often both days, we'd be out on the North York Moors snow-ploughing our way across the fields. The snow seemed to always be there, its presence not part of our decision to go or not. Amazing, how things have changed. The local club had a ski tow in a field, a simple massive loop of 11-millimetre rope pulled by a petrol engine and constantly moving that you grabbed and desperately hung on to as you were dragged up the hill. Not the longest of slopes, but easily enough to get some serious speed and some big air over the jumps we built. Standing in the queue for the lift at the bottom I witnessed that speed first-hand as my brother Chris lost control while heading directly for the queue – and for me. I'll always wonder if, at the last minute, he regained control and aimed for a direct hit, possibly theorising that if he smashed into me he'd be in the least trouble. Or, more likely, he thought that since he was definitely going to hit someone it might as well be me – to make up for all the hard times I'd given him over the years. Being four years younger and hence somewhat shorter, he had the ideal 'up and under' impact angle to send me flying the biggest distance and inflict the most damage upon me.

I came round some time later, probably out only seconds, but long enough for a crowd to have gathered – not around me, but around Chris as he lay flopped in the snow. I watched it build from behind the wall where I crouched, my head thick and with a sickness in my stomach that only comes with a serious smack to the head. Warm liquid poured from my mouth and splattered the white snow a brilliant red. It was coming out all too quickly. Tripping over with a ski still attached, I staggered towards the crowd who shifted their attention from my brother to the zombie that approached. Dragging my feet and stumbling in ski boots, with arms outstretched and moaning with blood pouring out of my mouth I would have been a perfect extra in *Day Of The Dead*, and I could see it on the innocent skiers' faces. My front big tooth hung down on my chin, still attached by a set of nerves, which no doubt added to my appeal. Fortunately, parents can see through the horror and both Mum and Dad were on hand for this ridiculous situation, my dental disaster and the very bad-looking, but actually infinitely less-bad hole in Chris's forehead that I'd made when I bit into it.

At the hospital a simple bit of sticky tape seemed to cure Chris's problem, but I was right at the start of mine. It began with my fear of needles. Before anything could be done my face was turned into a pincushion with injections under my tongue, in the roof of my mouth, up and down between lip and teeth and, worst of all, so far up each nostril that I'm sure they were injecting into my eyes. Thoroughly numbed, Doctor Number One attempted to snap off the dangling tooth with a sharp tug – but the nerve was having none of it. A pair of scissors appeared, but, before they could be used, Doctor Number Two suggested just 'shoving it back in' for now. Then the two doctors sewed my lip back together with some kind of black rope that ensured I looked as close to Frankenstein as possible. Finally, to hold my tooth in place, cover up the missing teeth that had been snapped off, and to stabilise an entire gob-full of now-wobbly teeth, I was issued with a plastic gum shield.

The fat lip was bad. Six massive stitches earned me my 'Donald Duck' name at school – that would stick for a while – but the gum shield was worse. Worn 24/7 for three months and then just during the daytime for another three, it coincided exactly with my last half year at school, just when things were looking up, just when girls might have started to look my way. Now they still looked …

The gum shield was awful, its transparent nature theoretically gave a natural appearance which utterly backfired at lunch time where it became packed with food and looked horrendous. My first few months were liquid only, I brought in soup to school and watched as everyone scoffed burgers and chips, but I didn't eat because I looked so shit with soup-coloured teeth. For half a year I skipped lunch and got skinny as a rake and I never smiled. Even when the shield went forever, the dodgy front tooth always looked grey and wonky and my fat lip stayed fat. Dental work went on for years, with the front tooth finally sorted sixteen years later. I developed a kind of half smile, a lopsided, not-quite-smiling look to disguise my teeth and lumpy lip. It has stayed with me forever. I still stifle the smile now and am never smiling in pictures. Now you know – it's not because I'm miserable.

5   MAGIC IN THE AIR

Considering my feeble personality I rode out the fat lip saga relatively well, but it was still an ordeal and kicked out the foundations I'd built towards becoming a recognised person – as opposed to a spod on the fringe of the playground. I took a step back, hiding away during school and just riding out the last few months before the summer holidays. The outdoors was waiting for me without judgement or discrimination as I poured myself back in. As spring turned into summer I found myself more and more absorbed, with climbing grabbing me in a different way to previous years. It was way more intense; a noticeable change in attitude that caught me by surprise.

Back in the eighties, most people got into climbing at a relatively late age. There simply weren't many people climbing back then; it wasn't a school thing and climbing walls were barely invented. There was certainly nothing like the dedicated centres we have today. So starting off could be a chance encounter, or seeing some inspiring pictures and hunting out a local club. I was one of the lucky ones who had it all there from the start and I'd basically done all my learning before I woke up and decided to actually get into rock climbing. I can remember the real starting line, the point when climbing took over – I was fifteen years old, just finished school and off on a six-day walking/climbing/camping trip around the local North York Moors with my best mate, Dave. We'd known each other for years, pretty much since we were born, and his family were good friends with mine. Though we didn't go to the same school or live that close to each other, our interests were the same, shaped through family experiences in and away from the hills. Slightly older than me, but more chilled, he accepted my drive and we made a great team. Waking up at the base of the cliffs each morning I just wanted to climb. We climbed all day, and, going to sleep I thought about climbing. Back at home I read about climbing. My mum was the Cleveland Mountaineering Club secretary and every month we got *Climber and Rambler* magazine posted to us for forwarding on to the club base. It was my monthly highlight and the front cover pictures still hang in my gallery of memories, more defined than any childhood photos. I still look back on them occasionally, the editions from 1986 burned into memory forever. Reading the text feels like I'd learnt it by heart, although the turmoil of those years now makes me laugh. Climbing was a confused teenager, just like I was, struggling to move forward and holding on bitterly to narrow-minded opinions. The battles between die-hard traditionalists and the new breed of bolt-clipping competition climbers are totally hysterical, but then at the time I looked on wide-eyed as the war raged …

The transformation from dabbling child to full-blown addict seemed monumental, but looking back it was relatively small – before my real starting point I was already at stage four out of five on most people's scale of climber.

Moving from secondary school in Redcar to sixth form college in Middlesbrough when I was sixteen introduced a whole new bunch of people. At school I was absolutely the only person who had any interest or knowledge whatsoever in climbing, but at college things took a monumental turn for the better with two other real climbers in the same year. Dave was one of them and it seemed a massive stroke of luck that I'd at last have a solid mate at school who was also a climber. There was also Tim, a new character with a stubborn personality who liked to get things done. Driven and psyched he carried me along and together we stepped forward into the climbing world at a pace neither of us expected. Tall, and with a shock of spiky black hair to match his sharp humour, Tim was one of the dudes, instantly high up in the ranking. But college is different to school; the small increase in age provides a huge increase in maturity and the fact that people actually choose to go to college massively influences the type of student. I was still the square guy with the fat lip, but these negative aspects were overruled by the bond of climbing, the general mismatch in our personalities irrelevant. Others joined the gang, Kev, Jon – and particularly Ste from my secondary school, who wouldn't have given me the time of day back then but now quickly became one of my lifetime best mates. It shows how tricky school life can be. Whilst I shuffled along Ste had carried a top lad status with the right combination of cool ingredients. We barely spoke for five years and then a mutual interest brought us together to make a great team. A relaxed character with a strong desire to travel and explore, he always seemed to be striving for and finding the good things in life. Good ideals to look up to.

As a climber I was the most experienced of the bunch and the best climber by far, giving me a status above spod for the first time ever. When we gathered to plan our Wednesday afternoons out, or a weekend away, I was included in all the plans, even driving the adventures and motivating the others.

Initially everything was local, but I moved up a gear with the climbing on the North York Moors. Old desperates became part of the solo circuit on Tuesday evenings while my parents swapped leads on VSs they'd done a hundred times before. Harder routes became viable. *Magic in the Air* is a three-star classic from Nick Dixon that had made it into the brilliant *Rock Climbing in Britain* coffee table book at number 81 out of 100 – it was our Moors representative of hard climbing alongside all the other amazing routes from around the UK and I held the soaring line up the imposing crag of Highcliff with pride, even though I hadn't done it, or even considered doing it. Now a potential ascent came into view. This huge arête is totally unprotected, but death potential had been avoided by using a side runner at half-height, pre-placed by climbing an adjacent E3. This was apparently justified by the snappy nature of the rock at the top; not that I really ever questioned Nick's style, Nick was my hero. With my new climbing psyche I was drawn to the route, top-roped it cleanly in the first session and then found myself psyching up for the lead. At sixteen this would be my first E5 and probably a turning point in my climbing. It felt like a big effort and took a couple of consecutive days of practice to feel I was good to go and then some serious co-ordination to get me and Tim in the right place at the right time for my lead attempt. This was no longer part of 'just happening to be at the crag with my parents'. This was my gig, but at the same time I could clearly see the essential role the belayer played. His confidence in me was crucial, as was mine in him. I may have been leading but this was a team effort.

Dropped off by parents late in the evening near the town of Guisborough, we struggled up through the forest laden with gear, the plan being to camp out and climb the following day. My mind was filled with an unfamiliar state of consciousness, absorbed by the route despite relatively minimal practice. An attempt was now imminent, I'd committed to it. Tim pushed the conversation: 'Think I might try and top rope *Moonflower* tomorrow, have you done that one?'

'Yes.'

'I heard it's really good, what's it like for the grade?'

'Fine.'

'Do you think you'll try and do anything else after *Magic* if you get it?'

'If you get it' – IF. That was still a big question. I'd practised the route a few times, climbed it without a fall, but it was still hard and scary up at the top. The side runner definitely helped and would most likely save a trip to the hospital, but it wasn't guaranteed and being way out to the side guaranteed at least a full body grating on the rough ironstone intrusions if I fell from any of the hard climbing. We pitched in silence, then unpacked the rest of our bags, mine looking alarmingly empty considering there was supposed to be a bulky sleeping bag still in there, which, of course, I'd forgotten. My mind was too cluttered. I'd also forgotten any kind of decent food and so suffered a cold, hungry and uncomfortable night under all the clothes we had. Unsurprisingly I didn't sleep well and though Tim's early and well-slept enthusiasm irritated at first it soon rubbed off and I shook out my stiff limbs at the base of the route.

'Go for it man, you'll cruise it.'

'Maybe.'

'Not maybe, you top-roped it clean on your first day, of course you'll cruise it.'

Yarding up the adjacent E3 to place the side runner made for a good warm up and felt easy. Confidence boosted, back under the route I eyed the line and shut myself away for a moment, but there was no need to go through the moves again. I'd done that already, many times before. I psyched up, had to take a deep breath and then went for it. It felt like a big step into a world of hard climbing.

In the end it was easy, faultless, almost an anti-climax, the power of focus and the effect of familiarity displayed to me for perhaps the first time. It immediately flung open the doors to what was possible. If this hard E5 felt so easy, what else could I do? What if I could apply that level of focus to on-sight climbing? The whole event was almost confusing (though considerably more exciting than confusing), and with this route there came the next step: the side runner, which was now losing its argument in justification. There was no doubt it would go as a solo. Then *Magic in the Air* would really be complete: a pure line of impeccable quality, a match for the famous *Master's Edge* in the Peak District, but without any man-made holes for protection. But the thought frightened me; I didn't want to think it. For that day I shook it off, yet it wouldn't go away, nagging at me weeks later when there was a gap in my consciousness. I knew I could do it, theoretically. I hadn't fallen off on top rope, hadn't fallen off on lead, so why would I fall on solo? Next time I visited the crag I looked closer at the dynamics of a solo, mainly the ground at the base of the route and the distance that separated it from droppable moves near the top. It looked hard and the distance far. I started to question why I'd even considered the solo. What was my motivation? Dispensing with the side runner made for a perfect and pure line without doubt, but I'd already climbed it really. I'd done the moves from ground to top without falling. In fact, come to think of it, why did I even feel I had to lead it? What really was the point of the risk, other than accepting the challenge that others had laid down? But in essence that was it, a challenge wrapped up in the simple and most basic rule of rock climbing: that a route should be led from the ground with the leader placing protection, if there is any, on his way to the top. This route remained tarnished, in a way, with the pre-placed side runner, which was impossible to place on the actual ascent. In a way it could be argued that it hadn't even been 'climbed'.

It became clear my motivations for a solo were for a first ascent. I'd already done the route in terms of movement, then accepted the challenge thrown down by the first ascensionists – the next step would be to raise the bar for the future. But in a way this seemed a trivial step and almost derogatory to Nick. It would be an ego-massage, making a microscopic mark in the history of climbing. But this tiny mark was something I craved, a little bit of recognition. My lead ascent would go totally unnoticed in the climbing world, as indeed it should being a mere E5, but a solo would make people sit up and think. They'd see I was good at something.

Tim didn't think it was a good idea, couldn't see the point. Neither could the rest of the lads. It was already one of the hardest routes on the Moors and they didn't want to see me hurt myself for nothing. Anyway there were trips to organise, things to be done and places to go. I was needed for these, to organise and drive the plans, to make them happen. Their sentiments made an impact and I realised that the recognition I sought I'd already achieved. Gone were the insecure school days being at the bottom of the heap. I'd ended up in a good place. I didn't need to be top dog or a cool dude or the best climber or an E7 soloist. A team player position was just fine, with everyone bringing different things to the table, everyone equal in their own way.

The prize of a solo was clear, but no longer shiny and gold and the consequences of failure shouted to be heard. Leaving the crag I knew deep down I'd never solo it, I didn't need to, the penalty of failure, though unlikely, far exceeding the glory of success. After all what is success and how is it measured? Everyone has their own set of criteria and I was beginning to understand my own. I'd taken what I wanted from *Magic in the Air*. It had given me a real challenge, physically difficult and tampering with a level of risk. The process had been intriguing and the actual ascent an enthralling flow of complex movement. I was happy with my performance, happy with my achievement and I felt good about my climbing. It was all I could ask for and summed up everything I'd be looking for in this funny little sport.

Magic in the Air   23m E7 6b ✳✳✳
The magnificent soaring arête. Originally climbed with side runners (at E5) but has since been led without, making it a very serious proposition.
Nick Dixon, Paul Ingham, summer 1982. Using pre-clipped side runners in the traverse of Stargazer for protection and graded E5 6b.
F.A. without side runners Francis (Monty) Montague 1991.

My first real climbing holiday in the UK was a two-week trip to Pembroke when I was sixteen years old. 'Real' meant totally self-sufficient, with no adult help and no adult supervision, no watchful eye and no safety net, a safety net which we'd been oblivious to for probably all of our childhood lives. Without it there were a few close calls. Setting off up *Yellow Pearls* at Trevallen, I was pretty psyched on what was one of my first big E5 on-sights.

Yellow Pearls is a good choice for people who get scared easy and are climbing wall fit – not that I was wall fit because walls hadn't been invented. I was, however, easily scared and so the promise of lots of bomber gear made the choice between this and other more scary routes rather easy. Trevallen cliff is the ultimate seaside sun-spot for the hard trad climber. No walk-in, easy abseil, non-tidal and with bagfuls of real quality Extremes, generally with good gear. It gets the sun all day so it's possible to get a tan to match your ego – but beware conditions. Anyway, despite the sun I set off because I didn't understand conditions in those days. If it was hot and sunny, surely that was perfect? Good job the gear was good, or at least seemed so at first, consisting of those keyhole type slots that can take anything from a Rock 3 to a Rock 9. They go in fine, but won't sit, and rattle around and seem to somehow fall out again for no apparent reason. I glanced down at Dave, my belayer and partner, also on his first 'real' escape from parents. He was looking relaxed, soaking up the heat on the sun-drenched platform and standing way back from the cliff to get a better view and avoid neck strain. Fair enough, we were on holiday and, as usual, here upon my request, meaning he'd be struggling out on *The Hole* later, the easiest route out from this cliff and the escape route he'd had to bear more than a few times already. So I could hardly complain, even if his position wasn't ideal from a belaying point of view. And anyway, he was aware of my struggle and kept the rope slightly tight, no doubt in an attempt to reduce the length of any fall. Unfortunately, it was tight enough that every time I placed some gear and pulled up the rope to clip it (which was quite often considering how hard it felt), the piece below would lift up, slip out, and then make a perfect arc as it slid down the rope to neatly whack Dave in the nuts. Pity there were no Hex 15s in there. Having placed about ten wires, but with only one left in place, I launched into the crux and committed myself to a crap, round pocket. If you've done the route you'll know that pocket; incut and sharp, but shallow. Unfortunately the launching style of move was utterly inappropriate for my combination of belayer position and rattling protection, which was instantly jerked up and out of its placement and slid down to join its friends on the wrong end of the rope. Luckily I was still young and hadn't delved too deeply into my nine lives and managed to claw my way up onto a shoebox-sized ledge to get my breath back and have second thoughts about trying hard routes in future. At least there was at last potential for good gear. Problem was, all my good gear was now neatly racked on Dave's harness. All I was left with was Rock 1s, weird old things, and a single Moac. Thank God for Moacs – they seem to go in anywhere. Pity you can't get them anymore. My one and only was given to me by Nick Dixon when I was thirteen, my first bit of gear, and the proverbial life-saver. Rattling it into a vague crack, I thanked the lord, and Nick, and sketched up the blank wall above to eventually claw my way over the top and ponder a change of underwear.

Pembroke was good for us: familiar from family holidays, hard, big and technical enough to force a steep learning curve, but friendly enough to just about stay on the right side of the line between ambition and disaster. We made the trip down a number of times each year, becoming more experienced and broadening our aspirations with every visit. By our third trip to Pembroke we figured we could hold our own in the world of sea cliff climbing. Four of us, myself, Dave, Tim and Ste, had planned a trip to fit in the college summer holidays, hitching down to spend a few weeks ticking the classics and dossing in an old barn beside the church in Bosherston. We'd all wanted to do the route *Blue Sky* for ages and made a beeline straight for it as soon as the weather seemed set. However, like true punters we hadn't even checked the tides, which were high that day and submerged the base of the route. More relevant was the huge sea that was running, blasting waves way up the cliff face and rendering the first half of the route completely under water.

You'd have to say it was pretty noisy on the half-height ledge. We hung around for a good while until, eventually, it was time to climb. The wind was pretty cold and our old sit harnesses weren't designed for sitting in – but what a spectacle! Perched 80 feet above a raging sea, watching it was mesmerising: a mass of angry water exploding halfway up the cliff with white ice fingers stretching up to nip at our ankles. Dropping back, the wave would suck outwards and curl under, momentarily revealing the jagged barnacle-covered sea floor before smashing on to it and blasting back up. The view was straight down into hell.

The novelty had worn off. It was cold now, and we were getting wet. With four of us on a ledge designed for one, even the sea's display wore thin. Ste and Tim were climbing together as a team and I was with Dave. We were the first team to climb and it was Dave's lead. No point in shouting commands, they'd never be heard. We agreed on the usual – three sharp tugs on the rope meant 'climb when ready'. It's universal, not perfect, not as good as a comforting string of solid clear shouts – 'I'm safe, take me off', 'You're off', 'Okay, on belay, climb when ready' – but it generally works. Once the lead climber is out of view, belay duty for the second involves simply paying out rope, enough slack so as the leader can move and clip freely but not so much that if he falls he won't give you severe grief after taking a twenty-footer with gear by his chest. At seventeen years old we all had a fair bit of experience and this kind of complication was all very normal. Since starting college the four of us had taken every opportunity to climb together and we knew each other's moves and style intimately. Dave set off, moving smoothly until, after fifteen minutes or so and with half the rope paid out, it stopped sliding through my belay device for a few minutes before going up in regular one-metre chunks. Obviously he was at the top, secured to a solid belay, shouting that he was safe and taking in. But – you know how it is – without being sure you frantically drag the rope through the suddenly-very-snaggy device until at last your end of the rope arrives, already tied into your harness and then at least, if he wasn't safe and is still climbing, he can't go anywhere. Since this pitch was only 80 feet long and the rope was 150, I thought it fair to assume he was at the top – unless he was down climbing, continuing back to the tent, or had gone hideously off route.

The rope went tight, then relaxed. It stayed relaxed. Then the tugs came. Three, or at least probably three, a collection of tugs. Slack again for a while, then more tugs, coming more and more frequently and leading into a steady tension like he was trying to haul me up. 'Jesus, Dave, give me a minute!' I fumbled with the equipment at the belay, unable to get out my beloved Moac. It was jammed solid. Saying a quiet farewell I eventually left it and days of youthful innocence briefly appeared, like the life of the Moac flashing before my eyes. Another team in the future would find it and take it, unaware of its value. More tugs, and at last I was away. Stepping out was intense, a sudden increase in gravity born from awe of what was beneath. I'd switched off from the immensity below whilst Dave had been climbing, but now it filled my field of view and forced extra precision and care with my movements. Steep and powerful climbing took me immediately away from the sanctuary of the ledge and the exposure stabbed home – but on a rope this was just a thrill. Reaching a crozzly jug with my right hand I felt the security of the hold, the jaggedness biting into my skin. Reaching up with my left was an easy move. Then the jug broke. I peeled off backwards, tipping over, my feet apart and above my head, the rope between them, the blue sky above and the route zooming away from me. It was puzzling: there seemed to be a lot of time to ponder when the rope would stop me …

A massive bang, then nothing, then water – a lot of water. My view was like the periscope of a surfacing submarine: underwater, then a glimpse above, then underwater again. I was observing a surreal situation, but completely detached from it. I'd not figured out what had happened, or what was happening. I was simply watching something going on. And then suddenly I was dealing with it. Washed out into a crazy sea and still not dead, noise and cold and pain flooded my brain. I knew what had happened but not why. Somehow I'd ended up miles out, well away from the cliff, where staying afloat was strangely desperate. I didn't seem to be working very well. My brain functioned, but my kicking legs and flailing arms were losing against the downward pull of soaking clothes and alloy weight belt. From the ledge Tim and Ste had already lowered an impossible-to-reach rope, but in their panic didn't notice the one passing just by their heads that was already conveniently tied to my harness – the one that should have held me. I shook the rope and they twigged, grabbing it and pulling hard. This seemed wise, then suddenly like a very bad plan as I was dragged towards the cliff and the froth and roar and crashing of water started to engulf me, sending me completely out of control and into an underwater panic.

My final views were like those of a surfer who comes close to the wave of his life, and misses it. The break is just ahead, the crest blowing back in his face and the hollow of the wave inches away, almost taking him in but then pulling frustratingly out of reach. I can remember the next moments like they were yesterday: being thrown at the cliff and frantically scrabbling for anything, then somehow finding the definition of a 'thank God jug' as the water below sucked back to reveal jagged rocks and certain death. I hung, waiting for something to happen, and then the water was crashing back in again, up and over my head, the jug now below me with my body dragged upwards, then outwards, then down and I'm hanging on the jug again. Now there's a rope, it's tight and pulling me up, I'm helping the haulers, scrabbling on barnacles and slithering on seaweed until at last I'm in some kind of control.

Somehow the half-height ledge arrived. They both looked pale and scared, Tim set off in seconds, speed climbing, trusting the gear that was still in place from Dave's lead. I tried to calm down. Bits of me weren't working well, my left arm was dead and my left leg very floppy. I pinched myself all over, knowing I'd landed on my back and panicking I'd paralysed myself. Luckily I could still feel stuff, so I guessed a broken arm and leg. I felt absolutely no despair at this, more relief, that these were my only injuries despite such a lob. I should have been totally mangled and yet had pretty much got away with it.

Then back to reality: sorting this mess out. We were now back where we'd started. Three sharp tugs on the rope, a break, then more tugs. I could trust it this time. Until then I'd not even considered why I'd ended up in the drink – and figuring it out could wait: a VS with half a body out of commission took all I had. Dave was on the top with a helicopter landing behind him, a surreal sight, the massive bulk of the yellow Hercules helicopter gently touching down amongst the hurricane of the rotors. There was no need for explanations. We never discussed it. What would have been the point? It could happen to anyone, it was no one's fault and I never held it against him.

I didn't even get a window seat in the chopper, it was the full stretcher, drip and neck brace for me. It seemed somewhat over the top – when the guys rushed out of the helicopter I was standing having a piss, trying to get the last bit out, like when you board a holiday plane and don't want the inconvenience of having to go to the loo. I apologised; maybe I should have hitched to hospital. In the emergency ward I cringed as my harness was sliced, but they seemed to know something I didn't. There were X-rays and checks at top speed and good news: nothing broken, no bones anyway. But a lung had been punctured by the impact, so it was down to business. The scalpel sliced my bare chest between my ribs, just below the nipple and I opened up like a mouth, red lips parting cleanly before the blood came. In went the 15-millimetre clear plastic tube. They warned me that it was going to hurt, and shoving it in was a tough job, pushing me upwards towards the headboard, a doctor holding onto my legs to stop the slide. I watched, like observing something from a horror movie. It reminded me of when the alien breaks through the stomach in that film. Then a pop and the tube went from clear to red and a glass bottle to the side began to fill up. Apparently, for that bit of the operation, the insertion of the lung drain, there could be no pain relief, but I'd felt little as it had all just happened too fast. Now though, as my body started to catch up and fired impulses to my brain, I was glad as the needle went in and, within seconds, I was gone.

Waking up was shocking. Images of the whole event tumbled together as I tried to place unfamiliar surroundings. Slowly they re-ordered, fragments coming together to paint a picture of a full-on 'experience' which I'd somehow got away with. The fall, a helicopter, a hospital and some kind of relatively minor injury which wouldn't be causing me too much trouble. But my brain seemed to have been transplanted into a solid wooden body, or else still in my own, which had died, because I could barely move a single muscle. In fact, the only movement I had was in my right hand. It was utterly alarming. Instantly I went into body-check mode, assessing the damage. I should have been okay; I'd got myself out and I was in one piece – that much I remembered. Mentally scanning my body, I analysed each part. Somehow I could feel myself, registering nerve signals from immovable limbs as they replied to desperate requests to operate. I'd survived. I was going to be okay. Visually taking in my surroundings I absorbed the scene: safe, comfortable, a place to recover. The power of adrenaline is incredible; I had been able to push on after the accident, even walking and climbing to safety, but now I'd gone into total protection mode. I'd shut down, I couldn't do anything. For three days I remained rigid, my back swollen and black and blue from my neck down to my knees. Nurses had to roll me over for the pee bottle and feed me when I asked.

But it wasn't so bad. I'd kind of lucked out at the hospital. As it was busy with patients I was placed in the old persons' ward, where, bored by the over-eighties' problems, the young nurses fussed over me and tended to my every need. It was embarrassing at first, but as my body relaxed I began to enjoy my 'hotel' break. Double food and extra chocolate for dessert, my own TV and plenty of attention meant I hardly wanted to leave. But I recovered quickly, and after eight days of holding it in, I managed at last to walk to the toilet alone and take my first dump. I'd not had the courage to ask for the bed pan. At just eighteen, and with the pretty nurses barely older, this was a request too far. Yet walking to my en suite was tricky: as well as feeling crippled, I had to drag around the huge glass jar that was my lung drain. Similar to a wine demijohn, and partially filled with a red mix of blood and other stuff, it was pretty heavy and, resting on its own wheeled cart, had to be kept on a short leash since it was still joined to my body via the plastic tube that was inserted into my chest somewhere just below the nipple. An occasional lapse in concentration and the jolt on the tube was excruciating.

Dave and Ste and Tim came to visit, peering round the door with anxious faces. After a week or so we could talk and laugh like the whole thing had happened to somebody else. We didn't analyse; there was no need. They stayed on to climb for a little while, but unsurprisingly their motivation was somewhat dampened and they soon hit the road. After their final visit I felt slightly alone, left behind by the healthy ones – though I knew I would not be far behind.

After ten days I was good to go. Amazingly I hadn't broken anything; my only injuries a punctured lung and some likely mobility repercussions in later life that I obviously forgot about completely. My parents came to collect me, extremely relieved to find me in one piece, but also pretty annoyed since I'd told my mates not to phone them, preferring to do it myself when I was ready to leave. 'No point letting them worry, or having them come all the way to Pembroke only to have to wait for me to recover.' At the time this seemed a really great idea, almost kind, and I patted myself on my black and blue back for being so thoughtful. Now, as a parent, I can see it was pretty obviously the absolute opposite of what they would have wanted. Still, I did save a ton of hassle on their part and saved everyone from the horrendous telephone call: 'Hi there, I'm one of your son's climbing friends, he's just had a serious climbing accident and is in hospital after a helicopter rescue.' In the end it was all very civilised. I just called them up from the hospital and began as if nothing had happened. 'Yeah, it's been a great trip, lots of good routes, and, er, the last one did actually go a bit wrong, but it's all fine now. No need to worry, I've been in hospital for ten days and I'm all fixed and, er, I don't suppose you could pick me up because the doctors don't want me to hitch home … '

I'd actually enjoyed my stay in hospital. I'd had a lot of time to think, something I rarely did. I'm much more of a 'doer', filling time with activities rather than pondering over problems or the meaning of life but my enforced week of lying down had allowed a more in-depth analysis of not just what had happened on the Pembrokeshire cliffs, but also of what I wanted from climbing and how much I wanted to risk. A glimpse at injury showed that it should be avoided at all costs; hitting the ground hurt and it was pretty obvious that I'd been ridiculously lucky. Parameters of risk were analysed: climbing was my main event, and no prize was worth losing it for. But I was already playing a cautious game. No matter how I pitched it the accident had been due to a breaking hold. Experience and common sense suggested the hold was solid. It was just bad luck, impossible to foresee. So I noted the incident, filed it in the 'close shave' folder and basically tried to forget about it. The only conclusion I could find was that I needed to be a little more careful still, like the accident was part of the game, an acceptable risk and almost to be expected. There really wasn't anywhere to move in the sport as I followed a narrow path of style and ethics. My aspirations didn't shift and my lesson in risk was taken lightly.

Starting college had been the catalyst in my climbing. Coinciding with a coming of age, new friends and a new scene, it finally allowed me to express myself. We pooled information and ideas and I suddenly felt unconstrained in my desire to climb and explore. It became obvious that I needed to be fed with new destinations; we all did. The Moors is okay for a potter around, but has nowhere near the quality and quantity of other areas. I had images painted in my mind of Scotland, Pembroke, North Wales and Cornwall – all places I'd been to as a kid, but never with a climber's head on. Now I had the freedom to get there on my own steam, sixteen years old apparently being an appropriate age to hitch off into the distance. Not that I asked my parents if this was appropriate, I probably just informed them that I was setting off, tomorrow, alone, to hitch 400 miles from Teesside to Pembroke.

Hitching was *the* mode of transport. I'd like to think that I was quite a good hitcher, as I seemed to get a lot of lifts in double quick time. Standing in the spread-out queues of hitchhikers on the M1 slip roads, I'd often get singled out and picked up after only minutes of waiting. It's a crazy thought, that. There would have been maybe ten people at every service station around the country all looking for a ride. Thousands of people every day. Hitchers were an integral part of the transport system in the eighties and early nineties. Now hitchers are looked on with fear and those that you do see have probably broken down, missed the bus or run out of steam on a long walk.

I'd usually be alone, because two scruffs with massive rucksacks immediately slashed your chances and, for a start, lorries only have one extra seat. The key to it was to somehow show you were a nice person with a purpose to your travel. That way it cleared the dossy scrounger badge immediately. The 'hanging rope' was probably the best method, guaranteeing an immediate bond between you and any driver with even the slightest interest in anything climbing related. Standing with a thumb out, the huge rucksack would be dumped in front of you, upright with your rope strapped under the lid, the colour carefully chosen to be as bright as possible. Colour was the number one consideration when buying a rope for the hitcher, placed well above safety and even price, because hitching was the way to go for saving money. Totally free, I can't even guess the amount I must have saved on transport. Hitching made travel possible. It wasn't just about getting from A to B – I met some really cool people, thousands of them. We talked a lot and I learnt a lot. It probably helped my personality too, being able to talk to literally anyone for hours on end has to be a handy skill when you're in a fix. Some people were incredibly nice, taking you out of their way, even buying lunch, but I never got laid as some people claim in their stories and the only famous person I ever met was Barry Grant (Paul Usher) from the soap opera *Brookside*. Tim had a ride with Jim Kerr from one of my favourite bands, Simple Minds, of which I was incredibly jealous.

Hitching may have had no cost financially, but it wasn't all plain sailing, or everyone would've been doing it. Time was the biggest cost – you'd have to be pretty relaxed with your schedule, and in order to keep things really cheap on a long journey, you had to be prepared to cope with some grim nights' sleep. My most regular 'hotel' was a small space under the motorway bridge at Birch Service Station on the M62. Basically, living on the east coast of England meant that pretty much every journey I did involved crossing from east to west and, from Teesside, this service station was roughly a day's worth of hitching away. My hotel room was a small triangular gap formed by the footbridge as it left the ground. It had a concrete base and was fairly hidden by bushes and pretty much ever-dry. In its favour it had an en suite service station attached, though against it was its location, way up on the moors with a good chance of rubbish weather. That's always a problem for the hitcher, because no one wants a soaking ball of water in their nice new car. Sometimes I'd stop there early, even if there was still some light in the day, as it was a safe bet and you never knew what was coming up. Bridges were the best choice when you were caught out as shelter was the number one requirement and waking up in the rain marked a disaster for sure. But sometimes I'd have to make do: an old sheet of eight-foot by four-foot plywood dumped on the ground right beside a service station on the M5 did the job. Propped up at one end by a few sticks it even sheltered me from the pouring rain, though not from the stares of all the travellers as they stopped off for their over-priced morning coffee and toast. Possibly the worst doss was under a school, some kind of wooden building raised off the ground by a half metre or so. In the dark and pouring rain, climbing over a fence to reach this luxury pad – which was even comfortable enough to allow a lie-in – seemed like a great idea, but as the school kids poured out for playtime and sports I realised I was in quite a fix. I doubted the teachers and kids would have appreciated some dishevelled tramp sleeping under their school, so I had to stick with it until after break time, hiding in my sleeping bag and trying not to move. Then, after a half-arsed pack-up in my tiny spot I legged it through the playground without looking back. Most journeys were a two-day job, although Cornwall or Scotland could be three. Regularly stuck on some random middle-of-nowhere road there was plenty of time to catch up on my diary and fill in the details. Looking back, half of my life seemed to be spent standing by the side of the road, or sitting in someone else's car:

September 1987

Rain on my face woke me at 8.30 and I lay there awhile but people were beginning to see me and I felt like a tramp. First lift was with a piss-head, dirty lorry driver in a crap truck who talked sexist rubbish but took me to a good spot. Next an executive stopped and took me into the centre of town. After some scran the next lift was off a forty-year-old boffin type who already had another hitcher in the car who was a seventy-five-year-old bookshop owner. They waffled on and made me feel stupid. The driver took the book guy all the way home and we went in for a cuppa and a look around his library, but it was going to be a long stay so I bailed. Back on the road a total lad picked me up, but he was knackered, I couldn't believe how tired he was and he kept falling asleep – he even asked if I could drive for him (I couldn't drive back then). Eventually it became insane and he was swerving all over the M6 at 75 miles an hour. I had my hand on the wheel most of the time and at last escaped at Penrith. I wonder if he died straight after setting off again. Five seconds later a doctor picked me up and explained the best drugs to take to die and how much alcohol was needed. Apparently a bottle of vodka is enough on its own for most people. He dropped me at Scotch Corner, a bastard place from where to hitch and I waited half an hour in the pissing rain until a Welsh guy stopped who was a painting seller. He dropped me in a crap spot that needed a two-mile hike to fix in the rain before getting picked up by a Norwegian weirdo hippie type playing amazing music. Next lift was with a climber who had done loads of cool things like Resurrection and Left Wall. They left me at a motorway roundabout, so no stopping. There was no way I was ever going to get a lift especially as it was dark now so I had to walk four miles in the gutter to a service station which nearly killed me. By the time I made it I was starving but it was shut and I had no food. I found a sketchy bivvy under a bridge but didn't sleep much as there were lots of people walking by, but since it was pouring down and windy it would have to do ...

A relaxed agenda was crucial, but also a high tolerance to boredom – there could be some long waits. My longest was four hours on the M6, but I've heard of people waiting a whole day in the same spot. A high tolerance to boring people and all-round idiots came in handy too. Lorry drivers were often painful, being sexist and racist beyond belief, but it was their cab and I just had to bear it. I met all walks of life. One chubby guy in his rep-mobile seemed rather nervy as we cruised down the M1 on my way to Sheffield. Stopping at the services he leaned over to the dash box for a map, rubbing his flabby arms against me. He was sweating like a pig and couldn't string a sentence together. Then, spreading the map wide open and across into my side, he reached under the map and fumbled his way across into my groin for a quick grope, looking into my eyes hoping for a positive outcome. He didn't get it but I weighed up the situation: fat and way out of shape, I reckoned I could take him if it came to a battle, which was luckily now out of the question as he gibbered out his apologies. I could have just stepped out but he was going to Sheffield and so was I. So we carried on with a slightly awkward conversation and he dropped me off right where I asked, which was not actually where I lived, just in case.

Maybe my worst lift came straight after one of my best, whilst on the way to Pembroke. On the M5 a total heap of a car stuttered to halt beside me and I slid the pile of sweet wrappers, sandwich boxes and old beer cans off the passenger seat and climbed in beside an obvious total stoner. Kangarooing off he pulled out a massive bifda of the finest variety which, after a few puffs, I knew would have rendered me totally incapable of any kind of activity whatsoever, never mind driving a car. His journey was a good chunk of mine, but he had to stop off en route to collect some 'stuff'. Alarm bells started ringing as it became clear that 'stuff' was, in fact, a large bag of weed. The situation was turning dodgy, but as we drove into a rather nice estate and met a well-to-do family man I felt much more at ease, particularly after the obligatory testing which left me well and truly off my face. Back in the wreck our conversation was rather one-sided, with this stoner obviously some kind of expert while I stared blankly at my map with no idea where I was or where I was going.

'I'll drop you here,' he suddenly announced, 'great spot this, you'll get a lift in no time.'

I staggered out, thanked him loads and collapsed in a heap by the side of what turned out to be a motorway intersection – a big no-no for hitching, it being motorway terrain and off-limits to pedestrians and, most of all, hitcher scum. Being spotted here by the police meant a guaranteed ride in a police car with a good chance of some kind of real hassle, depending on their mood, and even a conviction if they were feeling proper gnarly. In my current state any kind of police interaction was fairly low on my list of desired experiences and as darkness descended I hitched for my life, since according to my map the closest non-motorway road was a four-mile hike along the hard shoulder. When a big BMW rolled in beside me I flopped into the warm leather and babbled out my relief – but this guy didn't want me to talk. Short and bald and wiry he had a lot to say about what he'd like to be getting up to with young boys in showers. This was his crazy fetish and he wanted me to know all the details. I tried to steer the conversation away in a different direction but he was having none of it and as the street lamps on the M5 disappeared and darkness really set in my paranoia reached whole new levels. When his hand stroked my leg it was time for action. Next junction would be fine thank you very much, Junction 14 on the M5. He stopped, no questions asked, no hassle, nothing. Like he'd just been telling me a story and it had reached its natural end. I got out into the pissing rain and he roared off. At last I could assess where I was, especially as my stoned daze had unsurprisingly evaporated. Unfortunately it was clearly obvious to the seasoned hitcher that I was totally screwed. Raining and dark and at a junction that was never used by anyone I made the decision to hike to the M48. Laden down with a full trad rack, two 9-millimetre ropes, half a tent (very useful, the other half taken by Dave who did the journey in a day), sleeping bag, stove and all the other junk, it was four hours before I got my head down behind the bins at the services at Junction 1 of the M48. Next day the rest of the journey to Pembroke was a breeze: two lifts, and I was there in time to climb. Hitching was like that; unpredictable.

My thumb took me all over the place for the few years I was at college – Pembroke, the Lakes, Cornwall, Scotland, even around the Verdon in France – but plans to visit North Wales never seemed to gather any momentum. Ironic, as that was the area I wanted to visit most, alongside Sheffield. Both were infamous climbing venues steeped in history and well-known for being *the* places to be. Not only was the climbing awesome, but their scenes were going off, full of all the most colourful characters doing all the cutting edge routes and having the best parties. At last we organised a trip to Llanberis and secured it in the diary. It was Tim who finally made it happen. Having left college for Leeds University a year before me, I missed his driving force at home in Teesside and he developed in leaps and bounds within his new climbing environment, not just in his performance, but also in the social department. In fact, perhaps more in the social department. This was always going to happen, his razor wit and skilful storytelling guaranteeing he was always centre of attention. I visited him in 1989 to watch Leeds '89, the famous world cup climbing competition – the first ever world cup. The whole thing blew my mind. The atmosphere was electric. Everyone was there, all the best climbers in the world and, sitting close to the front, I was rubbing shoulders with Simon Nadin and Ben Moon. Jerry Moffatt was the winner, a fairy tale finish on home ground and his nail-biting final performance firmly established the legendary status of this first competition. There seemed to be so much going on in this climbers' city and the competition was just another event in a huge climbing scene packed with famous climbers and with brilliant cliffs all within a stone's throw. Tim was immersed and had already made the hitch to North Wales a few times, the central position of Leeds opening up way more doors than the far flung North East. We arranged to meet in the famous Llanberis Pass.

As usual my dad dropped me off on his way to work, saving me the first 10 miles of country roads. He pulled over into a lay-by at the start of the busy Teesside Parkway and left the engine running. Stepping out into the drizzle I dragged out my bag, dropping it into the wet grass, then leaning across the passenger seat we shook hands as we always did, a gesture we seemed to have adopted, formal for most people but having a much greater depth between father and son. He looked into my eyes. 'Take care son.'

'Yeah, of course. I'll be back home in about ten days. I'll try and phone.'

'Yes, keep in touch. Your mum worries … '

He pushed a small parcel into my hand. 'Some food for the journey.'

'Thanks, see you later.'

Sandwiches for sure, he'd have made them this morning, along with his own. I pressed the door shut rather than slamming it, then waved him off, watched him circle the roundabout and disappear into the vast city of the ICI chemical works. I looked down at my potential lunch and prised open the package. Cheese and ham, my favourite, and a chocolate bar too. Winner! Then I folded the sandwich back up and stuffed it into the lid of my pack and set off, scoffing the chocolate, to my usual spot on the slip road: a small, clean bit of tarmac by an iron drain where I could drop my pack, a spot where I'd stood hundreds of times before. I was more excited than I'd ever been.

It ended up being the standard two-day hitch with a dreary doss under a bridge near Manchester Airport, but as the mountains of North Wales rose up from the horizon I could feel my excitement rising. My first visit ever. Llanberis had somehow slipped off my parents' list, being too far for a weekend from Teesside and too near for a week-long holiday. Or maybe just too wet. As I approached and the craggy ridges and rocky walls filled the windscreen, the hairs on the back of my neck bristled. Passing Capel Curig and Plas y Brenin and then up to Pen-y-Pass was a sightseer's dream with perfect views as the sun poured down from a crystal clear blue sky. Dropping into Llanberis Pass any conversation I might have been having immediately dried up. The giant boulders beside the road welcomed me as I knew they would, familiar from countless magazines and books, a climber's landmark like a historical monument. We pulled into the lay-by beside them and I hovered out of the car, literally floating on the majesty of my surroundings. This was a place I'd dreamt of for years. Sitting on my pack in the blazing sun I tried to take it all in: the Cromlech, the Grochan, Dinas Mot, Cyrn Las, masterpieces hanging in the most exclusive gallery. Every cliff oozed history and quality in equal measure. *Right Wall, Lord of the Flies, Cenotaph Corner* and *Cemetery Gates* smiled down on me, their lines as familiar as the corners and walls of my bedroom. It was truly overwhelming to visit a place that had captured my imagination for so long. Llanberis Pass: the foundation of British climbing.

It took me a long time to recover. Eventually I set about making myself at home. Scrambling over the stone wall by the lay-by I scanned for a good pitch and lush, flat grassy patches invited me from across the gently babbling stream. Now almost dry, crossing was easy and the smell of the water and the moss and the grass heightened the senses. No one else was camping, but a small ring of stones marked an old fireplace and a paradise spot with a 360-degree view. Tent pitched, there was still enough light in the day to explore, and without a second's thought I set off to get a closer look at the Cromlech.

An hour later, back down at camp, I sat on the biggest boulder and watched the sun slide down the edge of the craggy valley and eventually fade on to the horizon. A perfect end to the day. Well nearly – it would have been better shared with Tim. He hadn't turned up yet. We'd arranged to meet here in the Pass via a few letters and some passed-down-the-line messages using his shared hall of residence phone, but we both knew that our mode of transport would scupper any attempt at exact timings. No worries, but that night, stretching out over my pathetic half-size Karrimat in a pitch black tent, I wondered whether Tim would make it by tomorrow. My mind was awash with images of routes and guidebook descriptions.

Left Wall
A brilliant route at the top end of its grade. A contender for the most popular, most fallen off and finest Extreme pitch in North Wales.

Right Wall
This brilliant climb is still a big lead and should not be underestimated. The original way up the wall, it is a route-finding masterpiece, the holds only coming to light at close quarters.

I tossed and turned like a child on Christmas Eve. The morning couldn't come fast enough. Somehow I finally slipped into dreams to sleep like a log.

From the depths of my sleeping bag a voice pulled me into reality. 'Helloooo, Helloooo.' It wasn't Tim, very definitely not. 'Fifty pence for camping, Hellooooo.' I hadn't expected a camping fee, but handed it over regardless, too sleepy to offer any kind of argument. 'The Old Woman' as she became known, lived on a local farm and would do her rounds every morning to collect her pennies, regardless of the weather and how few people were staying. As it turned out, the word on the street was she had no right to collect money, because she wasn't offering any service, but at the same time it was her land that I was sleeping on and she did have the right to chuck me off. Fifty pence seemed like a reasonable compromise.

Scraping the sleep from my eyes I waited for her to shuffle away before poking my head out of the fly sheet. It was still there, the panoramic vista of climbing paradise. Over on the Mot the shadow line crept down the cliff soaking it in red, corners and grooves standing out in extra 3D. By the river I splashed my face, smelling the water and taking in its earthy taste before settling on a big, round stone and waiting for the sun to bring warmth to the day. This camping spot and the few small flat patches of short-cropped grass on either side of the road became my regular place for literally hundreds of nights over the coming years. I feel at home there and alive. It feels like I belong there.

Waiting for Tim was painful and poring over the excellent Paul Williams guidebook only made it worse, highlighting how much climbing there was to be done. Today, instead, I'd walk up Snowdon. I did the full horseshoe and was back in time for lunch. Still no Tim. The next day I soloed a three-pitch HS on the Cromlech called *Better Things*, as well as *Spiral Stairs* and *Flying Buttress*, both V Diff. A proper climbing day out. Next day I soloed *Main Wall* on Cyrn Las and a little E1 called *Little Groover* near the Grochan. Still no Tim. It seems ridiculous these days to not simply pick up the mobile and find out exactly what was going on. In fact, I'd have known already with minute-by-minute information from endless texts. These days we are addicted to contact and demand constant updates. Back then I had no way to find anything out, I'd not even thought to ask his parents' number – why would I? So I carried on with the sun beating down, day after day for a whole week of perfect climbing conditions.

I sampled the slate for the first time, soloing *Seamstress*, *Seams the Same* and *Fool's Gold*. The style grabbed me, it seemed to fit my strengths and not punish my weaknesses, being ideal for the flexible, strong-fingered type but without requiring much endurance or big muscles of any kind. An entire world of climbing opened up before me as I roamed the quarries and took in the aura of this incredible climbers' playground. What a place. Every climber needs to go there.

After a week my time was up. I packed my bag and took out the trusty 'hitching sign', a clipboard to hold an A4 sheet of paper onto which I'd scrawl in big black letters the direction I was attempting to go. Lift-givers could then instantly separate themselves into potentials or wrong-direction drivers. It was a good tactic, forming a miniscule bond with a driver if he recognised the town name on my sign, 'Oh, I'm going to exactly the same place that he really wants to get to … maybe I should give him a lift … ' The key was to choose your sign name carefully: not so far away that your odds would be nil, but not so close as to pick up local traffic and a waste-of-time two-mile lift. The town of Betws-y-Coed was 10 miles away. That was a start. 'Sheffield' would be pushing it a little. I was off in seconds, friendly outdoor people passing through.

Tim arrived just after I left. We'd somehow got our weeks mixed up.

Our next effort in North Wales, a few months later, was more co-ordinated. It had to be as Tim had taken my beloved tent, an old A-frame Vango, to arrive a day or two earlier. However, as I struggled out of some beat-up Llanberis local's car into the pissing rain and a howling gale I wished I'd not loaned him the tent, as there it was, smashed to bits on the other side of the river. This was not quite how I remembered the Pass, but was in actual fact its default state – as I'd learn over the coming years. Tim was still in the tent, making do and trying to limit the damage and take the strain off the ripped flysheet. It was a crappy night to say the least, but somehow the morning dawned fair and after a rather poor DIY tent repair job we hitched down into 'Beris to dry out and make a plan.

A big breakfast in Pete's Eats swelled the confidence even more than the stomach, which is saying something, and we decided that even though it was after midday, *White Slab* on Cloggy was a totally feasible goal. And so, with much young enthusiasm and very little intelligence, we staggered up the railway track to the Black Cliff. It was further than we thought, we were slower than we thought and we arrived later than we thought – 4 p.m. – which didn't seem so bad. After all, it was July and there was plenty of light and the route was not long. Well … ten pitches. After that huge walk-in, the swirling mist and spots of rain that appeared from nowhere weren't going to stop us. The first few pitches were kind of nice, pitches 3 to 10 were done in pissing rain and then 8 to 10 in the dark and pissing rain. Luckily, we didn't take a headtorch or the whole experience would have been much less memorable. Summit celebrations were somewhat dampened as we realised the hideous waterfall we'd just slithered up was the easy bit of our day. Finding your way off the top of Cloggy in the pitch black is not easy, especially when you've never been there before and don't know the way. As a result, after two hours we found ourselves in the wrong valley, which we'd never been to before and didn't know how to get out of. Luckily, and by total chance, our stumbling took us to a signpost and then, via an hour's march, back to Llanberis village. This was where we'd started our ridiculous quest but, unfortunately, was nowhere near the base of the cliff where we had left our bags. Walking up the railway for the second time that day, dressed in tight-fitting rock boots, harness and full rack was very grim – but not as grim as walking back down again having failed to find our stuff and still dressed in the same unsatisfactory attire. We'd got right up to the base of the cliff but it was just too dark and too rainy. How can Wales be so wet?

The five-mile trudge all the way back up the Llanberis Pass to our tents at four in the morning was also very grim but, without doubt, the grimmest part of the whole experience was getting up the next day, crawling out of the shambles of a tent, pulling on our soggy climbing shoes and walking all the way down to 'Beris and then back up to Cloggy yet again to get our bags. The important thing was no one was hurt, except for our feet. Mine swelled to a size 8 from a 6, while Tim's turned green from the shoe dye. The colour took weeks to go away, though he probably didn't wash them. It was an excellent lesson in how a headtorch can get you out of a fix which, of course, I ignored entirely. But back then when the Petzl Zoom was as good as it got in torch technology I could just about excuse myself.

North Wales had everything I needed: mountains, beautiful scenery and more climbing than I could ever manage. Why had it taken me so long to visit? I was completely psyched. The only problem was the distance – the double-day hitch from Teesside (Tim could usually manage it in a day from Leeds University). But even that made no difference and we began a campaign of visits that would span a number of years. We made a great team. He led around E2, which translates to around E4/5 when following a leader on the blunt end of the rope, so there were no battles over who got the 'lead'. With so many classics around, this can be a common problem in a team of the same ability. I'd happily give him lead position on *Left Wall*, *Cemetery Gates* and the *Corner* in return for him following me on *Resurrection* and *Right Wall*. We knew the place like the back of our hands, soon ticking off all the best routes on both sides of the Pass.

Once on *Lubyanka* up on Cyrn Las, waiting for a team ahead of us, we watched the leader struggling to place his first bit of gear at the top of a massive shield of rock. Standing on the slightly detached pinnacle he fumbled with a rack of micro wires at full stretch only to drop the lot which ended up down the back of the shield and out of reach by about five metres. He spent a while staring forlornly at his kit before giving up and retreating. I went for a look. Having absolutely no small wires whatsoever I had to pretty much solo the start of the route, although this hardly registered as all I was thinking about was how I'd manage to extract the rack of wires. I spied the prize down the 10-centimetre-wide crack far below. It was tantalisingly possible to reach, though certainly not without aid unless you were Mr Tickle. Next day I suggested to Tim that we did a route on the same crag, cunningly chosen to pass the same shield. Back at the same spot, this time armed with a nut key on the end of a loop of string, I went into fishing mode. The wires took the bait in seconds and up came my prize: ten brass-head wires. They were from a dodgy unknown brand but so what? This was a major addition to the rack.

A (very) long time later (like fifteen years) I was chatting to a guy in Pembroke and somehow we got onto the subject of losing kit. He explained how his biggest disaster had been dropping a full rack of new wires down a crack up on Cyrn Las. Maybe I should have come clean, but to be fair, they were rubbish in the end and I'd given them away to someone else years ago.

The camping area by the Cromlech boulders is truly idyllic and makes the perfect meeting spot. It has everything you need: centrally placed for all the climbing, amazing views, a water supply and, most importantly, it's cheap as chips to stay there. Using it as our base camp, Tim and I had some great adventures. We went to Tremadog and Gogarth and slate, but mainly climbed in the Llanberis Pass. We got better at co-ordinating our trips, usually arriving within a few hours of each other – although maybe that was just luck. Hitching from two separate places we usually fixed a date and went whatever, regardless of the forecast. Twenty years on and armed with cars and accurate(ish) forecasts on our phones, we can go at the drop of a hat so long as work is not fixed, or sack a trip off if it looks wet, or even go for a single day. Llanberis Pass is famous for its changeable weather and it was tough to hit a dry spell. The incredible beauty of the valley soon vanished in pouring rain and howling winds, and in bad conditions all the plus points of the camp spot were suddenly overshadowed by the very wet and miserable five-mile hike to the shops, cafe and pub.

> *By 2 a.m. we were both wide awake to the sounds of sheeting rain and gale force winds; I was amazed the tent didn't just disintegrate around us. After a very sleepless night we peered out at 7 a.m. to find a total lake in the bell end and before we knew it we'd extended the lake into the inner tent. Everything was totally soaked. The water was so deep in the tent that a stray bowl of cereal actually floated away.*

Enough was enough, the boulders may well be a heavenly campsite but, strangely, it had lost its appeal; time to split. We leapt out and did a sprint pack, wearing shorts to try to save some dry clothes. It was hopeless. We might as well have thrown everything in the river and let it get washed the five miles down to 'Beris to save us carrying it. The tent in particular was looking pretty worse for wear and it was almost tempting to leave it or dump it straight in the bin by the side of the road. But you never know what's coming up, so we strapped up the raggy mess and hitched down into 'Beris to dry out and make a plan.

Down in the village there was potential for a doss. Being ahead of me in the university world by a whole year, Tim had moved on and was down with the student scene. He knew how it worked, he was cooler than me and knew what to say. I was feeling left behind, living in the arse end of nowhere and sliding back off into spod status, all my mates adopting different clothes, haircuts, music tastes and even complete vocabularies every time I saw them. Tim had visited Llanberis a few times without me and had become a fringe member of the Llanberis scene, famous worldwide for its partying and full spectrum of colourful characters. 'Beris was home to Johnny Dawes and John Redhead, and many others were passing through and leaving their mark. Slobbed out in Pete's Eats there would be many 'hellos' from the locals and sometimes they'd sit with us and share the gossip. I rode on the back of Tim's personality, pretending I knew what I was talking about, that I was also down with the scene and well on for a party tonight and a spur-of-the-moment trip to Tremadog in the morning. We were starting to feel involved. As the rain poured down onto the drab grey streets we passed time with tattered magazines or the new routes book, waiting for someone we knew to come by, as we knew they would.

Ali popped in for a brew and then took us back to her house to escape the rain. She said we could stay but we couldn't because it was already full, so we took a lift to Bob's house in the hope he'd ask us to stay. When we arrived everyone was wasted. At one point there were six of us with a joint each. I had too many drags from the strong one and had to sit in the toilet for a while to get my head straight before I could rejoin the gang. Later on Dwarf arrived, and what a character, he stumbled in, collapsed over a chair and greeted us with the phrase 'God I'm fucking wasted.' This summed him up perfectly in one sentence. Eventually everyone staggered off to bed, so we just assumed we could stay and lay down on the floor, a brilliant night's sleep as the rain lashed down all night long.

Once we were 'in', North Wales took on a whole new dimension. Rain meant hanging with some truly amazing characters. The scene was as colourful as it had been painted. Frequently, Johnny would appear and talk for hours on end about stuff we couldn't fathom. Just being in his presence was overwhelming. Then he'd disappear on some quest to conquer 'the move' on some horror project he was trying. Plenty of the climbers didn't even seem to climb, but were just being carried along by the fun of it all. One morning a bunch from the house necked a load of magic mushrooms and went off 'slate tobogganing', where they'd try and slide down the massive scree slopes on a huge slate slab. The slate became our local crag, minutes from wherever we were dossing, it would dry in seconds after rain.

Slate was cool. Everything about it: the route names, the style, the fact that it was somehow anarchic, like you weren't supposed to be there. Dodging officials and climbing over barbed wire fences was the norm in this over-grown playground. It was the equivalent of kids playing on a building site – but on a monumental scale. The whole place is a massive quarry blasted out of the beautiful mountain hillside. It should be a scar on the landscape, but it has a haunting beauty that, personally, I think adds to the vista but maybe that's just me and is because of my love of climbing.

The first commercial attempts at slate mining at the Dinorwig Quarries took place in 1787, but business boomed after the construction of a horse-drawn tramway to Port Dinorwig in 1824. At its peak in the late nineteenth century the quarry was producing an annual outcome of 100,000 tonnes. Dinorwig employed over three thousand men and was the second-largest opencast slate producer in the country. Slate tiles from there roofed houses all around the world. Although by 1930 its working employment had dropped to two thousand, it kept a steady production until 1969. Since its closure, part of the quarry has been taken over by a hydroelectric power station, adding to the history in a way, but most of the vast expanse of exposed slate has simply been abandoned, the scale of the quarry far too massive to even consider any kind of clean-up. And so it lies there; nobody really wants it and nobody can fix it. Slowly but surely the quarry will crumble, the walls and miners' huts will collapse and the pipework and rail tracks will rust away. Dust will cover the mountains of rubble, grasses will take root and eventually the quarry will disappear but, for now, this is a gift to climbers. There were bolts and even entire chipped routes with few people complaining, since, after all, the whole quarry was chipped out of the ground in the first place. And, alongside these, were fierce ethics with fully trad routes on minimal marginal gear, or 'designer danger' with a bolt placed just out of reach, its sanctuary reached only after a 'death' move. Why not place the bolt a metre lower? This is slate – anything goes. There were dynos for metal spikes, runners on ladders and teeters along rusting pipes. There were walk-ins through collapsing tunnels and routes fell down on a regular basis. Protection was all about skyhooks, Friends on two cams, tiny RPs and slings over imaginary spikes. *The Medium, Manic Strain, Raped by Affection, Fruity Pear in a Veg Shop Romp* – the route names said it all and tales of their ascents fell into legendary status. While attempting *Dawes of Perception* Redhead had a lucky escape:

'Just as he was about to clip the bolt his foot rolled off a minute smear. Inverting, he hurtled down the slab, ripping the Friend out and breaking

its trigger wires, snapping two RPos and ripping out the six other wires. Towse reacted instantly by jumping out over the lake – he dropped 10 feet. This act saved Redhead's life. After a fall of 50 feet he stopped upside down a mere 2 feet above the rock fangs, the creaking flake had held, his only injury a broken finger.'

  Second ascent attempt.

I fell for it big time. It suited me and I seemed to have the head for it. I could also crimp hard, which was by far the most important asset when wobbling up a slab 20 feet above a marginal RP. My first E6s on-sight were there. *Flashdance-Belldance* was a big one for me, my first E6 and a good option in that it was basically two E5s on top of each other, *Flashdance* leading into an E3 at half-height and *Belldance* breaking out from it (the E3 is *Comes the Dervish*). *Flashdance* is very bold, and, in fact, a solo with my substandard gear. *Belldance* is harder and very bold too, but theoretically not death due to the very good protection at half-height.

  After Flashdance I couldn't resist. E6 was calling. Razor blade edges took me to the roof and a relatively simple pull over, but a confusion in the guide between Tim and I took me back into the middle of the slab which was totally wrong. I made some hard moves, totally committed myself and realised I was totally wrong. Thin flakes snapped off and moss laid on the edges, untouched by humans. However, I could see a potential line. A desperate rock-over to a nothing edge with a 15-metre pendulum potential over a slab took me to more nothing holds that I'd prayed would be good. I got really worried here but had to press on, but moving awkwardly I lost my feet and had to resort to a totally desperate slap and then it was all over, on-sight E6 with death finish. I was well chuffed.

  Walking out we met Bob Drury and he'd seen me on the whole route and was well impressed and kept on going on about how crazy I was and what a crazy finish I'd done. By the time he left my ego was so high it was on Mars, and Tim kept on telling me I was in with the big boys now.

Slate is a hard medium: there is little below E1. Often the moves are not difficult but are in a dicey situation. Where the moves are safe, especially if a bolt had been placed, they tend to be desperate. Slate was like that, it was developed by the slate-heads at the time and it was their gig. Movement on slate requires an understanding with the rock, knowing when to place faith in friction and when to burn rubber ('To climb so fast that your shoes start smoking.' Paul Williams guide, 1987). You need your own 'slate head' too, often running it out forever in crazy positions, maybe on easy ground knowing there was no option to fluff it but at the same time knowing you wouldn't fluff it. Slate demands a new skill set, there are few intermediates and little friction. Short climbers are punished by long reaches and tall climbers by bunched rockovers. For the aspiring hard man, slate is exciting, as famous desperates mingle alongside amenable classic plods. From your line of jugs you can glance over to the blank non-line where an outrageous E7 is supposed to go. I was blown away by how hard the hard stuff looked and it was here that I planted some seeds for the future, building threads of a relationship with cutting edge routes totally out of my league. When the time was right I would call on connections I'd already formed to give me that little bit of extra drive and psyche that is so essential when pushing to the limit. We watched Johnny Dawes on *The Very Big and the Very Small*, which was to become the world's hardest slab in 1990 at 8c, and we stared for hours at *The Quarryman*. Lying near the gaping drop of Twll Mawr (Big Hole) we'd toss rocks over the edge and watch them spin away forever. *The Quarryman* rose from the depths of the hole following an outrageous line on the huge back wall. This was *the* slate route, at the time cutting edge, and made famous by the first real climbing film *Stone Monkey*. *The Quarryman* epitomises everything that is slate; it has it all. Even today it is the stand-out route in the quarries. It blew me away and it was my dream to try it, but that's as far as it went – a dream.

Climbing with new people opened my eyes to hard climbing and what was possible, both for the heroes and also for myself, though overall I chose not to see that much. There were a lot of big names here and a lot more passing through who glossed the magazines on a monthly basis. At the cliff I could match them, or at least wasn't far behind. This was puzzling. What separated us? What made them superstars whilst I was a bumbly? Though I could see the potential to climb hard I couldn't make the leap, not yet. My background was rooted in the rule that 'the leader never falls', or put another way, 'the leader never goes for it'. Though I'd pushed the rule slightly I rarely rocked the boat. I didn't commit to hard moves, even with bolt protection, only really pressing on if I thought I could reverse. Being strong, fit and technically good is one thing, not that I was, but at the end of the day climbing hard is all about trying hard and going for it. I watched as the dudes slapped wildly on projects and took whippers across the slate walls and I could see it was a 'strength' that I didn't possess. They had tenacity and focus, the ability and drive to explore the limits, and a complete and intimate understanding of the safety chain. Everything seemed different to my world of climbing, the pace and flow of movement, the speed of placing protection and clipping the rope. Even the belaying was different, totally attentive and a real team effort with encouragement and advice if needed. Slack was paid out for a clip in two huge armfuls, the belayer anticipating the exact moment it was needed. At least we took that on board – no more snaggy clips for us while we screamed for slack.

I could see the difference now, what separated me from the hard climbing world, and the gap was huge. It's not like I could flick a switch and suddenly become awesome; it doesn't just 'happen'. Seeing it was crucial, a visual display telling way more than words could ever convey. Now I knew the secret, it was just a matter of learning how to use it.

I could have lived in North Wales. With so much going on, so much climbing, and a scene that suited my personality it would have been an easy move. But I'd committed to Sheffield University and, despite Llanberis being fairly close to perfect, I'd never questioned my decision. Like North Wales, a hitch to Sheffield and climbing in the nearby Peak District still held out against a visit, waiting for the right moment despite being probably the closest and easiest place to reach from Teesside. A bunch of my college friends went to university a year earlier than me and a good few had gone to Sheffield, making it an easy visit. Actually, let's be honest here, they hadn't gone earlier than me, I'd gone late. I hadn't got the A-Level results I needed to get to Sheffield University to study mechanical engineering. My results of B, D and D were apparently enough to enrol on the four other university choices I'd made on the application form, but I'd clearly made these choices simply to fill the form as rather than taking a place at Newcastle or Manchester or even Leeds, I chose to stay an entire extra year in Teesside and re-sit my A-Level exams. There was really only ever one choice – I was desperate to get to Sheffield. In some ways this worked in my favour. The extra year was a piece of cake in terms of studying and I can't imagine I got anything less than 99 per cent in the exams (I got As). This had given me the time to climb a lot and visit lots of places as my friends populated all corners of the country. Ste, in particular, had laid the path for me in Sheffield, and being psyched for climbing he made a trip to the Peak an easy ride. He had all the knowledge and I just held his hand. My first visit had me gibbering with excitement, like a kid at Disneyland. We caught the bus to Hathersage and hiked back up the road towards the crag.

> Looking up from the road I could see Millstone and could pick out London Wall. Before I knew it I was standing right under it, amazing but there was no way I was going to try it. Moving on we passed Scritto's Republic which looked impossible and then Master's Edge and the death E5s. Everything looked really hard or impossible, and everything had death potential.

The Peak was all I imagined it to be and more. The scale seemed colossal and history poured out from every crack and groove. From high up on the tops around Stanage there seemed to be famous crags everywhere I looked.

Burbage South looked even better in the sun and I was itching to try everything. We started on Millwheel Wall (E1) which I nearly did but bottled at the top. After rigging a top rope I realised I should have been brave. I then top-roped an E3 6a next to it and was amazed to do it. Either I was climbing brilliantly or the grades were easy (definitely the grades). We wandered around and I did my first 5c on-sight on gritstone. Next I just had to try Offspring after seeing it on the film Stone Monkey. The top-rope was rigged and I lowered into place where Johnny Dawes had started in the video. The first move was hard but suddenly I was in position for the leap. I psyched up and then leaped and there was the top. I realised the route was no way E6 6b, it must have started up from the ground up a vague arête. I lowered down but couldn't do a single move. That put me in my place.

(The route I top-roped was, in fact, the exact line of *Offspring*. The direct was unclimbed and was later to become *Captain Invincible*, E8 6c.)

Before even setting foot in Sheffield I knew I wanted to move there and my visits from Teesside totally confirmed this. The Peak was amazing, but perhaps, more importantly, I'd sampled a ready-made scene that I could drop straight into. My good mates had been there a whole year, they knew the score, they were invited to all the best parties and they knew the bouncers at the clubs. There would be no fresh-faced fresher bollocks for me, no 'Hi there, I'm Steve, where are you from? I'm doing engineering so I must be a dork.' There would be no need to make friends with people who were obviously total knobs while standing lonely at a party. I'd be straight in with the dudes and the dudes knew all the crags, all the routes and the scene. Leaving home to go to university is probably a fairly stressful time for most students, but as the time drew closer I felt like I was about to embark on a massive climbing holiday for the rest of my life.

Sheffield is the Holy Grail for climbers, our Mecca, drawing us in. Climbing seems to hang in the air, its presence surrounding the roads and houses and seeping from the gritstone walls that edge parks and cobbled streets. There is a smell, definitely, in the same way there is a 'sea air' near the coast. There is the smell of the Peak and gritstone, especially in the autumn. I arrived as a student just as the leaves began to turn and carpet the streets in orange and gold. Out at Burbage the bracken died off to brown and helped colour the cliff edges in inviting soft shades. It was everything I had dreamed of. In all my years of climbing I'd only climbed around Sheffield twice, taken out by Ste and his uni friends. Now that I was there, now that I lived there, now that I belonged there, things were different. These were my crags now, my locals. I felt elevated in status without even ticking a route.

At the university freshers' fair, where all the clubs showed their wares and enticed new recruits, I confidently made my way direct to the climbing club, bypassing everything else without a glance. Running, tennis, drama, art, cycling … nothing was registering in the interest spectrum. Battling through the punters to the desk I waited my turn behind people who were clearly only signing up to tick boxes and get laid. Eventually I made it. Question one: 'are you already a climber?' Good question I suppose, separating the wheat from the chaff. Question two: 'what grade do you climb.' More forward maybe, but I answered honestly without knowing whether it was best to big myself up or go in low. 'About HVS maybe, on-sight, solo on the grit. I did *Flying Buttress Direct* last week.'

'Ah yeah, normal entry level then. Not bad as a start level. Sign these bits and we'll see if we can squeeze you on some meets coming up.'

'Entry level' seemed slightly harsh. I guessed he thought I was showing off and put me down and in my place. As it turned out HVS was somewhere beyond entry level for this particular so-called climbing club. In fact, any level would have been good, even climbing the stairs, as most people seemed to struggle to actually enter into any kind of climbing whatsoever. My first and only club meet was away in North Wales and was basically some kind of drinking mission where the evening's activities determined the pecking order to be adopted on the cliff. Being the loudest and most pissed was apparently an indication of climbing ability, though at the cliff, despite still being loud, there was little that impressed. A day at the crag was got out of the way as fast as possible in order to get back to the real reason we'd come away, which was to get smashed and tell exaggerated tales about climbing experiences that most likely were only ever dreamed up.

It was a rubbish start but I was still mad for it. Between the autumn showers I cycled out from Crewe Flats halls of residence to Burbage and Rivelin. Burbage, North or South, became my standard destination. It was the easiest cycle ride, with Stanage, Froggatt or Curbar being just that bit too far, and held enough history to keep me more than occupied. I soloed my way through the classics and occasionally pushed into the Extremes, *The Sentinel* and *Millwheel Wall* giving me a flutter and *Pebble Mill* being a step into the big numbers (E5).

That first year autumn held on well into November and I slowly became fluent in grit, leaving behind the sandstone of the North York Moors. Early trips in my teens with parents to Slipstones, Almscliff and Brimham in the Yorkshire Dales had been a sharp slap in the face, the gritstone feeling untranslateable, a world of subtlety that I couldn't fathom. Now slowly it was coming together. I almost managed *Blind Date*, or at least the start, UK 7a and a benchmark. *West Side Story* was close too, a different proposition back then for repeated attempts without pads. When the winter hit, climbing started to become hard work, with good days rarely coinciding with the weekends and always seeming to coincide with other more important or inescapable social activities. As the first term wound into Christmas it was all about parties and staggering around wasted.

There was no winter transition to indoors as there *was* no indoors, not like now. The stone walls of Broomgroove Road university building and Crewe Flats squash court were my only options and I spent countless hours traversing across the quarried gritstone blocks. The builders had done a great job, accidentally creating a crimpy technical masterpiece at around 7c. Both made for perfect training, in fact, perfect climbing. Catching winter sun, sheltered from the wind and minutes from where I lived these 'outdoor crags' gained a special place in my heart. I still chuckle at the thought of shaking out pumped arms and glancing back to see a bunch of foreign students standing beside me, on their way to class and wondering just what the hell I was doing. When Crewe wall was knocked down some years ago I was gutted, but Broomgrove lives on for all.

Over the coming year I fell into a turbulent love affair with Peak gritstone. We were up and down. I gained strength, tuned into the friction and began to understand the flow, but was frustrated and never felt that I'd found my true love. Part of the problem was transport and, without a car or enough knowledge of what was right on my doorstep, I fell into a rut. I never discovered Cratcliffe or The Roaches, never came close to the traditional limestone, and the sport limestone remained so firmly in the magazines that it might as well have been in a different country. Without knowing just how close they were I never pushed to go. If I had known I'd have made it happen: hitching, cycling, on the bus, whatever. I'd have dropped into a scene and it would have started from there. But the spark that was there just didn't quite light the flame. The easy pickings on my closest crags I took early, leaving me with only the tough ones – those that needed a different level of psyche to what I'd summon up during an afternoon's wandering with a bunch of chilled dudes. Ste from college was usually in the team, as well as John Bedford (the ultimate stoner) and

Tony (the ultimate healthy cyclist). A fine selection of randoms totally unsuited to each others' company but brought together by the rock. I'd lead, they would follow. Two ends of the difficulty spectrum compromising in the middle as I dragged them up E2s and the odd E3. Occasionally I'd push into E5, but it was a self-induced psyche with no real interest from the team. Sometimes it's tough to continually find the motivation when the psyche has gone and the time is edging towards a beer and a chill.

But the real problem was style, both in the climbing itself and my approach to the routes. On-sight was what I strived for – first go, no inspection. Set off from the ground and aim for the top, taking on the full challenge and figuring it out on the way. This is traditional climbing in its best form, but this style is tough on gritstone, where the complex friction moves are desperate to read first go. It takes real expertise to understand if a smear will stick and then to trust everything to the bite between rubber and rock. In addition, the nature of the gritstone edges means that as the climbing difficulty rises, the danger keeps pace. In fact, it usually outstrips it and I was struggling to find routes to test my on-sight ability without unacceptable levels of risk. The Great Slab routes and *Green Death* would all go if I just plucked up the courage, and I'd eyed up the finishing holds on *Edge Lane* and *Mint 400* many times before giving in to the down-climb.

Sometimes a top-rope would be rigged to play in safety, but this was an admission of failure, unlike for many people where it's the start of a process and the only considered sequence of events. This process is the 'headpoint': leading a bold route from the ground after top rope practice, like a redpoint but with the bolts replaced by danger. I'd climbed in this headpoint style before, *Magic in the Air* on the North York Moors was a great experience and there had been a few others around Teesside, but critically these little projects had been 'relatively' safe. They had been about pushing myself in a scary situation, but never facing a death fall. I'd watched the North Wales boys going for it on slate and in the mountains, pushing themselves to the limit and taking huge falls, but always being saved by the rope. It was intense and scary but I could understand it; I could see it was a skill I could learn. The really bold stuff on the grit was at another level, with high up and hard-to-read balance and friction moves above guaranteed full body smashers. I didn't really get it. I wanted to, and worshipped the heroes who seemed capable of operating at their physical limits whether there was a rope from above or no rope at all. It allowed them to take something more from climbing, making it an intense exercise in remaining calm and focused in an extreme situation. This was a different skill I knew I simply didn't possess and would never be able to learn. The buzz of keeping it together didn't seem justifiable relative to the risk of everything turning pear-shaped. That was basically it: keeping it together. It was all in the mind, with moves rehearsed until wired. As a climber you knew you'd not fall off before you even left the ground. You had to know, because if you actually thought you'd actually fall you were staring straight into hell. For me, the chances of a fall had to be so close to zero that I had to question the point of doing it at all. Perhaps the crazy heads could push it further, maybe a 10 per cent chance of a fall would be worth it and give the desired thrill. I've even heard of people setting off above guaranteed death without even being capable of the climbing, hoping the extra incentive would somehow get them through. I looked on in both amazement and disappointment – for me it was the wrong sport. I'd surrounded myself with a style of climbing at which I'd never be any good.

I would top-rope a route once I'd decided it was out of my league, just to see what hard climbing was all about and whether I should have plucked up the courage after all. Many of the big routes from the stars, Moffatt, Pollitt and Dunne, carried a status that placed them in the out-of-league cabinet regardless of difficulty. *Messiah* shocked me with its difficulty. It would never have gone first go – I could barely do the moves – and *Parthian Shot* could never have been considered. Just playing on these routes was humbling, but it was the Dawes routes that always carried a real aura, standing proud like abstract artwork and drawing the eye from surrounding corners and arêtes. Lines painted by water and wind that required movement by skill and flow. You could see why Johnny had been drawn to them; just pulling on holds was not the answer. It took soul searching to feel worthy of play, like you had to be invited by nature. You needed to be up to scratch, to flounder and polish the surface would be an insult to the rock. *The Braille Trail* was top-roped cleanly first go but the lead was never on. A route like that deserves more respect than repeated top-ropes to a guaranteed outcome.

Some routes I should have saved for the lead. I blew *Perplexity* and *Balance It Is* with a rope from above. Fortunately most I did save and years later, after gaining greater strength and skill, *Cool Moon*, *Mint 400*, *London Pride* and *Top Loader* were all on-sighted smoothly.

Alongside the danger lay some difficult but protectable gems much more suited to my style. It was just a matter of seeking them out and building the psyche. *White Wall* and *Strapadictomy* were some of the first, and, with their safety nets, *Profit of Doom*, *Coventry Street* and *Bat out of Hell* were all easy. *London Wall* was the perfect challenge, ticking all my boxes: physically hard (it's about a 7a+ sport grade) with good but hard-earned protection. You can place as much as you like – if you can hang on long enough. So the key is to continually assess energy reserves and difficulty against acceptable risk. It's the leader's choice whether to burn energy and make it safe but risk failing through fatigue, or to run it out, accept more danger and perhaps have more chance of success. I managed the on-sight after a fight and wanted more of the same but, overall, grit was the wrong rock type for my passion. I looked back on my early days in Pembroke and Wales with fondness, and forward to the hard sport routes that filled the pages of the press.

Hubble went down around this time at the limestone sport climbing cliff of Raven Tor – a very different style of route to the gritstone epics. Ben Moon's big statement to the world, it was the hardest route in the known universe at 8c+, the first of its grade and absolutely miles ahead of its time. Probably 9a and Font 8B+ it still sees few ascents.

I watched Ben's event from a distance via *Climber* and *High* magazines, even though it was all going down just 15 miles from where I lived. I viewed it like the first lunar landing, overwhelmed by what had been given to mankind, a monumental advance that was the result of masses of hard work and dedication. It inspired me on a new level, a new style of climbing that grabbed hold of me and inflamed my desire.

Sport climbing had been cool for a while but rattled under my radar. It didn't quite seem to fit with my ethics and, perhaps more importantly, looked way too hard. Now, having sampled gritstone and its big bold lines and left with my tail between my legs, I shunned my original aspirations and took a sideways glance into the world of the hard and safe.

Ironically, it took one of the most bouldery routes ever climbed to make me sit up and take interest. *Hubble* was a million miles from what I was doing and about as far away from my physical strengths as was possible, and yet I could see some kind of connection. It was what I looked for in climbing. It had always been about the movement for me, to really be climbing, tackling great hard routes. Not routes wrapped up and dominated by fear, but packed full of immersion and flow.

Once first year exams were out of the way and the summer holidays stretched out before me I knew exactly what I wanted: Pembroke, my old haunt, packed full of long routes, good gear and hard climbing. I had a few persuasive words with Ste, still carrying baggage from my accident a few years earlier, and after we'd signed on at the Sheffield dole office we hitched straight down. With time on our hands and as motivated as ever we were guaranteed to have fun.

Ste racked up, a jumble of unmatching gear placed haphazardly on his second-hand harness. It was the racking system of a climber more used to gritstone, used to having time to sort out the mess from comfortable ledges and placing bomber gear in predictable cracks before short sections of on-off friction wobbling. Watching him closely, it struck me that maybe he was not really a climber, more of a good mate who'd been dragged into it when too many of his friends had been too keen. I always felt it was my passion that I'd pushed on to him, adamant that climbing was the best sport in the world and assuming everybody else must surely love it. But for Ste climbing was never the main event and there were a few close calls. His first rope was state-of-the-art, a sub-9-millimetre trad rope that I kind of persuaded him to buy, mine being all fluffy and nicked from my dad. We took it straight to Burbage and set up a swing on the Cioch Block. After just one swing each (a good one though, getting miles above the ground) we retrieved the rope to find it totally trashed in two places, with only three strands of the core left. Ste had no choice but to chop his new rope into three fairly useless 15-metre lengths. Climbing and Ste just weren't cut out to be a couple.

It hadn't been easy to get Ste back to Pembroke, and that's forgetting the double-day hitching nightmare that was guaranteed. Our previous big trip, two years ago with Dave and Tim, had been eventful to say the least, with a couple of incidents that could turn anyone to somewhere more comfortable. Halfway through the trip Ste had to point out the amount of mud on the back of my neck which had built up from dozing in the dirt under the priest's old house. We bought some soap and scrubbed ourselves in the river near Bosherston. Then a week into the trip Ste took a block on his foot. I saw it sail through the air, the size of a shoebox, dislodged from high up on *Deranged*, a classic E2 at St Govan's Head. Watching it aim directly for Ste, the calculation of size, lack of helmet and type of injury looked bad. Somehow it missed his head but seemed to land square on his foot. As I ran over to assess the damage it was clear it wasn't good, but there had not been a direct hit or the whole foot would have gone. A bunch of stitches at Haverfordwest hospital were required, plus a week of not being able to wear a climbing shoe and not being able to climb, which I doubt was a major hardship. Ste had to endure sunbathing on the beach, snapping photos, and spending evenings with us getting wasted in the barn and stumbling over to the St Govan's Inn for endless games of pool. It was probably more of the holiday he wanted to be honest. Later on at the end of the trip I made sure it was definitely the end with my monster fall from *Blue Sky*. This experience had been pretty harrowing, though at the time I hadn't considered the effects on the others involved. I'd got away with it, kind of, and assumed we'd all just forget about it and live happily ever after. But it's often the observer who has to deal with the aftermath, the one who really sees the horror unfolding. Memories run deep and are never erased. As I brushed myself down Ste was carried along with a different point of view.

Now we were back at St Govan's Head, the sounds and feel of the place seeping into us as we gazed upwards at the vastness of the cliff. To our sides, rock stretched out for miles and behind us the jumbles of house-sized blocks, usually pounded by Atlantic waves, were sitting relaxed in a gently lapping millpond. Over the last few days Ste had been climbing well, we both had, encouraging each other into big leads. As usual I was doing the pushing, pushing myself, pushing Ste, because I thought that was what he wanted, what he needed to take his climbing to the next level. As a steady HVS leader it was time to take the next step, the big one into E1, into the Extremes. This is a milestone in every climber's life. I wanted Ste to make the step, to feel the elation and accomplishment. I even chose the route, *The Arrow*, E1 5b, a total classic. I'd done it before, a few times. It begins with an easy wall rising out from a jumble of car-sized rounded boulders. After about 4 metres comes a wide ledge, the start of the route proper. Here it kicks in with some steep climbing leading to a bulge at around 8 metres. Reaching around this is probably the crux of the whole route, stretching up for a small ledge. Then it's a romp to the top, 20 metres of impeccable and well-protected climbing.

At the big ledge Ste fumbled in protection. It was taking a while, bits going in and being taken out again to be replaced by smaller and smaller bits. Eventually, the placement was abandoned and a new one sought out. I vaguely remembered the same problem, having to force something in way out to the side, unhappy to commit to the moves without something decent between me and the ground. Something stirred in my stomach, a feeling of unease. This came to me occasionally, but here, in Pembroke, and here with Ste, it was stronger and more foreboding. I observed it, but didn't act on it. I hadn't been to Pembroke since my accident on *Blue Sky* two years ago and now my memories flooded back. They often did, sometimes in slow motion when I had time to spare, often speeded up, fast forwarding through the events like a warning.

My mind snapped back as Ste struggled with his jumble of wires, the need for attentive belaying suddenly more important. I'd got away with my accident, a mere punctured lung and a few weeks recovering in hospital. I should have been dead. The fall and the impact were enough to do the job, and when they didn't, the sea should have taken me. My body had been spared and did recover, but my mind was still on edge, aware of the vulnerability of the human form. At the time I didn't think it had affected me much and that I could just sweep it under the carpet and carry on as normal, but every now and again I'd feel the fear surround me, a sharp awareness of consequence rather than assuming everything would always go according to plan.

Ste had done as well as he could with the rack he had and was now left with the psyching up, assessing difficulty against protection, reward against risk, choosing whether to set off. Apparently it was worth it, in that moment at least, and he committed to the bulge, aiming quickly for the small ledge. He reached it, but faltered. There should be good holds there, but he'd not found them. 'It's wet here.' I was suddenly alert, hands gripping on the 9-millimetre ropes that I fed out in precise amounts, my mind focused on both the climbing movement and the single lonely wire that was suddenly looking wholly inadequate.

Disco leg.

'It's really wet, I can't get onto this ledge, watch me here.'

'With you mate, good holds coming … '

Ste was getting really worried, he tried to move up but couldn't, so he went into reverse mode but that wasn't working either. I watched his feet flicking around, his toes searching for a hold – none. Now I began to feel the fear down the rope and I could see his panic, thrutching hands, shaking. Suddenly he was in real trouble, shouted that he was going, and then he was off. I watched in slow motion as he peeled off backwards and waited for the rope to go tight but it never did, the wire leaving the rock like it had been held on with Blu-Tack.

First impact was with the ledge, some kind of thud and then a limp body, all limbs coming at me, filling my whole view. He landed within inches, almost on top of me, then bounced into the boulders taking the hopeless wire with him. It was the sound that was intense, like dropping a full El Cap rack on a concrete slab from 1,000 metres. The crash echoed in my head as the view of Ste face down beside me sunk in. No movement.

I rolled him over in fear of what I would see. Two eyes staring up with nothing in them, but a deep hole in between that said it all. There were white bits and other bits sticking out before the blood came.

First thought – dead. Second thought – not dead. There was a twitch, but this was not survivable. A horrible hopeless feeling enveloped me as time took on a whole new meaning and I observed the inevitable. Then suddenly there were people around. A pad went on to stop the blood flow. By now it oozed and trickled around us, small streams of dark red appeared in the distance. It covered everything, there was just so much of it; more than there could be in a person. Someone was off to raise the alarm and I held onto Ste, feeling useless as others did essential jobs. More people around us now, nervous about getting involved, but I appreciated their presence. I didn't know what was going to happen. There had been a lot of groans and then a few words, but all disconnected, nothing to give encouragement.

'Talk to him, keep him with you.'

I questioned him about irrelevant stuff, anything, trying to get an answer even if it was just a moan, fearful that if he dropped out of consciousness that would be it.

The clatter of the helicopter could not have been more of a relief, quiet and distant at first but ramping in volume to explode as the bulk of the chopper cleared the cliff edge above. They'd arrived in amazing time, being on nearby training exercises. As the stretcher dropped in and activity suddenly went into a frenzy Ste began to fit, shaking uncontrollably and wailing.

It was really awkward getting him onto the stretcher so in the end everyone just picked him up and lobbed him in. The guys fastened him down and I sat right in front of him, staring into his face. All the bandages had come off now and I could see the hole between his eyes. He was unconscious and his breathing wasn't encouraging, sounding like he was breathing through a half full snorkel. Blood still poured from his head and from his mouth and nose. He wasn't moving at all now and couldn't respond at all. Then suddenly the winch took him out and up and away and I was pretty sure that was it. The end.

Many hours later we were given the news. Neutral I guess. Not dead, but not stable. Of course, they were doing all they could. Time passed slowly and the hospital waiting room grew more uncomfortable, but there was nowhere else to go. More news: not going to die. Probable brain damage. What kind of news was that? Good, neutral or bad? I wasn't sure. Now we had to wait. They would keep him in an induced coma for nearly a week, to let the swelling go down. We'd know nothing until after that.

His parents had to be told. I couldn't do it. I passed the buck to my dad. Totally unfair, but the job was beyond me. My mum and dad happened to be in Pembroke at the same time on a CMC club meet and we'd kind of co-ordinated our dates, knowing that they'd be useful to be around, a kind of climbers' version of taking your student washing home every half term. It had been my dad who had been first on the scene; he'd been watching us climb from the top of the cliff. He'd helped stabilise the bleeding, run to raise the alarm, come back to help with the rescue, driven me to the hospital and now dealt with the horrible task of telling Ste's folks. He'd been critical in every part of the event. He probably saved Ste's life. Ste's parents came straight away, holing up next to the hospital and by his side every possible moment, looking for something, a clue as to what might be left. They didn't blame me, of course. That's what they said, but how could a parent not blame?

Seven days later and he'd been conscious for two. Very shaky at first, but still 'there'. We watched for signs, stressing over jumbled sentences and out of sequence memories. But slowly Ste was coming back. Another week later he was flown to Teesside Hospital. I hitched up to visit, I could have stayed in Pembroke, but there was nothing for me now. Something had changed forever. Climbing took a back seat for a while. It was easy to let it go with so many other things in my life at that time: parties, travelling, hanging out in bars. I ventured out occasionally to the cliffs, but it was an ordeal. I wasn't enjoying it. My climbing was lumpy, hesitant and without any ambition, but worse was my place in a partnership. The fear of someone hurting themselves was always lurking, I became the world's worst belayer. As soon as someone suggested they were up for something bold I'd be onto them. 'Looks wet mate, gear looks bad too. Getting late as well … '

My definition of acceptable risk changed again. I felt like I'd been on a path my whole climbing life, searching out what I wanted from climbing and trying to fathom an acceptable level of risk, balancing it with the elation of success. This was another lesson, but a big one, perhaps the final lecture I'd need to discover my own meaning of the sport. We go through our climbing lives taking risks, balancing them against rewards, but few of us really know the actual outcome of failure. We can vaguely imagine it. We try to discuss it – 'That's ankle-breaking height for sure', 'A fall from there will be really nasty', 'It's certain death for sure on this route.' – but we brush it off, because we haven't seen it, we can't relate to it. It doesn't seem like it will happen. But I had seen it. It was real.

I'd be quick to set up a top-rope, and still enjoyed the movement. The climbing part of me still longed for it but the traditional climbing environment was no longer leisure. I let it go.

Ste made a full recovery. He lives in Sheffield, and has three happy kids. I see him a lot and we were in Pembroke again last year. He hasn't climbed since the accident.

Moving to Sheffield was probably the pivotal point in my life. There aren't many events that come close to paving your life compared to choosing where to live. You move from one place to the next and your entire world restarts with a different set of parameters. Much of 'you' is already set, but from your new ground zero you build friendships, careers and passions. Everything will be shaped by what is around you. I like pondering over this, wondering how different things would have been if I'd opened my suitcase in Leeds. I'd still be a climber but would I have taken a similar path; was it something I was destined to follow? I might have been a bumbly all my life with an eight-'til-six job in an office, or maybe I'd have got a head start, found a way into the scene much earlier. I might have been hanging with Ben and Jerry at the Tor and ticking the hard sport routes way back in 1990.

It was ironic that my choice of Sheffield University was based entirely on my desire to climb, but I then spent most of my university years doing almost no climbing at all. From my viewpoint, there wasn't much climbing to be done, not once I'd reached the edge of my rigidly enforced comfort zone. I was blinkered and lazy; un-ambitious and easily led. There was a much bigger world of climbing on my doorstep but I never managed to be at the right cliff with the right routes and the right people at the right time. Looking back I realise I should have tried harder.

But the accident in Pembroke was also pivotal. Perhaps not in paving my life, but in redirecting my climbing. Though as it's turned out, it could be argued that climbing is my life. At first it wasn't so obvious, I'd find myself at the familiar cliffs of Burbage and Stanage, perhaps through habit, but my intent was weak and excuses to leave easily found. In a way I went out just to validate myself, 'Hello, I'm here, I'm still a rock climber, but got to go now.' Gradually I let it all slip, it was easy to step away and I found new non-climbing doors opening before me with inviting stuff behind them.

Once I'd come to terms with what I assumed would be a temporary fall-out with climbing, the fun could really start. Living together with a good bunch of mates on Freedom Road in Sheffield was a first term riot. Autumn came in a rush, soaked in dampness and shrouded by mist and I didn't give climbing a second thought – but then second thoughts were hard to come by considering the quality of this particular magic mushroom growing season.

We picked them by the field load and visited whole new worlds probably too many times. Our cellar was coloured in ultra violet paint and lit with a UV tube and a strobe. The Orb provided the soundtrack. Parties came thick and fast with our poor neighbour, Gladys, fortunately deaf, telling us each time to, 'make as much noise as you can'.

But I'd chosen the wrong university course for the professional waster or potential dirtbag climber and could never get completely involved. Sheffield University had a top-three reputation in the UK for mechanical engineering and it made its students work for that, obviously keen to hold its position. Nine until five, five days a week with a shit load of homework, additional holiday studies and a heap of exams. From February onwards, basically as soon as the weather came good, life was all books and thermo-dynamics and material science. As the year wrapped up, with everybody else heading into summer and juggling in the park with cans of Stella and a picnic blanket, my work placements began, a whole holiday evaporating in a sweaty office in Portsmouth. Full-time, five days a week, no escape whatsoever. Without a car, weekends were barely better than work days.

My final year surprised me with the amount of work I was willing to endure. Strangely I seemed focused and determined on getting a good degree despite the fact I already knew without a shadow of doubt there was no way I was ever going to use it – not if being an engineer meant wearing a tie and sitting in an office wishing most of my life away. I'd learnt that much from my work placement at least, though I'm not sure it was the desired outcome. I stuck with the studying and, walking out from my final exam, I was without doubt the cleverest I've ever been and ever will be, with a ridiculous amount of knowledge somehow wedged into my tiny little brain. Unfortunately it would all tumble out before I'd even made the cycle ride home, but it was an incredible feeling and I knew I'd done well. When the results came I was happy with my 2:1, but slightly miffed with an overall score of 69.8 per cent when the pass mark for a first class degree was 70 per cent. When the breakdown dropped onto my doormat I couldn't help but notice my outstandingly low mark in 'Solar and Wind Energy', the lowest mark in the entire year in a subject that was a complete piece of piss. At around 30 per cent I couldn't imagine how I'd got less than 80 per cent, and, in fact, I'd known so much stuff that during the exam itself I left a few pages' gap after the first question before moving on to the second and third so I could come back and add even more knowledge … ah!

I went to my tutor, ironically the solar and wind lecturer who was most puzzled by my score, until noticing the overall mark. Then it was suddenly case closed, nothing could be done, apparently all the papers had been

shredded immediately. I coped with that. It's only a number after all;
an interesting comparison with the world of rock climbing grades.
Compared to the boffin mature students on the course I didn't really
deserve a first class degree anyway. It's only later that you learn about quotas
and ratings and how the system works and that PhD students with
hangovers mark your work and give scores based on handwriting, and that
papers are definitely NOT shredded after marking.

During my final term a funny thing happened: The Foundry opened –
the UK's first dedicated climbing facility. It was awesome. Just down the
road from where I lived and packed full of brilliant routes. Not a training
facility in my eyes, but a whole new crag, with steep and hard routes to test
me without a hint of death. The rock stars were there too. I saw Jerry Moffatt
from a distance and hid in case he saw me. When Ben Moon said 'Hello'
I couldn't think of anything to say and just stared blankly at him before
running into the toilets. I watched Simon Nadin fall off a 7b and then
I moved in when he'd gone. Putting in the fight of my life I got the on-sight
and so for an instant was better than him (and he was a previous world
champion), even though it was probably the last route of his day and
probably his hundredth day on. The scene was great: loads of people,
all motivated and friendly, and I was hanging with dudes who seemed
capable of crimping on nothing, banging out problems on the famous
'Wave' using holds I could barely even see, never mind pull on. Inspired,
my physical strength skyrocketed. With renewed psyche from grabbed
sessions between revising I felt I was discovering climbing again, but
with a whole new twist. The addictive movement was pulling at me,
even though it wasn't even on real rock, and I welcomed it like an old
friend. But the real excitement came from leading up insanely steep terrain
without a jot of fear. Or at least that's how it seemed. I still backed off when
a fall looked likely, shouted 'take' when my arms gave out and would grab a
quickdraw rather than accept a lob – but the fear was completely different
to my usual whimpering on gritstone wobblers. Just as I'd trusted the top-
roping system as a child I now trusted this indoor leading system completely.
Being an engineer I understood how it worked, knew the strength of the
materials, knew there would be no failure, just as I understood how natural
protection could come out and bits of rock could unexpectedly snap.

The break from climbing had probably done me good. For a start I'd
focused on my degree, but it had also been a time of reconciliation,
allowing my aspirations in climbing to orient themselves without
being influenced in one direction or another. The Foundry was the jump
start I needed and allowed a glimpse of a style I'd only but dreamt of.

It was my entrance point back into climbing and with bold, traditional climbing completely removed from the equation, at least temporarily, my view shifted. It became simpler and clearer and so much more suited to my personality. It became obvious. Suddenly I was as keen as ever. Old magazines were found under the sofa and re-read, and new ones were hotly anticipated. Guidebooks were dusted off and objectives came back into view. I wanted to climb all the time and was surprised at how much I'd shut it out. It seemed such an integral part of my personality.

I wanted hard stuff, to push myself physically, I wanted to be strong and fit and to throw myself at the outrageous terrain decorating the glossy pages of the magazines.

I took out an extra student loan on the very last day of my student life to pay for an immediate departure on a six-week trip to the south of France and when I came back to Sheffield I signed on at the dole office. It was the first stage of my apprenticeship in being a full-time, dirtbag climber. And, of course, every strong and serious climber needed a cellar. By now the secret was out: it was impossible to get strong without spending countless hours hanging from little bits of wood in a damp Sheffield cellar above a moulding mattress dragged out of a skip. I blagged some half-inch ply sheets from a building site, lugged them home and chopped them up with a blunt handsaw. I cut some holes for handholds and then set about fixing the boards to the wooden roof joists. This was going to be awesome. I could see my grade flying. Balancing one end of the panel precariously on a heap of tables and pushing the other up against the cellar roof joists with one hand, I slowly pinned the boards into place with a shoddy screwdriver. Twist by twist the roof took shape; closer and closer to awesome power. Tough work – a bonus maybe? Free training before I'd even started. My arms were getting a thorough work-out. In fact, I'd never been so pumped. All this screwing work was screwing with my forearms. It must have taken all day to place a good few hundred screws, standing on my tiptoes. Talk about power endurance training. Next day I was still pumped and, strangely, also the day after, though the pump seemed to have kind of moved out of my forearms and intensified into my elbows. It was a different kind of pump too, actually more of an all-out pain, a kind of pain I hadn't experienced before and the kind of pain that was becoming increasingly obvious as the kind of pain that means 'you've just fucked your elbows up completely.'

In true climber style I tried to cure the problem with a few sessions down at The Foundry. I'd have used my new awesome training roof facility except I couldn't support my own weight or hold my arms above my head for more than about three seconds. Funnily enough the climbing sessions didn't work – a lesson that, despite being taken probably hundreds of times since then, I've still never quite managed to grasp. It may be obviously stupid, but it still seems sensible to ignore any symptoms completely in the hope that they will just disappear by themselves. Eventually I realised the game was up when I couldn't even lift a kettle or sleep properly, but even then it took a cycling accident to finish it. Pedalling hard down the super steep Hoole Street in Walkley I hit about 55 kilometres-per-hour before pulling hard on the brakes as I closed in on my rented house. This hurt my elbows like hell, but not for long, as the front brake cable snapped and the wire loop between the brake cantilevers dropped neatly onto the heavily knobbled front tyre stopping it instantly. As would be expected I continued at roughly the same speed, up and over the bars and then through the air in some kind of Superman pose, flying down the middle of the street with no kind of landing plan whatsoever. The resulting bad back was relatively minor, but put me out long enough to realise that my elbows were well and truly broken and that no amount of climbing wall therapy was ever going to fix them.

I saw two NHS physios, but as one strongly recommended deep 'frictions' to break scar tissue, and the other insisted I avoided any massage at all, they didn't really help. They both reckoned that doing absolutely zero exercise whatsoever for a very long time was the best plan, along with the old 'hot – cold' treatment to stimulate blood flow. The elbows needed be subjected to a temperature differential to kick start the blood and so I'd sit with a bag of frozen peas on one side and a bowl of red-hot water on the other – which inevitably would get tipped into my lap or left on the floor and kicked over later in a stoned stagger in search of late night munchies.

So my ambition of becoming a dossing climber had got off to a less than ideal start. Other dubious career paths appeared on the horizon – not that I was looking for them. A job as a 'calculator operator' brought in £2.60 per hour, a ridiculously small wage for a ridiculously crap job, basically adding up numbers all day on an oversized white calculator with big blue buttons. This wasn't really what I thought I was cut out to be doing. I needed something to fill the gap of climbing, but didn't really want to go down the proper job route quite yet, confident that my career as a climbing bum was my destiny and that I'd need to follow it for at least a few years. Conveniently, I didn't have to look any further than right in front of my face to find a solution – the parallel and actually pretty-similar life that my university mates were all still living. I'd been bouncing along the edge of it for the last three years of my life. This was the party life and right now it was getting pretty interesting. Acid House was flooding the scene and we were there right at the start. The 'Cyclone' was our baby, a big dance party rave in a hired room on the university main campus. Five hundred ravers freaking out to their own tunes, all spun right in front of their luminous painted faces. We organised the whole event, printing fliers, hiring lights and smoke machines, selling tickets and mixing the trance. We even handed out ice-pops, quick-frozen in a bucket of liquid nitrogen nicked from the chemistry lab. It was the ideal distraction for a while, knocking out these events every month or so and generally being too knackered to worry about my ability to hang on little crimps. Life was either extremely busy, extremely funny or fast asleep. In the end we got banned. Of course we did. It blatantly should not have been allowed.

From there the Sheffield scene split, either travelling into Asia for half-year stints or working in Holland in order to save enough money to travel into Asia. I put on my sheep costume and headed over to Holland. Looking back I'm pretty alarmed at my complete inability to even think for myself without the direction of climbing, as it's painfully obvious that Holland is about the bottom of the list of places that I'd like to live. Fortunately I realised this, though not for some time and it would be a lie to say I didn't have fun figuring it out. A team of us lived in a big rented flat, working in the flower fields by day and getting boxed by night. We earned exactly enough to spend all our wages partying, which seemed like a pretty good formula at the time, especially considering how funny life was. Still, after a while, laughing your head off for hours on end for no apparent reason can only be so much fun and I began to notice just how flat the world was, the highlight of my day being the slight downhill cycle ride on my way to work over the largest bridge in the area.

Back in Sheffield I still had my sheep costume on. Travelling seemed a good idea. It had a purpose – a gap year. That was surely long enough for my elbows to fix and, anyway, I did want to travel. Or at least I'd convinced myself that. India and Nepal are probably fairly poor choices for the climber (we are talking pre-Hampi days), but without rock climbing in the equation the mountains of the Himalaya shone through. The whole travelling sketch would be easy. I'd not be alone as I'd be travelling with my girlfriend. We'd been together for a couple of years and, with similar interests, had been funnelled into the same travelling route, along with a whole bunch of the Sheffield posse who'd be out there at the same time. We'd all be criss-crossing our way through Asia, meeting up now and then, only to branch out on different paths if we wanted, or to hang for a while if we didn't. It was uncharted territory but how hard could it be? We'd take it as it came and, all good mates, we'd hold each other's hands if they needed to be held. For the New Year of 1993-4 there would be no less than eight of the Sheffield posse, all giving it some on the beach dance floor at the New Year Party at Ko Pha Ngan in Thailand.

They say going travelling is going on a journey of self-discovery. That studenty thing needed for late teens or early twenties kids who don't know who the hell they are and have basically bumbled their way through life without daring to open any doors. Though my travelling wasn't a journey of self-discovery I was definitely looking for something. I'd lost my way. Right up until the end of university I'd followed some kind of path, not looking too far ahead, but somehow sure it continued into a happy place. I didn't need to 'find' myself. I felt I already knew the score and was confident in my ability to make things happen, even if it hadn't quite worked out and my nicely-defined path had petered out into a confusing maze. I'd been naive and relied heavily on rock climbing as a backbone to direction. Climbing gave me a purpose, a meaning to life no matter how vague my path through life became. Now, without climbing I stumbled into dead-ends and passed blindly through unmarked junctions. I'd lost my direction a little, but travelling was just about filling in a gap. Somehow my clouded state felt temporary – soon it would right itself and, out of the fog, I'd pick up the track again, clear and defined, and continue happily forward along it into the rest of my life.

13 INTO ASIA

Delhi Belly – the guaranteed illness when visiting India. No one can escape. However, being a scuzzy climber and well-used to eating in the dirt amidst the germs and stuff I figured I'd be fine. I prided myself on my cast iron stomach that never got sick, so it was a surprise to find myself slumped in the aeroplane toilet squirting out my insides even before I'd touched down in India. A great start to my half-year travelling trip. As we bumped onto the lost-in-the-past runway in Delhi my first and only thought was to find a toilet fast. This was to become a rather common theme during the trip and once home. I'd copped Delhi Belly big time, and no matter what I tried I just couldn't escape it. From then on every day began in the same way: the moment I passed from dreams into the real world the clock would start. I'd quickly shake myself awake and would have about 30 seconds, a minute on a good day. Easily long enough on the very rare occasion where there was an en suite toilet, but pushing it in sketchy guesthouses and scummy hotels with their shared facilities and long narrow corridors. Even worse when camping. By 5 seconds my clothes would be going on, 15 seconds and the sandals were velcroed up, eyes still not open. At this stage there was no apparent reason for the mad rush, but then it would start, a giant internal tsunami surging forwards and totally unstoppable. This massive stirring was the final warning. From there I'd have 10 seconds and the contents of my bowels would be out, no questions asked, a steaming brown gush of hot bubbling horror immediately jettisoned into whatever was available. Then I'd stay for a bit, slumped against the walls, exhausted from the efforts and dealing with any second waves. During the day I'd need to be on my guard. Inevitably I'd need to go, so it was a matter of being aware of your surroundings; being in the (toilet) zone at all times. Subconsciously I'd clock potential spots. Put simply, it was better out than in – this meaning 'in pants' as opposed to 'in body', as that option was definitely not available – and this was regardless of who could see. Switch off the pride button and squat down. Amazingly I never shat my pants once, a truly outstanding achievement, possibly my best to date and way harder than any 9a+ redpoints.

You'd have thought, and definitely hoped, that upon returning to the Western world you'd leave all this shit behind you. Unfortunately

I imported mine home, a smuggled disease, though the doctor could apparently find nothing wrong. Handing him my sample jar of light brown sludge, 'nothing wrong' didn't seem the likely outcome. If 'nothing wrong' meant 30-second morning sprints then I was truly concerned for those with a real illness.

At our house on Crookesmoor Road, two months back into the UK, I began my usual ritual as my dreams drifted aside. Trousers on and T-shirt, no time for socks, and I'm away to the bedroom door. Then I'm hitting the corner on the corridor at top speed and still accelerating into the home straight, only to slam on the brakes and stop with a skid at a locked bathroom door, bursting into a hot sweat at the sound of the shower starting up. Jo was up early, or I was late, and showers took way over the 20 seconds which I estimated was my maximum time limit. Ninja toilet skills kicked in and I was already into the back-up plan, so far not used or even considered: the yard round the back of the house had great potential. Leaping down the stairs and careering into the kitchen I felt the first wave and auto-clench was engaged as I reached for the back door handle and turned. Locked – shit, no key. Now really stuck. The house fronts onto a main road and there are people outside for sure, people that care, not like in India. People that will be alarmed and disturbed at the sight of some half-dressed scrag leaping out of the door and squatting in the gutter. The front door is locked anyway and my key is upstairs and my stopwatch has just hit five seconds. Urgent now. The pan on the worktop shouts out from the heap of last night's washing up, still some pasta stuck to the bottom. Pants down and in it goes, just as I hear the upstairs floorboards creak as someone makes their way down. Panicking I stuff the cookware into the cupboard and cover the door just as Paul appears, 'WOOOAAAHHH, Jesus. What the f***? It totally stinks in here mate, like horrendous dead dog shit. Is that your arse?'

'Yeah, still bad. I'm going to see the doc again today. I don't think I'm fixed.'

'No shit. Get it sorted mate.'

No shit was exactly what I wanted. Paul made his cup of tea in silence, no doubt holding his breath, and quickly escaped the chemical warfare zone back upstairs. I grabbed my front door key, put a lid on the pan and took it outside, walked up the street a bit and dumped the whole lot in someone else's bin.

The whole thing was embarrassing, but worse than that it made me feel weak, not just physically but mentally too. I felt pathetic and feeble and dirty. These negative feelings had hit me right from the start, right back at the beginning of my trip. Crawling out of the concrete toilet room in the first 'hotel' on my very first night in Delhi I curled up on the dirty mattress and felt rather sorry for myself. Puking, shitting, moaning – horrible.

Being an experienced traveller, the thought of India hadn't phased me. France, Spain, even Italy with my parents was surely a solid grounding that would prepare me for anything. I'd been to the Verdon without my parents at only sixteen, even hitching a lot of the way there. India would be a breeze. I thought of that as I staggered under the ridiculous weight of my oversized pack and struggled along Pahar Ganj in New Delhi. I'd tried to do all the travellers' jobs straight off in one hit: travel from the UK, walk straight to the Nepalese Embassy to get a visa (turning down all rickshaw rides to save the 2 pence fare), then book a bus ticket to Nepal and, finally, find a hotel – all with the minimum of fuss and the maximum of Western efficiency. It was an instant shambles from the moment I cleared UK airspace. Nothing worked. The embassy was shut on random days, including the day I arrived, and the bus to Nepal only went twice a week and took forever. That's how it goes in India. Now as I jostled through the streets I was feeling hassled. The string of touts following me wasn't helping. 'You want hotel sir? I know very good hotel sir. Come sir. Cheap price sir … You want drum sir. Good quality sir. Good for music … ' I presented my air of 'I know where I am going', which was totally unconvincing despite the fact that I actually did know where I was going. I obviously stuck out in that ridiculous way that only new travellers can. I was hunting for the Bright Hotel, recommended to me and a place I'd stay no less than eight different times over the coming months. 'Bright' turned out to be possibly the biggest misnomer of all time, with 'Dull Hotel' being a more appropriate name and even 'Dark' being more than generous. A ramshackle jumble of rooms piled on top of each other, thrown together from an assortment of materials ranging from solid concrete to cardboard. Beds were just a plywood box and the toilets were usually shared squatters with a pipe and a tap should one fancy a shower. But on the plus side it had an incredible roof terrace and balcony overlooking the streets where endless hours could be spent watching the madness below. No words can describe the bustle of the Indian streets, an explosion of colour and noise with no reason or order. Completely packed, but with everybody trying to get somewhere and with random stuff thrown in to really mess it up: cows and elephants wandering around, old men dragging carts full of rubbish, motorbikes revving and blasting out exhaust fumes, and the odd truck that simply wouldn't fit. When the view all got a bit much the rooftop always had a fine collection of randoms who would gather: hardened travellers, alcoholics, chatty northern Europeans, artists and even musicians who would be happy to play whatever it was they could play as a soundtrack to the bizarre reality. The air would be thick with smoke and, in fact, many people seemed to have chosen to travel to India based entirely on the abundance of weed. But it was not for me out there. For a start the whole place was crazy enough, but perhaps more important was the possibility of getting rumbled by the police. Dealers and cops worked together and huge bribes were the only way to avoid a long stint in an Indian jail. If my current accommodation was classed as a 'hotel' I dreaded to think what life in the slammer would be like.

I finally made it to Nepal and it was amazing. But I'd got the trekking all wrong. Trekking is all about walking through incredible mountains taking in the vibe and scenery of the place. I'd apparently put myself down for the 'Sherpa' course which was all about stupid massive packs, getting your head down and travelling from A to B as soon as possible. Thinking I was 'Mister Mountain' I had packed everything that might possibly come in handy and, of course, had no intention of hiring any help whatsoever. Even if it was free I'd not have accepted and my kit was rubbish, heavy and massive, inherited from my parents and completely out of date. I didn't even have a duvet jacket, just a bulky fleece and a jumble of woolly tops. My sleeping mat was a roll of foam with a pack size of about 35 centimetres in diameter and, since it was usually soaked in water, a comedy weight. My whole bag weighed about 25 kilograms and included my tent, stove and food. This shoulder-snapping weight was a blunt penalty for my stubborn intention not to stay in the countless cheap as chips guesthouses along the way. We stayed in them anyway.

I was glad to have some company and, initially, my travels in Nepal were spent with my girlfriend. Months earlier we'd excitedly planned our routes from the comfort of a sofa and saved up for essential kit, as recommended by Mr Lonely Planet. But all the guidebooks must have been written for the super-fit because I was struggling big time. Trekking in a pair made life a tad easier as we spurred each other on, but funnily enough we got seven days into our 21-day Annapurna Circuit before, finally, I accepted it was no fun whatsoever and that, actually, I wasn't going to make it. She was faring better; her bag was much lighter than mine because, a) she couldn't carry such a massive bag and b) she *wouldn't* carry such a massive bag, it being obvious to her that I was carrying around a load of useless junk. We bailed from the circuit to the Annapurna base camp which was just three days' slog away. It was a good call, a totally overwhelming place, with the vastness of the high mountains surrounding us. I'd spent days and days slogging my guts out, killing my body, and I'd just about reached the base camp at a mere 4,000 metres. The 8,000-metre peaks towered over us imposing their scale and I felt totally and utterly out of my depth. A sharp slap in the face and kick-in-the-bollocks-realisation that my personal opinion of myself as a tough mountain type was completely out of line. Here I was tiny, nothing, a tourist at best. It was depressing, but at the same time incredibly inspiring and motivating to even get a glimpse of the achievements of the real mountaineers so far beyond my own abilities.

After our Annapurna trek we opted for the Langtang trek, which was much better. More acclimatised, the four-day hike up to base camp felt easier, but it was still rough. Illness held us both back. I spent a whole day bent double, curled up in agony with the worst case of wind before a 30-minute long continuous fart. It was tough going. I was pushing myself hard and my body wasn't up to it. The weight fell off me, I'd left the UK at 65 kilograms and now I was down to 50. In the mirror I saw someone else, not just in appearance, but the person staring back was drawn and empty. This wasn't quite what I'd anticipated to say the least, just a month away from the comfort of our Sheffield home where we'd busied ourselves with exciting research and efficient organisation, poring over guides with bookmarks on must-see mountains. We'd had high hopes for a trip of a lifetime, some tough times perhaps, but ultimately a holiday of the finest variety. Right now I was unsure I'd been reading the right holiday brochures, I was struggling to uncover the highlights from the mound of hard work. At the Langtang base camp we stayed a few days to recharge, both of us detached from each other by the intensity of the journey and by the effort and illness. We sat apart writing furiously in our diaries, lost in our own thoughts.

Maybe I've always been a diary writing sort of person, otherwise known as a 'spod'. First entries were at around sixteen years old and were brief, probably started because it was 'cool' for some reason, but they soon ramped up into essays. The purpose I never questioned, whether it was a record for the future, a friend, or a place to pour thoughts and questions in the hope that an answer will appear by itself. Looking back, its purpose was never meant to be a record: catching up on missed days or even weeks was a pain in the backside, with half a sentence no matter how interesting my activities had been, and I've never read any entries anyway. On the flip side, when the chips were down I'd be there for hours and ten sides of A4 might be the result. It was a tool for the sad and lonely, depressed or confused, and I guess for those with some time to burn. I don't have a diary now. I'll give that a thought some day. I do have a climbing diary, but that's completely different – though in some people's view, when looking at an obsessed climber, it could be still for the sad and lonely …

Based at Langtang camp, at the end of the path and without my over-powering goal of getting somewhere as quickly as possible, there was time to chill out and actually see where we were. Ironically that's the whole point of trekking, though I seemed to have entirely missed it with my intense approach. Our base camp guesthouse was a really cool dorm thing with good basic (like really basic) food, a great communal room and a view to die for. In the blazing sun we'd sit out in deck chairs and soak up the mind-blowing scenery, but there was more to observe and take in than the panoramic vista. For a few months now, since the start of the trip, I'd noticed a change in our relationship, a gradual flipping over of the balance. I'd always felt the dominant one, though to be fair not by much, a healthy amount in my eyes and a close balance really, but now it had tipped the other way and by alarming degrees that increased on a daily basis. She was distancing herself from me and building a wall I couldn't climb. I could see it in her eyes. Looking at myself didn't help. I could see the reasons. I was a shadow, skinny and pale, weak and pathetic. I clung to her for support in measures that she couldn't give and my desperation repelled her even further. Out there with so much space and beauty and time and freedom we were becoming trapped in a relationship that, once strong, was now sliding out of control.

At first I ignored it, explaining the shifting dynamics by our radically unfamiliar and constantly changing environment, but as the days progressed they became as obvious as the mountains around us. Discussing it didn't help, both of us confused by alien feelings and unwilling to confront the situation head on. We'd skirt round the edges, changing topic when things got scary. We didn't want to extrapolate too far in case we suddenly reached the end of the road. The relationship we'd brought was the only normal component in this new world and essential to fall back on in times of need – but my need was greater and I was becoming desperate, surprising myself by the way I clung to her, and appalled at my pleading. Normally solid and strong, my personality was shockingly fragile and I could barely recognise myself. My new 'poor me' attitude did nothing to help, insisting it was 'all my fault' every few minutes only drove her further away. She seemed to be thriving in the mountains, fighting off illness and loving the food, the simplicity of dhal and vegetables suiting her tastes and she soaked up the fresh air, the surrounding views and the exercise and gained strength with every step. As people, we seemed to be evolving in radically different directions that highlighted previously unnoticeable and irrelevant incompatibilities.

I had no answers and just put up with it, but she was looking for a solution. In the end there was only one answer and we decided to travel in different directions for a while. She needed space, this was her trip of a lifetime as well as mine and I wasn't exactly making it a bundle of fun. I was desperate to argue but couldn't push it anymore, I knew she was right, and figured I'd soon be back on my feet. But once I was by myself the loneliness surprised me, overwhelming me and questioning my strength of character. I'd never have seen it coming, the extent of how lonely it's possible to feel, or the depths of depression into which I'd soon fall. Something was missing, that place I'd go when the chips were down, my escape route away from anything in the real world. Scrawling in the diary revealed it. In a past life I'd have simply gone off and climbed and it would have fixed everything. Maybe a simplistic view but that's how it felt. I'd have immersed myself in the movement and cleared my mind in the meditative trance. I'd have felt comfortable in my environment, an expert in the field; I'd know what I was doing and where I was going. But climbing was gone, taken away first through fear and then through injury. I felt deserted. Where was climbing when I needed it?

At least I managed to pull a bit of myself back in, at least for a few days, and set off on a solo ascent of Yala Peak, 5,500 metres, no big deal, some easy glacier crossings and a bit of snow and rock and rubble. This mini-expedition also justified carting around a Super Nova tent, a stove, fuel and food plus a ton of associated junk for a few hundred miles. My pitch at 5,000 metres was supreme, a camping spot to die for, and maybe I nearly did, waking up in the middle of the night, puking into the front of the tent and then spending the rest of the night totally confused and with a banging headache. Of course, being me, I never once considered any kind of altitude sickness, though it probably wasn't that anyway as I eventually woke up fresh as a daisy and set off for the summit armed with a pair of walking crampons and the single steel peg that was my emergency ice-axe should things get hairy. Straddling the tiny sharp summit I felt all of me again. Huge mountains towered over from every side but I'd climbed something slightly technical, a proper bit of climbing, and under my own steam. I was worthy of being there. Then as the sun dipped and faded and the crystal clear air seemed to gain a thickness as it cooled I started down, with the sounds of glaciers creaking and groaning around me, down away from my high point and back into the depths of the new reality into which I'd travelled.

I needed some exercise, I'd done a lot of walking over the last six weeks but that wasn't enough. The mirror proved it, as did my clothes, which hung off me like shirts on a hanger. The city of Kathmandu couldn't help with my exercise withdrawal, there not being an abundance of Virgin Gyms or any comprehension of why anyone would want to do even more exercise than dragging themselves around the mountains. So I'd made my own gym, a selection of bricks to lift and a pull-up bar on the roof of my dilapidated guesthouse; hardly up-to-date equipment but something for my sanity as I waited out the lonely days for a bus to Varanasi in India. Taking up my personal stereo I flipped open a tape box and tapped out a mix tape, techno and trance, one of my favourites. I pushed the tape into the player, hit play and began a work-out, but it wasn't happening, I was unmotivated and had become so feeble there was no point even trying to recover any kind of strength. It would be a one-off session anyway, two at best, it would make no difference whatsoever other than to tire me out and probably make me even more ill. So I sacked it and retreated into my diary, the act of writing taking me far away into a world where I had control. Spreading out the day-planner the weeks and months stretched out before me for what seemed like eternity. There were a lot of blank spaces before the lonely but longed-for coloured-in date that represented my flight home back to the UK. The timescale seemed unfathomable, a lifetime away. I've no idea why I didn't just sack it all off and book an earlier flight. Something held me back – probably the inability to make any kind of decision. At least a few events punctuated the blankness, most noticeably my entry into Thailand, an excursion not planned as the main event of this huge trip but now a glittering lifeline. Some of my Sheffield mates would be on the paradise beaches at the end of the year and together we'd quickly worked a reunion into our schedules. As I'd excitedly booked extra flight tickets in the Stone Age travel agent in New Delhi a few months ago it had seemed like a bonus adventure. Now the meeting with my friends stood out as an oasis amongst the pit of travelling hell in which I was stuck.

Christmas Day in Thailand rated pretty low out of all my Christmases so far, even below the one where I'd got totally pissed on Christmas Eve and spent the whole day in bed, missing Christmas dinner. A bunch of us met up in Bangkok and made our way to Koh Tao, swapping turkey and mince pies and snuggling round the fire for hot chilli, blazing sunshine and crystal-clear snorkelling. There were five or six of us, all packed full of new traveller experiences that needed to be shared – except for mine. I remained quiet, feeling I had little to offer. Seeing my old mates again was awesome, breathing some fresh air into myself. Tina and Chris helped reset my horizon and still remain best mates today, but sitting down for a Thai curry Christmas dinner brought everything home. My friends brought laughter and happiness, they were taking positive experiences from this whole travelling jaunt, growing as people. Other couples strengthened their bond and together they flourished. Jealously I looked on as they held hands and stroked each other's sun-bleached hair. Amongst familiar company I felt more lonely than ever.

The small slice of normality amongst surreal surroundings highlighted my inner isolation. I felt better with strangers as there was nothing to relate to, but amongst strangers I felt lost and without purpose. I had to pull myself together; there was a lot of fun to be had and I was missing out. For a while I thought I'd cracked it, filling my diary with solutions and promising myself that I'd stop being so pathetic. All I had to do was be myself, but I just couldn't do it. I was ill, weak, lonely and filling in endless days doing nothing I saw of value, sitting around wasting time. Thoroughly miserable I disappeared into myself, incapable of opening up to anyone. My confidence was in freefall and everything ahead was a nightmare out of which there was no escape.

Just after the Full Moon Party on Ko Pha Ngan everyone began excitedly planning their next adventures. The news of their travelling, or rather being left on my own, was like a death blow, leaving me totally without direction. I had no idea what to do or where to go. Stuck on a paradise island with a whole lifetime's worth of amazing experiences, I could have easily just sat miserably in the same spot for the rest of my life, sitting in the sand by yet another beach fire and feeling groggy from too much booze and weed. But that's where I met Waster with his story of the climber's paradise and his map to Tonsai Bay.

Without being stuck alone after the departure of my mates, Waster's story may well have washed over me like every other meaningless traveller's tale. There's no way I'd have made the break away from familiar company, but left to myself I knew I had to eventually pull myself together and there were many days to fill. Climbing had dropped so far off the radar that I had to press the re-boot key when Waster mentioned the awesome cliffs of Tonsai, my muddled brain so clogged full of rubbish that it hardly remembered what rock climbing was all about. I absorbed his information, then researched it further in a clearer state of mind to make sure he wasn't making it up. Waster really had thrown me a lifeline. I doubt much else would have made any impact, but the pictures I found in the travel books of cliffs and the mentions of a sport climbing paradise stirred the deep-rooted obsession, lifting me up from the depths. Digging into the bottom of my pack I uncovered my climbing shoes, an old pair of green Asolo Runouts. Underneath these was my half-filled chalk bag crumpled into a plastic bag. This was the only climbing gear I'd brought, an afterthought really, stuffed in at the last minute just in case. Though I expected not to use them their presence was essential, proving my identity as a climber. No real climber ever leaves home without their climbing shoes. Dusting off the sand and dirt that had made its way into the bottom of my pack I cleaned the rubber sole and squeaked up the rubber, feeling the friction under my fingers. Just having them around put me in a more familiar place, and as the simple travel logistics quickly fell into place I was back on home turf, planning another climbing trip just like old times.

The climbing at Tonsai and the whole package of the surrounding landscape and scene was monumentally further ahead of anything I could have ever imagined. I had more good times by far in a few precious weeks than in the rest of the entire travelling trip, but I still felt myself wishing it away, counting down the days until I could escape back to England. I felt guilty having fun, that fun wasn't allowed until the rest of my life was in a good place. I held myself back and withdrew in the evenings, conscious that I wasn't all there and, if I'm honest, rather unconfident in my ability to interact with others. All happy and bouncy and full of excitement, the other climbers overwhelmed me with their colourful future plans. I knew mine were grey and tied into upcoming travel arrangements, but amongst the limestone cliffs much brighter horizons appeared in the distance. The climbing had opened my eyes. The meditative nature of the movement and the way in which it lingers for hours and even days after a route pushed my depression aside, and the absorbing nature of the new style of sport climbing really grabbed hold. Sport climbing was not entirely new to me, but for the first time it made sense. I could see how it worked. I was rubbish at it but that didn't matter. I was falling for it, especially out there above the beach with the outrageous terrain and immaculate rock. The safety of the bolts turned the climbing experience into a complex mental challenge where I had to figure it all out before arms gave in to gravity. It was not, as many traditional climbers including myself had insisted, purely a physical challenge devoid of meaning and stripped of all the real values of proper climbing. It was just different, and different was just what I'd been looking for. I threw myself into it, climbing every day that my feeble body would allow – day on, day off, an acceptable ratio considering the wealth of other amazing must-do activities. My elbows held out. I'd all but forgotten about them and their tendonitis, a twinge on the occasional hard move serving as a reminder as to why I was actually there in the first place. They felt fixed and that alone lifted me to a whole new level. As my time on Tonsai drew to an end I knew I was leaving with a lot more than I'd brought and even though home was a long way off there was something shiny in the distance worth reaching out for.

After six weeks in Thailand my visa was up; time to go. Roaming the streets of Bangkok picking at street-market chicken legs, I felt just as depressed as I had done when I'd arrived. The last few weeks had done me a lot of good, but it hadn't fixed anything really. It was like I'd been on holiday and now I was back, Monday morning at work, normal drudgery, nothing to look forward to. However, I'd spent my last few weeks having the time of my life on a paradise beach in climbing heaven and I'd brought back a huge bag of souvenirs.

Next day I flew back to India, I still had nearly a quarter of a year to go before finally returning to the UK. The days and months stretched out before me, impossible to comprehend, like a prison sentence with no chance of appeal. In the end I just had to get on with it and, given time, adopted a new understanding of my situation, kind of stuck I guess, but I squeezed out some great adventures and experiences. The Sheffield team were still criss-crossing the country with plans and timescales, allowing me to adjust mine to fit the same agenda without imposing too much. Nobody really wanted to spend much time with me, that was obvious. I was hardly a bundle of fun, though at least not permanently miserable. Finding a little of myself out on Tonsai had lifted my spirits. At last I felt I could enjoy myself.

One evening, sitting in a scruffy cafe on Pahar Ganj in New Delhi eating chips, I overheard a few Brits talking about climbing with the cafe owner. Then one of them pinned a poster on the wall advertising India's first ever international climbing competition. I couldn't help but pry and we soon got chatting. It turned out that these two guys were helping with the organising and were in charge of the setting. It even turned out one of the guys was Tim's mate from Leeds and that I'd actually met him before. The posters they were putting up were to try and attract some international climbers, as so far the only entrants were Indians. Even though my only competition experience was watching Jerry Moffatt win the world cup at Leeds '89, I figured it could be a laugh, especially when they said they'd be setting the finals at around 6b+. They asked if I'd come along and help with the setting as they were a bit wobbly in this department, but said that I could still compete. It was true Indian-style with random organisation and rules all over the place, changing every 10 minutes to suit the situation. In the end I pretty much set the routes on a 13-metre high vertical stone wall with a tiny overlap near the top. The climbers were allowed to play on the routes before the comp and do whatever they wanted, with the 'competition' day being pretty much the same but with a start list and someone noting who had got the highest. However, it became very obvious from very early on that I was going to win by a very large margin and as such the competition title was quickly changed to India's first national competition. I was still allowed to compete and won the special 'best climber position', rewarded with a massive trophy presented to me by the Indian Minister for Sport. The bottom of this half-metre-high trophy fell off before I even got back to my guesthouse and I spent the following day getting it welded together again in some sketchy workshop for about 12 pence. Amazingly, considering its quality and size, I even lugged it all the way back to Britain, by which time it had gone completely rusty. I lobbed it in the attic, never to be seen again.

The trophy was an eye-catcher though and often sparked up conversations with other travellers wondering what the hell it was. Having met up with a friend of mine in Pushkar, Rajasthan, we were sitting scoffing a thali in one of the scruffy cafes when we got chatting to a young lone traveller. He had a lot to say and after a few hours of boring us to death brought over some sustenance in the form of a bhang lassi, a dope-laced yoghurt drink totally legal in the area. 'Bang' seemed to be an appropriate name, as that was exactly what my brain went off with after about 10 minutes. The young lad seemed totally unaffected, other than his speech doubling in speed, and, apparently disappointed in the effects, he ordered another round. I could only manage a few extra sips, mainly as I was concerned by my dissolving state of mind, so he downed the lot and suggested we went back to his room to chill. Unable to think straight we followed and half woke up in his room, a bizarre square box reached via a labyrinth of corridors. The room was exactly symmetrical with two doors opposite each other and two beds also opposite each other. The lassi was now apparently having an effect on him too, as he sat on the bed facing us and bombarded us with non-stop political views. It started to get scary and when he broke off to make a spliff we decided we literally had to make a run for it, as so far any suggestions of our leaving had been met with disdain. But which way to go? Which door to risk? Choose the wrong one and we might end up stuck in a toilet. We'd totally forgotten which way we came in, so we aimed to the left. Thankfully it wasn't a toilet or broom cupboard or even simply locked, but it wasn't the door we'd come in through either. It bizarrely led us out into another part of the maze of a building, revealing this guy's room to be just a square bit of corridor with some beds in it. After stumbling around for ages we finally tumbled out into the street, only to find it was pitch black when we'd expected daylight. Time had zoomed away into a new dimension. To make matters worse a dog and a pig were embroiled in a ferocious battle, the dog clearly not bothered if its bacon was cooked or not. Skirting round the scene with our backs to the wall we fled back to the cafe where we'd started the whole ordeal and chose our next drinks more carefully. Next morning I woke up still completely off my face. It was the same again the day after that and I began to really worry that I'd completely gone over the edge and would now have to live my life in a confused, stoned state, incapable of making any decisions whatsoever. Fortunately I was okay in the end, but haven't gone near a bhang lassi since.

As the end of the trip loomed it began to fill me with dread. Though my current situation was less than ideal it was bearable and, more importantly, familiar. I'd settled into a kind of limbo where my expectations, desires and state of mind matched the surrounding crazy country. Returning to Sheffield would involve dealing with the real world. Everything would be different. The foundations of my old, solid, little society had crumbled. It was ironic that I'd been desperate to get home from almost the day I arrived in India and now that I was going home I wanted to stay. So I lived out my last few days in Delhi, relaxing at the Bright Hotel and revelling in my 'Indian-ness'. At last I had fallen into place in this country. No one hassled me, no one offered Kashmir rugs or tried to clean out my ears. I was thin, brown, chilled and knew the score. Mostly I'd had time on my hands and rolled with the relaxed but chaotic attitude. When you've reached this state the country of India is the best place in the world to travel, but before that it's a nightmare. Boarding my Aeroflot flight to Manchester it seemed I was carrying a whole raft of happy memories and looking back now, twenty years later, mostly I can see the good stuff: the castles of Rajasthan, the tufas of Tonsai, the mountains of Nepal. The filtering power of the mind is amazing. It has to be I guess. If it filtered the other way then you'd end up wondering why you bothered doing anything.

Sheffield was just as I'd left it and my timing was ideal, with a room coming free back in the same old house with the same mates on Crookesmoor Road. These good friends soaked up my happy stories and gave me the comforts I needed but it was a real culture shock, much worse than first arriving in India. I couldn't find my feet in familiar terrain and didn't fit in anymore. The first few days were okay, luxuriating in chocolate and TV, but I quickly began to scare myself as the window between reality and the bizarre place in which my mind was still stuck began to mist up and lose transparency. Each morning I'd wake, and for a few moments, before my standard legging it to the bathroom, I'd be convinced I was still in India, in some random guesthouse by a desert or in the mountains. Then the truth would flood in and as I opened my eyes it was as if there was a line-up of people all ready to throw stones at me, suddenly releasing their load. Pelted by reality I'd crawl into the day and hunt for some direction. After such a long time away I struggled to find things to do other than ponder my current state of mind in the hope it would sort itself out. By the end of the trip in India I'd reached an acceptable status quo, bumbling through with no particular purpose, but now the very normality of Sheffield life painfully highlighted my issues and there was nothing ahead; no purpose.

Days dragged as I moped around the house alone. I missed my girlfriend. Spending some time together back in Sheffield hadn't fixed us. Way back in Nepal I'd hoped some time apart and a return to normality might have sorted us out, but it was clearly the end of the road. I was sliding back-wards and loathed myself for being incapable of even the simplest of tasks. I couldn't do anything, never left the house, never went for a walk, or a bike ride, and climbing didn't even register. The only thing to look forward to was getting wrecked in the evening, or maybe earlier. In a different state of mind things felt more normal. I'd wait out the hours until someone returned from work, but their company only highlighted my issues. I was feeling more and more detached, cast adrift from a normal society with a head full of questions that had no answers, the kind of questions that should probably never be asked. I've never felt so lonely and incapable of knowing which way to turn, like floundering in quicksand or running in treacle. It seemed endless. I needed to tell someone and get it all out because I couldn't work it out myself, but I knew I couldn't get it all out because I didn't even know what it was. It was too embarrassing to describe: pathetic, feeble, confused, and totally and utterly sad. I'd tried before, looking for a little support but at the same time keeping it together as best I could, hiding the extent of my feelings, trying to keep a brave and normal face. Basically I was falling apart. I knew that deep down, but this kind of thing just shouldn't happen to me and I refused to accept it, refused to admit any kind of weakness. Somehow I'd ride it through, but it was pretty obvious there was no simple way of going back to normal.

I needed a bit of space so reluctantly packed a rucksack full of stuff with the intention of staying out in the hills for a few nights. Then I set off on a

1 Me climbing *Ali Baba* (E2 5c) at the Wainstones.

2 Dad up at the Wainstones.   3 Learning the skills at Scugdale.
4 The view from home across the beach into the Teesside chemical works. *Photo: Chris McClure.*
5 Tom McClure (Dad).   6 My first climb.
7 At home with Dad.   8 Jean McClure (Mum).

9   *Terrorist* (E4 6a), Wainstones. My first E4 lead at fourteen years old. Note the EBs and Whillans harness.
10 On the lead on *Magic in the Air*. *Photo: Tim Nicholl.*
11 Hanging out somewhere at the bottom of the Verdon Gorge.
12 Hanging out on the moors: Dave, me and Tim. Tim has a broken leg here but it didn't stop him climbing.
    Photo: Tim Nicholl.

13 Two climbers on the mid height belay of *Blue Sky* at Pembroke. I fell from a few metres higher than the climbers and landed on my back on the lumpy protrusion 80 feet below!
14 James McHaffie soloing *Mint 400* (E6 6b) at Froggatt. A different proposition these days compared to a lonely on-sight above a 30-centimetre-square piece of carpet!
15 Me and Ste Smith on top of *The Arrow*, twenty years after his fall.
16 The elbow-destroying cellar roof at our rented house in Walkley, Sheffield.

17

18

19

17 India's first international competition wall. At least it was colourful.
18 Back to the UK and feeling totally out of place. Suddenly I didn't belong anywhere.
19 Tucking into a thali. Massive portions three times a day made no difference to my collapsing weight.
20 My second home for a while, Tonsai Bay, Thailand. *Photo: Keith Sharples.*
21 The problem with perfection is that everyone wants to find it! Tonsai Bay, Thailand. *Photo: Keith Sharples.*
22 Hitching in the Verdon. Tim and I pack up camp.

23 My first magazine cover appearance – *OTE* magazine, May 1998. *Photo: Ben Lowe.*
24 Early days sport climbing in the Peak: on the groove of *Mecca* (F8b+), while climbing the *Extension* (F8c). *Photo: Keith Sharples.*

25 *Mutation* (F9a). A route designed for me. *Photo: Keith Sharples.*
26 Vic climbing *Wide is Love* (F6a), in the Verdon Gorge.
27 Maria and Vic, relaxed above the Verdon.

28 *Northern Lights* (F9a), the start of it all really. *Photo: Keith Sharples.*
29 A star studded deep water soloing trip around Croatia. Chris Sharma, Tim Emmett and
   Leo Houlding, and an unlikely Jack Osbourne, living the dream. *Photo: Simon Carter.*
30 The diet starts tomorrow … or maybe not. Possibly my greatest asset is my weight, which never
   varies from about 56kg no matter how many cakes, biscuits, pies, chocolates and pizzas I shovel
   down my neck. *Photo: Simon Carter.*
31 The first ascent of *Ring Of Fire* (F8b+). Named after an earlier attempt where I landed legs wide
   apart from 40 feet … *Photo: Simon Carter.*

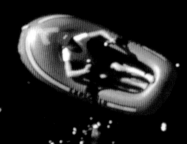

32 Bouldering beneath the real stuff in southern Greenland. *Photo: Nick 'Tufty' Boden.*

33 Massively dehydrated after making the first ascent of *21* with Miles Gibson. *Photo: Nick 'Tufty' Boden.*

34 Said Belhaj checking out the food snacks on the Petzl Roc Trip to Redriver. This was a single day's supply for four people!

35 The amazing cave in the Getu Valley of China developed during the Petzl Roc Trip. *Photo: Sam Bié.*

36 Finishing off the first ever on-sight ascent of *Dawes Rides a Shovel Head* (E7/8 6c), Raven Crag, Langdale. *Photo: Keith Sharples.*

37 Low down on *Rhapsody* (E11) at Dumbarton Rock. *Photo: Keith Sharples.*

38 *Rhapsody* at Dumbarton Rock – where sport and trad merge; a trad route climbed with sport focus and commitment! *Photo: Keith Sharples.*

39 Toes are the way forward. Seems obvious to me. A comfortable toe-hang rest provides enough recovery for the crux section above on an unnamed 7c at the Pirates sector, Costa Blanca. *Photo: Rich Mayfield, The Orange House.*

40 Abseiling from a motorway bridge in northern Norway as part of a Fat Face photoshoot. I missed my boat landing!

41 Hamming it up for the camera at Diamond Falls, Australia. *Photo: Simon Carter.*

mountain bike into the Peak, going as far as I could so I knew I couldn't bottle it and get back the same day. I ended up way out, high on the Derwent Edge tops scurrying around for shelter as the early darkness of a bleak March night descended.

Spliff break needed from sorting out my cooking junk. Things are at their worst now. I thought it was bad in Thailand and India but that was nothing. I'm sitting in this freezing cave and now the hard work starts. Well actually it's already started, no working jet in my stove. Bloody stove, always pissing me around. I'm pretty gutted as I wanted to stay three nights to battle through this, but with no stove it's going to be grim. Also there is hardly any water and it's lonely here, like really lonely, but I've got to start somewhere. I need to immerse myself into this problem and sort it out. I need to find out what the problem really is. I can't think straight, I can't string a sentence together in my own head. I don't know what I'm doing. I think I need to escape from everything I know, leave everything behind and start again. I need a plan. This isn't going to be easy.

Eventually it became obvious: I just had to run away from the Sheffield scene. The normality of my surroundings was painfully highlighting my crumbling mental state and, trapped in a vicious circle, I couldn't get a foothold on to any kind of escape plan. I thought I'd made some headway into dealing with the inevitable departure from my Sheffield home and surroundings, but when the end suddenly became clear and arrangements fell into place I just totally crumbled. I'd been somewhere near this point before, but this time I'd gone over my elastic limit and finally snapped. Slumped on the sofa in the living room in front of the usual mates sobs came uncontrollably. Through the tears I saw my friends staring at me. I could see their confusion at such an outpouring, but also their acknowledgement that this had been coming for a while. I was now detached from them, from all of this, I was on my own, it was the only way to move forward and with that I took a deep breath, stood up and took the longest walk of my life along the corridor passing familiar pictures and scratched walls. Opening the door out onto the main street and leaving my key on the inside, I stepped out, then ever so slowly pulled it closed until it finally clicked shut forever.

14 LEGO

After the much-avoided but totally inevitable departure from Sheffield I holed up for a while with my good friend Howard. Howard is a real-life Mr Happy, but he knew when to smile and laugh and when to just listen. When I closed the door of 229 Crookesmoor Road I felt like my world was about to completely collapse, that the last few bits of my life's Lego kit would be scattered and lost like the other thousand parts. Things didn't seem that different now. If I could have pulled myself together it would have been obvious that actually I'd only lost a few bits of my life and that what remained was still almost a complete set. Howard helped me see this and sorted me out enough to start thinking for myself.

The first thing I did was to run away to North Wales. I was on a sad and lonely man's mission to be alone and wander around miserably with the intention of 'finding myself', becoming enlightened, and returning all jolly and bouncy with a rucksack full of optimism. I took everything I needed, including an open-ended time period, though in reality not enough money to make it last more than a week. It was there I discovered 'shunting': the 'Billy-no-mates' answer to going climbing. I'd found the Petzl Shunt at the bottom of the Verdon Gorge years ago and it had hung around in the pit of my rucksack as a useless lump of metal with no purpose whatsoever. Now it was my best mate, allowing me to climb whatever I wanted, whenever I wanted, and never letting me get really scared (well, still a bit scared.) All I needed to do was reach the top of the route, fix the rope, abseil down, and then clip on the Shunt and climb back up again. The Shunt attached to my harness and slid up the rope. If I fell off I just sat there for a bit and then carried on. The down side, of course, is that the 'leading experience' is lost and I carefully avoided routes I hadn't done, or shunted routes I knew I'd never dare to lead. But the experienced and well-planned Shunter can cover a huge amount of climbing in just a few hours: *Colossus, Slipstream, Pull My Daisy, Poetry Pink*, all in a morning's work.

There was a lot of time to think being alone and wild camping up by the Cromlech boulders. A lot of long dark evenings spent listening to the swaying of the wind and babbling of the streams. I didn't really want to think, but the simplicity of life was lifting my spirits. Out there, in the countryside, away from everything and everybody, I knew who I was. I could be myself on home ground. There was no India or Thailand or Sheffield to confuse me, no worries of future plans, fitting in with friends or worrying about who I'd let down. I just busied myself with simple camping tasks and filled my day with climbing. Even using a Shunt the act of climbing was utterly absorbing, taking my mind far away from all its troubles and back into a place it knew all too well, a well-known and comfortable place that gave solid hope of everything turning out okay.

On the fifth day of my North Wales rehab expedition my fingers were battered, so I opted for a huge walk up over the Glyders and then down to Llanberis, then back up to Snowdon and over Crib Goch. It was a route designed to ensure much suffering which seemed appropriate for a sad loner type. Thoroughly exhausted after this massive effort I finally staggered back down to the boulders as the light faded. Foolishly I'd left my torch in the tent and I hurried along with past headtorch lessons ringing in my mind, but got away with it; I'd not been caught out this time. Reaching the camp spot I had a sudden heart flutter as I noticed that the tent didn't appear to be where I'd left it. Staying calm, but with a rising panic, I attempted to rationalise, assuming maybe someone had kindly moved it to a better place, or perhaps I'd simply pitched it somewhere else and forgotten. Pretty quickly it became obvious that someone had helped themselves. That finality was made clear with a blatant clue, and I'm not joking here: my toothbrush stuck up vertically in the grass exactly where my tent had been. This evil symbol, like a middle finger to my distress, was all that was left of all that I owned.

Sitting on the rocks as darkness descended I was feeling pretty sorry for myself. All I had was the clothes I was wearing plus a waterproof, a water bottle, a local walking map and a few left-over cereal bars, plus about £12 and, of course, no cash card and no phone. There was no option other than to bail immediately, even though it was about 8 p.m. and my chances of getting home that night were nil.

As expected it didn't go well. No one really wanted to pick up a lost-looking tramp in the middle of the night, and lost was exactly what I was. With no road map, I was taking lifts to local villages and getting out of the car with no clue as to where I was, having to wander around looking for road signs to places I might recognise. Eventually, at about two in the morning, sitting in a lorry driver's cab and looking at his map, I realised that I was actually going back in the direction I'd come, so asked to be dropped off at the next junction. This was rather ill-considered, as it was immediately obvious – as soon as he drove away – that this was the kind of junction that is never used by anyone; the kind of junction built for just one farm, or a tiny collection of houses owned by pensioners who never go out, especially at two in the morning. I'd blown it. It was the end of the road for that night and in total pitch black I stumbled around for ages looking or, more accurately, feeling for somewhere to sleep. (A torch would have been so handy … a rather familiar feeling. I decided there and then that I needed to permanently attach one to my head.) Fortunately it was dry and not too cold. I lucked out, kind of, and slipped into a ditch by the side of the road filled with leaves. Shuffling in I covered myself in leaves to stay warm and covered my head with my empty bag to stop spiders crawling over my face.

Next day I went directly to Teesside, after a small deviation due to forgetting I didn't actually live in Sheffield anymore. It took a couple of lifts before I suddenly remembered. To be honest I needed home comforts, the type that only parents can give. I should have gone there straight off in the first place. Ironically it was an easy hitch. Months later the police recovered some of my stuff, though it was only my manky old clothes tossed into a tree near Llanberis. All the good stuff was gone. Tent, sleeping bag, stove, full rack, rope, harness, boots – time to start again.

Back home in Teesside my parents welcomed me like parents do, slotting me back into my old life where Sheffield had no relevance. I had my old room, comforting surroundings, familiar smells and noises from good times. I could even erase the last four years of my life. There is never an ideal time to run home for support but, as it turned out, the timing of mine was perfect, with my parents about to go on a two-week camping trip to Briançon in the south of France. Of course, there'd be an extra tent, a place in the car, room on the ferry and no cost whatsoever. It was absolutely exactly what I needed and the perfect way to – finally – look clearly in the mirror to see just how much good stuff was remaining. For me to fall apart so catastrophically was way out of character. I'd never have seen it coming. Before we left for France I sorted out some of my travelling junk and, reading through some bumf on my anti-malaria tablets, made a chance discovery which may have explained a lot. A bit of research showed some interesting stuff.

> *Neuropsychiatric effects are reported with Mefloquine use. The FDA product guide states it can cause mental health problems, including anxiety, hallucinations, depression, unusual behavior and suicidal ideations, among others. When some measure of subjective severity is applied to the rating of adverse events, about 11-17% of travellers are incapacitated to some degree.*

I'd taken Mefloquine, along with Chloroquine, for the entire duration of my trip and the six weeks after returning as prescribed and, although I didn't appear to have caught malaria, it might have been worth bagging the pills off and taking the risk. Though I'll never know if the pills had done me in, they were a perfect thing to blame and now that I was off them I was back on the road to being myself. Maybe the ultimate placebo – knowing that I was on nothing.

Briançon is an amazing place. I have a few friends who live there and I'm very jealous. The town boasts over 300 days of sunshine per year, perfect skiing and ice-climbing in the winter, and brilliant rock climbing, mountaineering, mountain biking and pretty much everything in the summer. It's also the ideal rehab spot, especially combined with some really cool people and my parents, who totally sorted me out. There was a mountain bike to borrow when I needed and everyone was off hiking somewhere every day. I plunged myself into climbing, the mountains being so accessible. I soloed the 4,000-metre of Barre des Écrins, which felt a little dicey for such a punter, and then went on to solo the Ailefroide. This was dicier: I bivvied out alone under a stone slab before going for the summit, but got totally lost trying to find a rocky 'rake' (a diagonal thin ledge) that would take me through the vast rock face. At one point I followed a vague crack for about a hundred metres until it disappeared and I was left soloing V Diff terrain in big boots on crumbly rock and totally bricking it. After an assortment of epics I was on the summit at around 4 p.m., watching everyone else for miles around already well-established on their descents, little coloured dots on the vast fields of white snow. Four o'clock is far too late to be up high: the snow turns to slush and any glacier crossings become really dangerous, especially when you're alone. I took the same route down that I'd ascended, as most of the route was in the shade and the snow was fortunately frozen but, hurrying along, I tripped on a crampon and fell side-ways out of a bergschrund onto a vast, wide open and very steep snowfield. In a microsecond I was moving faster than running pace and with no axe I knew instantly that I was in real trouble, with this sledge-run ending abruptly at a few-hundred-metre free fall back down onto the glacier. Scrabbling at the ice with thick gloves made no difference, but then, with-out warning my leg went into a crack in the snow, my foot jamming on its crampon points and swinging me round through 180 degrees to be lying on my back with my head downwards. I lay there for a few moments as the ice crystals melted into my face and the icy water ran in over my neck, urgently planning my delicate extraction such as to avoid another tobog-ganing experience. I'd only actually slid about 10 metres, but it was obvious my escape had been a total fluke and that, in reality, I didn't really know what I was doing. I made it down just before dark and sacked off the snowy mountains for the rest of the trip.

However, the whole experience left me feeling alive and invigorated, even the unplanned sledging. The thought of careering over a thousand-metre cliff would have been almost appealing some months ago, but now I was inspired to move forward, life had a lot to offer, and there seemed a lot of very good things to do.

On the rock I knew what I was doing – apparently. Still carrying an element of Mr Miserable, some solo climbing seemed acceptable and so on a number of occasions I set off alone up three or four pitch sport routes on the limestone cliff of Le Fournel. One of these was around 6c, and to safeguard any fall, I took two long slings with one end of each attached to my harness. If the moves looked tricky I'd safeguard myself by clipping one of the slings into a bolt with a karabiner. With the slings being about one and a half metres long I'd be able to reach the next bolt with my other sling and then reach down and unclip the first sling from the lower bolt. This seemed a great idea, but clearly shows I had absolutely no grasp whatsoever of fall factors and impact forces and looking back now it makes me wonder how I managed to get any kind of engineering degree whatsoever. If I'd fallen above the bolt I'd have dropped onto the non-elastic sling which would have snapped straight away, giving me a massive jolt in the process, ensuring that not only did I die when I crashed into the ground some hundred metres below, but that I'd also really hurt myself before I'd even started falling. What's also scary is that, despite a lifetime of climbing experience and a good degree in an entirely relevant subject, I was still oblivious to how things worked, which makes me wonder what kind of risks the rest of the climbing population are prepared to take.

My two-week trip to France was so full that there'd been little time to dwell, and back home in Teesside I felt amazingly refreshed. The complete change of scene from Sheffield and jumping back into the outdoors had drawn a line under the whole affair, allowing me to leave it behind and move forwards. I was actually beginning to feel rather embarrassed with myself and my infantile behaviour. The more I pondered the more I realised I'd blown things out of all proportion, not just blown, but completely exploded on a pathetic scale. Sheffield life carried on just the same without me, of course it did, and when I spoke to my mates on the phone they wondered when I'd be coming back, like my huge nightmare was just some kind of little blip, which, of course, it was. At last I was starting to see the big picture. Still, I felt fragile and confused at how I could end up in such a state. I didn't feel the need to rush back to Sheffield, even though by now I'd figured that that was where I'd be heading. Home life with my parents was a rather nice rehab hospital and I'd just hang out a little while longer.

To fill the days I spent hours playing on my old garage climbing wall. This little wall must have been one of the first of its kind. Even when I was only about seven years old, so back in 1977, I had a desire to have my own climbing wall. I wanted to climb everything and spent hours climbing trees near our home. I had the local height record on 'The Old Airey', a massive tree, the biggest in the area. This had been achieved only because I weighed almost nothing and was able to teeter my way up 20-millimetre thick branches to leave a little string marker at my high point. Another local lad tried to beat it, but, still nowhere near my record, he fell off and crashed all the way down, breaking his leg on the way. Some of the railway bridges could be traversed but I wanted something closer to home, so my dad and I built Climbing Wall Version One. This was on the outside of the house and an epic to make. Fifteen-millimetre holes were bashed into the masonry between the bricks with old-style 'star' hand-drills, each hole taking forever. Into these holes we hammered bits of copper pipe that, sticking out 20 millimetres or so, would provide footholds, or 'footpegs'. The handholds were the brick edges, enhanced in places. But this climbing wall was only about 2 metres wide and, more critically, outside. Version Two was opened in about 1981 in the garage, a similar affair, but much improved with the use of some epoxy resin we'd been given from a builder. With this resin we stuck bits of assorted rock to the wall: limestone, sandstone, grit, slate, granite and beach pebbles. I spent a lot of time getting it right and the result was a pretty good traversing wall, even if I do say so myself. I drew up a topo and set myself hundreds of problems and circuits. It was intensely fingery, with many of the handholds being just the 5-millimetre wide edge between the bricks and the same for the feet. Having recently tried these problems again I'm thoroughly impressed with myself and with the difficulty, though to be fair most of the problems are a little bunched and designed for someone probably half my height.

This was perfect training and a perfect grounding for what was to come many years later. The style was totally appropriate to British limestone sport climbing, crimpy and gnarly with bad footholds on a fairly vertical face. My wall was all about pulling into positions, holding them, reaching smoothly to the next handhold and locating the fingers precisely. With such poor footholds, keeping tension throughout the body is essential. This is exactly what British sport climbing is all about. However, my wall would look somewhat out of place these days. Training has apparently advanced massively over the years and is now all about leaping between bits of wood or dynoing on 45-degree overhanging walls between massive sloping blobs. There aren't actually many outdoor routes like that and, interestingly, since the advancement of training, the standards at the cutting edge on UK sport climbing have pretty much stalled over the last ten years.

Anyway, the style of movement was based entirely on my experiences out on real rock, but was also limited by the wall we had, it being vertical (as house walls tend to be), and only 2 metres high by about 5 metres wide. I trained on this extensively, every other night for a couple of hours or so. It probably explains a lot, but is also a good advertisement for intensive but low impact training. I was really young and pushed right through puberty with this type of workout and suffered no finger injuries whatsoever. Even now, at forty-three, I have only had one finger injury which was only really due to bashing it into a handhold whilst route setting and bending it sideways a few years ago (and then not letting it fix properly). Many kids these days are broken by their mid-teens and even if they make it without injury their footwork is often all over the place.

So this was my training when I was young, but it was never training. This stands out as a critical point. I wasn't trying to get better and I wasn't using it to aid my outdoor climbing at all. I'd built the wall because I wanted to climb on something. My little bit of bouldering was a stand-alone activity that was more like a mental puzzle. I'd spend hours making harder and harder problems pulling on tiny pinches or millimetre edges, where catching the next hold was all about exact positioning and precise movement. If I couldn't do it, or couldn't manage previous problems, I didn't get all pissed off with 'being weak'. It was more like my head wasn't in it, like when you try a crossword and your brain isn't working, you just put it down and wait for another time. I climbed a lot, and always alone, but only when I actually wanted to. There was no one to impress and no desire to get better, just to play. I didn't beat myself up for having an off day, or get depressed over missing a session, worrying that I'd get all out of shape. The attitude I had was very pure and I look back on it with fondness really.

Life should be all about playing. As a parent you look at your kids and see how much they play and realise how much you don't. My favourite toy is Lego. It filled my life for years, beginning with big mega blocks, then moving into town Lego, space Lego and then the ultimate – technical Lego. I learned a lot from this toy, I was an engineer from the start I guess. The biggest challenge for me was to try and build a car with front-wheel drive and independent suspension, near impossible with the bits on offer back then. I spent hours, days, weeks even months on this project, refining my ideas, even altering bits of Lego with a saw and sandpaper, though this was an act that took much soul searching, bending the ethics of Lego design. With each finished project the whole thing would be dismantled to its individual parts. All laid out the canvas was blank, each bit ready for assembly. Most were just the basic building blocks but some were special; intricate hinges and suspension mechanisms. Sometimes new components would arrive, bought in with new kits, and older bits would be left in a tin, never used. I loved how the simplicity of it connected with the complexity.

Life is like a Lego set. Not in a miserable way; it's just made up of many components and assembled in a specific way. Each finished model is unique and shaped by the builders of life, but never really finished, with continual alterations and additions of new components with the passing of time. Like a Lego set it's possible to smash it to pieces, breaking it down into tiny fragments and randomly scattering the parts. A rebuild from scratch is nearly impossible; the step-by-step instructions long forgotten in the distant past. My Lego model of life had taken a hit, but as my view cleared, I realised that just a few of the components had been dismantled. The majority was really still intact, the shape of it, all the special bits, family, friends and health, that kind of stuff. It was just a matter of putting it all back together in a slightly different pattern.

In a way it was a blessing; humans have a habit of pressing on regardless rather than facing up to issues. I'd needed a bit of a kick up the arse, in particular with my climbing, as we seemed to have separated from each other over the recent years. I felt like it had deserted me but in reality I'd pushed it aside. My model of climbing had lost its shape and didn't fit together with the solid foundations or the way my life model was evolving. I needed to break the model and with the components laid out this gave the opportunity and freedom to put them back together in a new and better way.

After a while in Teesside I returned to Sheffield. Despite cutting many of my ties, Sheffield had become my home and in the end it was the only place I could go. Again the climbing was the draw, just as it had been before university. My experience of sport climbing in Thailand had rekindled the desire and now, as I cleared the muddled fog I'd been lost in for the last year or so, I felt an overpowering yearning for movement over the stone. Initially dossing at a mate's house, I quickly fluked a single roomed bedsit near Fulwood, which is as close to the Peak as you can get and still be living in the city of Sheffield. I could cycle to Burbage in thirty minutes, or drive there in less than ten (if I'd had a car). Isolated from the old crew I led a monk's life in my little box of a room, cycling to the Peak during the day and chilling in the evening by myself. Hardly an active social life but I was completely content and didn't even consider any relationships with the opposite sex. I just wanted it simple, and climbing was easily enough. Some new climbing opportunities started to appear in the form of mates

I'd not seen for a while. However, unlike myself, they'd all moved on and grown up a bit and most importantly they all had cars. It was obvious that my university days had been hindered by the lack of transport because suddenly the Peak District expanded massively, putting a whole new world of climbing within reach. Millstone and Curbar were no longer on the outer limits and became evening quick hits, and places like The Roaches and Stoney went from impossible to easy. At first I went out on the odd easy bumbling afternoon, more of a social catch-up and familiarisation with how to speak to humans, but this quickly gathered pace and eventually snowballed to a point where I couldn't keep up with the available opportunities. One friend led to another, and then a whole new team, and new teams beyond, all out and about. With no ties, no job and nothing to hold me back I jumped at the chances; my desire to climb combined with a desire to simply 'feel wanted' which, although sounding totally feeble, is probably about the long and short of it. I threw myself in, feeding off the positive energy like a massive sugar hit after a long-suffered starvation. Early summer good weather inspired weekend trips to Wales and the Lakes and long days meant evening climbing with the after-workers. I felt like I was caught in a whirlwind but just went with it. There was nothing to hold me back.

Unfortunately my elbows were still dodgy. Almost two years of no climbing and they were still aching after every trip to the crag. A few months ago whilst in Thailand they hadn't hindered me, but the climbing was low level and I'd only weighed a few grams. That apparent recovery had given me a huge mental boost, reopening the climbing door that I'd closed. Now I was more psyched than ever, had time on my hands that I needed to fill and I was pushing the elbows again. I poured all my energy into climbing, relying on it completely without any other kind of back up, and a feeling of dread was seeping in alongside the all-too-familiar throbbing tendon attachments. This time they annoyed me; I shouted at them to get better and I'd have bashed them against a wall if I'd thought it would have done any good. I chose to just ignore them. 'You elbows can just piss off and leave me alone.' Not a perfect recovery plan but I'd given them their chance. I'd rested and stretched and iced and even rubbed 'magic healing stones' against them and said prayers to God. That was it. Enough was enough. I just carried on climbing. Being out of shape was a blessing; still underweight and utterly feeble from India, I was well below par and didn't even try and hit the ground running, taking more of a snail's pace really. This was exactly what my elbows needed. Looking back it's obvious, and it's well-known that the body responds to requests. Sure we need rest to recover from injury, but at some point we need to work the injured site, otherwise it forgets what to do. I'd let my elbows go to shit and they had gotten used to doing nothing other than lifting pints of beer and operating the TV remote control. They didn't need to get better so simply gave up trying. With my gentle return to climbing they woke up and, at first, got pissed off and shouted back at me, but then realised it was time to get down to it and sort their lives out. After a few weeks the elbows felt really sore, after a month and they were crying out with pain but then, a few months later, I'd forgotten all about them. The tendonitis seemed to have completely vanished. With fixed elbows, improving strength, new mates and new crags, I was on a roll. From wanting to leap off a cliff to only wanting to get up one in just a few short months. What a transformation.

Flicking through the brand new edition of *High* magazine I was captivated by the images of honed athletes attacking desperate-looking moves. I was fifteen years old and it was 1986; sport climbing was exploding. The difference between it and the traditional climbing that I knew and understood seemed vast, and it wasn't just the bolt protection, it was a whole new fashion with bright Lycra tights, cool haircuts, state-of-the-art rock shoes and new-generation equipment. Plateauing out on the traditional routes, the top climbers had thrown themselves headlong into sport climbing. There was a lot of room to expand and standards were flying through the roof. Even the grading system was new, with the French system imported and the old UK system left behind for the big boots and breeches brigade. Images in the magazines were of tiny holds and outrageous moves, big muscles and contorted faces as a new breed of rock star strained under the appalling difficulty of the moves. Ben Moon, Jerry Moffatt, Mark Leach and 'Basher' Atkinson crimping and slapping their way up *Statement of Youth*, *Revelations*, *Cry Freedom* and *Mecca*. The cliffs were huge and outrageously steep: Raven Tor, Kilnsey and Malham Cove, all like nothing I'd even seen before. It was all about the 'redpoint', pushing right to the physical limit, the final fall-free ascent a flawless gymnastic routine of the utmost difficulty. It was an exploration of climbing ability totally different to anything I'd ever experienced and an entirely different world to my bumblings out on the local moors with their short vertical walls and ledges to shuffle along.

Though totally out of my league it struck a chord. I kind of understood how it worked and it fitted with what I was looking for. Even as a youngster brought up in a purely traditional environment and inspired by the great lines in the mountains, I could still sense this was a type of climbing I'd really enjoy. It was still viewed with disdain by the masses; it wasn't 'real' climbing, and a huge divide opened up with regular heated debates on ethics and many boiled-over tempers. The fear was that pre-placed bolts would appear all over the country on all rock types, ruining established climbs and removing the risk from climbing. The future generation would be robbed of their unclimbed rock as the greedy bolters gobbled up every inch of virgin terrain. But the sport climbers argued their routes were unprotectable and simply not viable as traditional climbs. In theory, the routes were possible without bolts because they'd actually been climbed without a fall on the redpoint effort, but it was insisted that the danger level was totally unfeasible. For someone to solo a line and declare it bolt-free would make the climb impossible for nearly everyone else, thus taking a much-desired challenge away from a steadily growing group of climbers. Sport climbers, apparently, weren't interested in changing the character of existing routes, they were only attracted to the blank and over-hanging limestone faces of the Peak District, Yorkshire and North Wales. A compromise could be reached but it wasn't going to happen overnight.

It was hard to know in which camp to sit, my elder peers strongly against it, my gut instinct suggesting that it looked rather fun. So I sat on the fence and watched the war rage from a distance, aware of this new and radical style and waiting for a chance to give it a go.

It wasn't until 1994 that I really discovered sport climbing in the Peak District. At twenty-four years old it was a complete revelation and the start of a performance-climbing phase that would change my life forever. It came at exactly the right time: hunting for stability from a fragile mental state, this new and absorbing style of climbing was the perfect medicine. There was so much to learn and, critically, I could see I was pretty good at it, which was a much-needed boost to my confidence. Praise flowed my way and I shyly soaked it up – but even though I could see I had a talent I never thought I was better than anyone else. I've always seen climbing as a relative sport where everyone operates on their own level, taking their own experience. The only difference may be the angle of the rock or the size of the holds. The ability to pull on little crimps is just one of many strengths and I look on in awe at others who far surpass me in tenacity, drive, motivation, flexibility and so many other ways, irrespective of their position on a graded list.

The massive sport climbing revelation was actually on my *second* trip to Peak limestone. The very first visit, in 1991 whilst still at university, had been a mixed affair, cycling out from Sheffield with minimal knowledge of any sport routes and even less of how to actually go about climbing them. The primary goal was a bridge jump from the big bridge near Chee Dale Cornice, the one that is always cluttered with abseiling kids. The jumping part of the trip was a total success, which is more than can be said for my first Peak limestone route later the same day, which was somewhat below a total failure. Scoping the line of *Sardine* at Raven Tor I was amazed at how easy it looked for an E6, with jugs all over and even the odd bolt. Setting off I already had the route in the bag, though within seconds I was getting pumped and couldn't get my head round why something so blatantly easy was proving to be so hard. All the jugs seemed to be made of glass and to make matters worse, they all looked like they were about to fall off. The first bolt, pretty high up at maybe 5 metres, was just a stud, a bit of threaded bar sticking out from the rock by about 10 millimetres. The hanger had either been stolen or fallen off. From the ground it hadn't looked important, an excessive placement on easy ground. But now, as I wobbled way out left at the end of the famous traverse, the looped wire of a Wild Country Rock number 2 over the stud was looking extremely unreliable, especially as there was no doubt whatsoever that I was going to fall on it. Swinging down to skim the ground I never took my eyes off the wire as it pivoted dangerously close to the end of the stud, only held on by a thread or two. Back in play I was basically way out of my depth. I hung on every bolt, frigged the moves and cheated my way to the top. It was a humiliating experience and I declared there and then that I would never, ever, not in my life, come back to this polished pile of total shite that pretended to be rock climbing.

But I was back, three years later, and I'd forgotten the crumbling polish. And anyway, I had nothing to lose with my climbing. With my bedsit as a base, time on my hands and eager to level myself, I was wide open to new experiences and every experience was from ground zero on this new white rock. It was Mike who took me out, a long-term mate, younger than me but part of our family gang from my teen years, a bunch of families that would holiday together in Pembroke, Cornwall and the Lakes. We'd always got on well and our lives followed a similar curve, gravitating to Sheffield for climbing in the disguise of a university degree. He was a natural at climbing movement, way better than me, but never took it as far as he could. Somehow he had a car, unusual for a student, and we drove out to Rubicon Wall, a destination beyond cycle range and too much of a pain to hitch. Skirting along the edge of the river, white walls hung over us and dots of chalk and shining bolts marked the routes, with tiny edges the only visible holds. I was so excited! This was a place of big numbers and famous routes, stuff straight from the magazines. It may have been my first visit but it felt familiar, like a second home.

A young guy was slumped on the rope belayed by his dad. Swinging out, he asked for 'the stick' which he then used to pre-clip his rope another bolt higher. Hanging on this bolt he then fiddled around with various holds before grunting a fair bit but barely making upwards progress. Sometime later, back on the ground, he offered his rope should I fancy an attempt. Having just done *Dragonflight*, a classic trad E3, I doubted my chances on this E6 6c that, even though only double the E grade, was quite clearly exponentially more difficult even if it was safe as houses. Throwing myself into the lead I performed exactly as expected, totally rubbish, and within seconds was hanging from the first bolt. I lowered down, only to be told that this wasn't the way it worked, you weren't supposed to try and climb it first go. The route had to be 'worked', the moves dialled and links made. Then eventually it would be time for the redpoint. I knew this, of course, I read the magazines. I knew of Mark Leach and his forty-two days on *Cry Freedom*, and of Basher and Zippy with their multi-day sieges at Raven Tor. I knew all about redpointing and working moves but to see it in action was weird and to try and do it was worse. Climbing for me was really all about first go or not at all, but I took the bait and from the rope, holds appeared where I'd never have found them on lead and the subtleties of grip position became clear. Trying the moves over and over allowed optimum footholds to be isolated and committed to memory. Strangely it was absorbing, distilling the climbing down into individual movement unclouded by fear. The bolts were close enough for me to reach from one to the next, allowing each section of the route to be inspected 'on top-rope'. Within an hour I was good to go and the redpoint fell first shot. *Let the Tribe Increase*, 7c+, my first real redpoint. Twenty-four years old, a bit of a late starter, but I was buzzing, a head full of moves and positions heightened by the physical pleasure of moving at my limit. But there was confusion too. I'd done this route, I'd ticked it, I could put a big fat tick in my Rockfax *Peak Limestone* guide, but at the same time I wasn't sure exactly what I'd done. My on-sight ethics could be bent to accommodate a redpoint ascent, but the extent of the practice, the way in which it was distilled down to the final 'performance', felt a slightly hollow victory. Still, I knew for sure I'd be back for more.

16 THE VERDON GORGE

I consider *Let the Tribe Increase* my first real sport redpoint. It was the first time I'd really embraced this initially bizarre procedure, even if it had been rather reluctantly and slightly shambolically. I'd worked the moves, examined the holds and eliminated ones I didn't need. Sequences were analysed and the most efficient methods for my size and strength committed to memory. Then, after adequate and considered rest, I'd blasted the route without fault and clipped the belay with a glow of pride. It was very definitely very different from anything I'd done before and very cool. However, this wasn't really my first: I wasn't a complete redpoint virgin. I'd red-pointed a sport route before, just once, way back in 1988 when I was seventeen and considerably more clueless about the whole sport climbing game. This had been on my first major trip away, an adventure to the Verdon Gorge with Dave and Tim using up most of our college summer holiday. We took the National Express, which took forever, and hitched the last bit to spend six weeks in poverty and climbing heaven. We climbed every day, skinny and brown, ticking off the classic full-height routes and the immaculate single pitch lines.

1988 and the Verdon was in full flow. Dragging oversized rucksacks, we threaded our way into Camping Bourbon, anxiously hunting a free spot like a timid late arrival to a music concert. A single patch winked, devoid of shade and limited on grass, pegs requiring a power drill placement and instantly bending beyond use. Glancing round we soaked it up: Pollitt strumming his guitar under the willow trees, Basher and Gore animating their projects and Moffatt's voice filling the campground. Later, tumbling from some rusting local's wreck of a car packed with sun-bleached ropes and frayed slings, we tottered over the limestone pavement for our first view of the gorge, the sharp edge looming, the depth making its presence felt. Slowly, hands welded to secure threads, we peered over and allowed the scale to strike: the river far below, the smell, the gentle updraft, the volume of rock *everywhere*. The rim bristled with activity. Climbers had come from all corners of the world and the immaculate walls were dotted with Lycra inching upwards, coloured ants in a sea of grey. We had arrived, the Verdon Gorge, the finest cliff in Europe.

Je suis une legende is a classic 7a+ right below the belvedere viewpoint. Very easy to top-rope and hence very polished and very hard. I'd managed it first go on top-rope with one rest. A cool name, *Je suis une legende*. Paul, another Brit who was camping near to us, had also climbed the route, and now repeated the name over and over, the words apparently applicable to him in some kind of way, so he thought. As he was older than us, we looked up to him slightly. He also knew how things worked; sport climbing and redpointing and stuff. But he was obviously a bit of a knob. There were a lot of climbers in the Verdon at that time and the campsite had an innocent and simple vibe long before the performance and grade-crunching days. Guitars, lie-ins, Lycra, beer and dope painted the scene. The big boys were there; magazine heroes and front cover stars, far too big for us; we hung around like flies, and when Basher passed us his dregs of beer we scarpered like schoolboys (which we were). Paul was halfway between us and them, the right age to be big, but only cool enough for us. As we were in a three, Paul adopted me as belayer in his attempt to become big by climbing a hard route with a suitably large grade. *Liqueur de Coco* was his target, into which he'd already put in some work; 7c+, and certainly 8a for my height. An immaculate line slicing the centre of a huge, mirror-smooth face. Tied in to the belay a hundred metres above the jungle, I watched as Paul organised his junk, still mumbling about his legendary status, before finally swinging into action and immediately falling off at the first bolt. He didn't look close to say the least, and his effort turned into a dogging mission, a shambles of rope hauling and aiding. Later, his 'redpoint' effort seemed like a total waste of time, though what did I know? He said there was good progress and 'it would go'. So I top-roped out after him, the most difficult route I'd ever been on at that time by a considerable margin.

Way above me, but between rests on the rope, I could see past the difficulty and through to the beauty of the movement. I was sucked in, pushing aside my traditions. Though on-sight was still everything, I was back on *Liqueur de Coco* next day, without Paul this time, and with Tim holding the rope I top-roped it clean first try of the day. It was a revelation, but the progression way beyond comprehension. I didn't know what it meant and, perhaps, where I could have taken it if I'd tried. Looking back it's more obvious now and a pointer to the future. If I'd known how sport climbing worked I'd have led it straight off without doubt. Back then in 1988, at seventeen years old and with no training and no idea, that would have been a good level. A few days later I led it straight off, placing 'draws as I went as we didn't know any better. Paul was gutted and he didn't hang with us anymore. I guess he realised he wasn't destined to be a legend after all.

The trip had us psyched for climbing, but we'd not yet found the sport climbing style. The Verdon isn't quite sport climbing. For sure there are bolts – there have to be, as most routes just wouldn't go without them – but the bolts are spaced and old-style in places, home-made from bits of angle-iron. We climbed like we were trad climbing, with double ropes and slings on spikes. In a way it was worse than trad climbing; as at least on trad you can generally place gear in cracks when you want it, but here, looking up at a UK 6b move and down at a 2-metre run-out and then beyond into a 300-metre drop, it all felt pretty airy. The Verdon has an adventurous feel; epics are likely. On the second to last pitch of *Pichenibule* I'd clipped a sling into a bolt on the belay, passed it through my harness belay loop and then back into the screwgate on the bolt. A classic Verdon hanging stance, middle of nowhere, impeccable, flawless limestone faces all around. Tim seconded me up and then led through into the distance. A tug on the rope from above was my signal to climb, the updraft making a shout useless from 45 metres away, but the screwgate was jammed shut. Nothing I tried could free it, and the more I tried the greater Tim's impatience grew, as indicated by the tightness of the top rope. Eventually, drastic measures: I pulled down on the rope, now as tight as a guitar string, and held it with my teeth while quickly untying the rope from my harness and retying it around my waist with a bowline knot. Then, loosening my harness, I climbed out of it and left it dangling behind. Next day I abbed down with a borrowed spanner and borrowed harness and unscrewed the bolt hanger and took the whole lot up. I've still got the hanger at home as a memory to the event. A good bit of improvisation I think, but the Verdon is like that, you need your wits about you to get out of the mess that you get yourself into.

Almost terminally pumped from the 7a wall pitch of *Nécronomicon*, I at last sagged onto the belay slings and allowed my breathing to catch up. Unclipping my belay device and rotating it into position I suddenly fumbled it, numb fingers and mind astray. Juggling in front of my eyes I made a grab, only to send it on a lonely 300-metre descent. Ping ... Ping ... Ping ... Each high pitched note a reminder of my loss as the device glanced off the bullet-hard limestone to eventually come to its grave on one of the huge tree-covered ledges balancing on the massive walls of the Gorge. Bollocks! This was bad news. One week into the six-week trip and there was no space in the budget for a new device, but every route began with an abseil, sometimes a long one and always a scary one.

This was a huge loss to my already pathetic rack borrowed from Dad, a tatty 45-metre 9-mil rope, a few oval screwgates, and about eight quick-draws made up from various lengths of sling or rope and big fat krabs for this funny bolted stuff. Hanging from the home-made double bolt belay in the immense sea of grey I belayed Tim up with an Italian hitch, though having never used one before it was more of a jumble of twists in the rope that looked tangled enough to hold him if he fell. I put it round my waist too, just in case, and, feeling rather inadequate, attempted to hide the mess under my shirt as he approached. Still, it was only a week ago that he'd belayed me from his plastic gear loop, only realising when I fell off and there was a nasty tearing noise – luckily I didn't weigh much. So we were quits there, but that still didn't sort my problem. Looking down I was sure I could see my now beloved device, the old Sticht plate style with a spring and bit of white string to clip into the krab to apparently ensure it wouldn't be dropped. Surely it would be easy to find, lying lonely and obvious amongst the scree. I didn't have to think much; of course I'd be going down to rescue him.

Alone as expected (why else would anyone want to come along on such a rescue mission?), I began the multiple abseil first thing next day after hitching to the cliff. The others rested since I had all the ropes and a borrowed figure of 8. It was strange, descending alone, committing and pulling the rope with no retreat possible. The only way now was down, but eventually the ledge arrived, more of a garden really, and I could relax before beginning the search. Of course, it wasn't where it should have been, or anywhere obvious, or in the bushes or trees. After an hour's effort I was giving up feeling stupid and sad, but a glint caught my eye under some leaves, not grey metal but blue – a quickdraw, and a nice one too. Funky colours with a luminous Petzl quickdraw tape. A worthy prize for my efforts perhaps? And then another one, pink this time, then a chalk bag, some old wires, a cam, more quickdraws, the odd boot and at last a Sticht plate, not mine, but just as good. In all a very good haul by the end: three figure of 8s, two Sticht plates, seven quickdraws, a Shunt, two cams, an assortment of chalkbags and a jumble of slings that I left behind. I even took back some odd boots figuring that if one fitted any of us we'd be halfway towards a decent pair of climbing shoes. Staring way up I could see the tiny ants slowly moving up the vast walls. So many routes up there, so many years of climbing, of course, there was so much stuff, nobody in their right mind would really bother to go to so much trouble just to get one bit of dropped kit from a moment's loss of concentration. Their loss and my gain. This vast ledge was only a few pitches off the gorge floor and I landed close to the start of *La Demande*, the classic 6a or E1 I'd done before. Home ground now, safety. A long walk back, perhaps, but I strode into camp with the swagger of a triumphant explorer, displaying my trophies to the lads who stared in disbelief. There was plenty of kit for our team now and the new quickdraws were loaned out to whoever was going for the hardest lead. The colours, weight and feel made our old stuff seem from another time, which I guess it was.

Maybe there was more to be found down in the depths of the gorge. There had to be – surely it would be worth another trip, to a different ledge of course. I chose the biggest, the one that must have the most booty, my greed far bigger than the thought or planning put into the second exploration. The first abseil should have put me off: two old bolts linked with some frayed tat. A dirty gully with loose blocks, it didn't look travelled, and I had to search around for the next anchor, praying my ropes would reach. A very long free-hanging abseil led to the third pitch down, and I had to swing hard and keep it going to hit the belay. Was there one lower? I didn't want to risk it and run out of rope. Pulling the rope, the end swinging away and up out of reach, felt very committing. It was coming though and more and more rope coiled over my legs and around my feet as the end slid upwards. Then, inevitably, it stopped, jammed. An inexplicable phenomenon somehow preventing me from getting back my rope. Sometimes it comes free, with enough force, suddenly escaping its trap, but often it doesn't, and this time I just knew it wouldn't. The thing is, you don't know what's keeping it in place. Is the knot permanently wedged securely in a crack, or on a dead twig on the point of snapping? Of course, it couldn't be trusted, but what now? There were hundreds of vertical metres below me and no actual route back up. I wasn't sure I'd even told my mates where I was heading and this place didn't seem too well used. Hidden away in a chossy gully, there was no one around, no climbers to alert, perhaps a helicopter could find me but that couldn't be an option: far too embarrassing, and what if I had to pay for it? Time dragged. There seemed to be plenty at first to solve this puzzle and come up with a safe, comfortable and obvious escape, but home was a long way off. In the end I came up with a plan, like making up the final word to fit a crossword just to have closure. I tied the pulled end of the rope to the anchor and put myself on belay, as if to abseil, but instead set off upwards, paying out the rope as I went, my factor two fall looking less and less attractive with each move. But I also had a prusik on the jammed rope which still hung from above. If I fell surely this would hold – after all I'd not been able to pull it down. But if it did come free, well, I could grab my belay device as

I crashed into the gully below and possibly save the day. My goal was 40 feet above me, dangling 10 feet out from the crumbly limestone corner I was inching up. The free end swayed gently to and fro, beckoning. If I could get a prusik loop round this end, I'd have one around both ropes and I was in, safe. After maybe an hour I was level; the end was just hanging there, now utterly motionless and almost inviting a leap and a grab. But I had a better plan, using a stick, cunningly picked up en route to reach out into the void and pluck at that tiny bit of tape on the end of the rope, now waving and flicking from side to side having been knocked from its sleep. Easy does it, the spindly bushes I leaned out from groaned, dry and brittle, already barely clinging to the rock in this vertical desert. Another swipe; the rope is really swinging now. I can't reach it, but surely this will work. And then I have it; a knot in the end and a prusik loop on in seconds. All that's left is the stomach-churning swing out above the void, away from my friendly gully and then upwards with prusiks on both ropes to discover the cause of my epic. A crack, of course, right on the edge, the knot firmly buried and impossible to have released from below. The weight of a car couldn't have freed it.

Later, down in the garden, I unenthusiastically began the search, but strangely I'd had enough. There was nothing anyway, not even bits of tat. Looking at the topo it was obvious: the few routes above were 7b+ or worse, not a collection of 5s climbed daily by masses of beginners, all fingers and thumbs. And being a topo, of course, it didn't indicate that this ledge was actually fairly close to just being part of the vertical wall, with spindly bushes clinging desperately to an unlikely sloping heap of scree that was clearly about to avalanche itself over the edge of the cliff. I descended, wishing to find a helmet as rubble rained down from above until, at last, I reached horizontal ground and safety. This was a no-free-kit-day but nothing really comes for free anyway, it's given and we take. I'd just got lucky last time and luck you can't push.

Occasionally luck does strike, but it's not always good. In the Verdon storms can fly in with no warning. Some years later, hanging with Tony a pitch from the top of the gorge, a comedy black cloud moved in from nowhere. The colour of death, it threw jagged lightning in all directions like a scene from a comic book. Tony scrambled his way up the pitch and I was on belay in seconds, the rain coming now and the sense of urgency rising into panic. I sprinted the 40 metres of 6b in seconds as lightning rained down with its primary target being the sharp rim of the gorge on which we were now both converging. Leaping the edge we bailed imme-diately, leaving everything in a drenched heap, only to be utterly floored moments later by the loudest crash I've ever heard and a flash so bright as to be made by some kind of nuclear explosion. Back on our feet again and we were now in a war zone, sprinting for our lives through the torrent of rain. Luckily the road was close, seconds away, and also the car into which we dived, at last safe. Ten minutes later we heard the sirens and then the ambulance screamed by, only to stop right behind us. Four cyclists had been sheltering from the rain under a tree. One went out to move his bike – a moment of good luck for him at least – but the other three were killed instantly by a massive strike. It was all a bit close. I used to find thunderstorms good fun; now I don't.

From the first day at Rubicon I was hooked. I'm not sure if it was the style or the difficulty that drew me in. To be climbing right at the limit without fear was alien and addictive, but the numbers were also attractive. I'd grown up with numbers: E6 6a; E7 7a; 7c+; 8b; 8c+. Grades shouldn't be everything, but they are everywhere in the climbing world whether you use them as a guide to a nice day out, to find a test to the max or a way to get sponsorship. Grades were attached inextricably to ingrained images from the magazines of my youth: *Climber, High* and *Mountain, Lord of the Flies* E6 6a, *Requiem* E7 7a, *Zeke the Freak* 8b, *Chouca* 8a+, *Hubble* 8c+. I'd followed the progression and I knew what they meant and now I was skirting along the edge of big numbers. *Tribe* at 7c+ wasn't really that big, but it was really big for me, and I'd climbed the route fast and could see the potential for something much harder.

1995 was a good year to really get started, one of the driest summers for ages and when I turned up at the Cornice in Chee Dale I was blown away by the quality – a French-style sport crag only thirty-five minutes' drive from my house. I pretty much lived there for a few months, climbing day on, day off depending on when I could blag lifts – and lifts were easy as there were loads of people going out all the time. There were weekenders, after-workers and those who worked odd days, not to mention non-workers, all mad for sport climbing. Being at the crag was like being down the pub, with good banter and new people to meet at every visit. It was the inverse of my university climbing days on the grit; suddenly I knew tons of people who were all really psyched and transport was a piece of cake. Crucially I wasn't always alone and struggling to find motivation for hard stuff – there was encouragement everywhere, driving me forward onto routes previously placed in the 'reserved for superstars' box. Most of my climbing was still on-sight, as there are loads of mid to high 7s in Chee Dale and these kept me busy and excited. I was still translating 7b+ into E6, and E6 was a dream-world grade for me, but I was doing them at every visit, first go.

The only spanner in the works was, of course, 'work'. Money, we all need it. I didn't need much though. My bedsit was peanuts, £125 per month which was paid by my housing benefit anyway. There was no gas and no phone, hot water was included, and there was no council tax back then. My only bill was electricity, a pound-coin slot meter downstairs. So I never used the heating and just used a few pence a day to cook. I didn't drink or smoke, so my only bill was a bit of shared petrol. Dole easily covered everything, especially as I had time to cycle around buying food from Netto and cheap pound shops. I didn't need a job, I didn't want a job. Looking back I'm hardly proud of this, but on the flip side I like to think of this period as a kind of YTS scheme, or even government sponsorship, and to be fair I reckon I was a very good investment. With their help I could climb when I wanted and became well and truly hooked, and I've gone on from there to make a career from climbing and paid my taxes every year without fail like a good honest citizen. So there you go Mr Tax Man if you're reading this.

But I didn't start off making money from climbing, that part of my life was still a long way off. During my six or seven months on the unofficial government support scheme a few jobs appeared on the potential list. Being on the dole meant you had to be 'actively seeking work' and that meant not turning down interviews and not turning down job offers. The dole office took me aside as I signed on to say they'd found me a job that 'suited my requirements'. This was both a disappointment and a surprise as I was pretty sure I'd carefully tailored any applications to ensure no job would ever be suitable. A researcher post was going at Sheffield Hallam University investigating vehicle brake disc and pad units. It was flexible and with a short-term contract and there was an interview lined up that I couldn't escape. Sitting in the secretary's office amongst the candidates I felt clearly outclassed as they dropped qualifications and work experience into play, but totally relaxed, as out of all of these suit-wearing boffins I was the only one who didn't actually want the job. Rolling into the interview with trainers and jeans I played myself to the panel and surprisingly they seemed to like my game. We ended up talking about climbing and travelling and they almost offered me the job there and then. A few days later I got the letter I'd expected, the job was mine, could I start next Monday? As it turned out I had a few climbing trips to Chee Dale planned as well as a weekend in North Wales, so I told them I'd start in a fortnight. This set the scene for what turned out to be a great job.

My boss was Alan Wirth, ridiculously short and round, but a great character, and a firm believer in the working climber's favourite motto, 'as long as the work gets done it doesn't matter when you do it'. We got on well. The vehicle brake lining company, Mintex, were working with the university to optimise their lining material and it was my job to analyse how the lining and metallic disc brake interacted. I was given samples of disc and pad to view under a scanning electron microscope. Then, based on what I found, I'd suggest new materials for the brake lining and set up real and lab-based experiments to see what happened. Basically it was my job to help you stop faster and more safely. I'd landed on my feet big time. First of all I actually liked the job and suddenly I had a relative fortune (a whole £7,000 per year), but most importantly it didn't impact on my climbing. A little jiggery-pokery here and there and I was out at 2 p.m. Tuesday and Thursday – so long as I worked until 8 p.m. on Monday and Friday. It was all I needed; I didn't even need all the six weeks' holiday as the Peak had everything I desired.

The flexibility within my job was probably crucial to flying through the grades. My time was divided about 50/50 between trad and sport, with limestone trad far more appealing than the gritstone. Not that I didn't like the grit as an actual type of rock, it was more about the scale and style. Gritstone routes tend to be bouldery and short and often scary. Limestone routes are longer and more sustained. Protection is intricate and difficult to place, but at least there usually is some. Basically on the limestone I would be in the 'zone' for longer, absorbed in the climbing process, something that didn't often happen on the grit. Places like Stoney and Chee Dale even had similarities to the awesome traditional climbing at Pembroke, but sport climbing was taking over as the trad routes were ticked off. Sport is also very time efficient, with a lot of hard climbing possible in a very short time. Sport routes don't need complicated equipment and they can be led in minutes. In fact, they have to be led in minutes or you'll run out of steam and fall off. An anchor is clipped at the top allowing the leader to quickly lower to the ground. No walk offs, no rope coiling. The two climbers in a team don't even need to do the same route, as often a sport cliff has routes of varying difficulty side by side. In a way a lot of the experience of climbing is lost: that summit feeling, the traditional environment, dealing with danger and commitment, sharing a route with a partner. All these things are replaced with real absorption in the movement and the exploration of physical limits, as well as having a full-on workout sending those exercise hormones flying. And all uncluttered by fear. I'd had a lot of years of dragging friends up E2s and walking down in the rain with soggy ropes and, of course, many a nice day out as well, but sport was new and it drew me in.

As well as on-sighting I played on the hard routes. My first 'grade 8' was *Zeke the Freak* at Rubicon, done in a day on 31 September 1995. I know the exact date as it's in my climbing diary. The old mega-detailed diary for the confused and sad young person had been well and truly ditched, replaced by the climber diary. This is the little book containing routes and mini topos and training ideas and lists of injuries. Most climbers have them, especially the psyched ones, and I was one of the psyched ones.

Book 1, 28/8/95 - 8/11/96
First entry:
The start of it all. My years of injury finally came to an end in February '95 and a trip to El Chorro a few months later was the real start. Since then I've discovered the Peak District and the limestone. Sport climbing is clearly what I am cut out for! Never before had I realised my potential! I need this book to keep track …

It was an exciting time. My first season of sport climbing and it lasted forever. I redpointed *Masculine Power Trip* at the Cornice in Chee Dale on 12 December. If you know that route and where it is, and how wet it usually is, then you'll be amazed. The year hung in right until Christmas and gave me the best possible start. Ironically the next year, in 1996, the Cornice didn't dry out at all. It remained permanently under a covering of damp green sludge. I'd just assumed it was always dry, just like the crags are abroad. How naive! In reality the Cornice is usually wet, I'd just fluked it in my first year. However, that meant a move to Raven Tor which suffered less seepage, a crag I'd avoided as the routes were simply too hard for on-sighting. I like to think that as I moved into sport climbing I followed a steady and sensible pathway, building a solid pyramid of routes with a stable wide base. That is the desirable way to progress through the grades, make sure you are solid at one level before moving on to the next to avoid getting your fingers burnt (or injured). However, looking back in the diary I was quite alarmed to see what I was throwing myself at. Before even ticking *Zeke* I'd been on *Mecca* 8b+ and a whole lot of 8a and 8a+ routes without any success and without any real effort to try and climb them. I guess I was just playing. I wanted to see what the really hard stuff was all about. It's not perhaps the best method, and often you will see punters like me floundering on routes out of their league and wish they'd take a reality check. My climbing time was split between routes that I'd on-sight and routes that were basically a bouldering session on a rope. It doesn't sound ideal. However, if I was asked the fastest way for most climbers to improve (which I do get asked a lot) it would have similarities. I'd suggest roughly half a person's time, depending on experience, should be spent climbing routes within the comfort grade and half the time should be spent getting stronger and more powerful. This ensures movement skills are constantly increased and the comfort zone expanded, whilst at the same time making physical gains. Although the on-sighting wasn't always quite within my comfort zone I was following pretty much my perfect plan without realising it and, crucially, I was learning about potential and tenacity – two extremely valuable lessons.

I recently noticed a thread online asking:

'Do people who climb E11 7a have natural born talent? Can the rest of us just train harder and be them?'

Obviously there were a lot of answers, but it was assumed that 90 per cent of people could achieve the upper reaches of the sport, so long as they just put the effort in and only 10 per cent had the extra genetics that take them to the very cutting edge. Potentially this is good news, meaning that if you just get off your arse and try a bit harder you'll probably be a super hero. I'm not so sure about that, I reckon nine out of ten people would never get up *Rhapsody* (the first E11 in Britain), no matter how hard they tried. Perhaps nine out of ten people who are already totally suited to top-end climbing could do better: athletic, driven, the correct body shape and so on. Maybe this bunch can do well and can go from HVS to E11 with a few trips to the gym. However, being fit and 'strong' is just part of the equation, with climbing demanding many other strengths including flexibility, technique and experience – and that's before we even start on mental strengths. Tenacity and drive can certainly go a long way and there are many examples of people who were perhaps not the most technically gifted who took the sport to the limits. Tenacity and motivation are the most important strengths for any sportsperson. Watch how hard the world champion tries in the finals and watch how hard the top end climbers train. Watch as a top performer slaps out another move when for sure they are off, and then another, and another.

I was learning about tenacity. I watched other people, and I tried harder myself. Extra effort took me further without any gain in physical strength. I was amazed how far I could push. Tenacity is without doubt my major strength, allowing access to all my physical ability, and potentially more, somehow magically finding some extra power from nowhere or stealing it from someone else. This strength has been a major blessing as it's allowed me to remain lazy and lardy. I've got away without proper training and can get up stuff that defeats others who have really put the effort in. I feel like a cheat. Even now I still surprise myself on a regular basis, struggling on individual moves only to then bust through a route or boulder problem with relative ease, but only when it counts, only if I start from the ground, it won't work on links. I can't open the tenacity tin unless I have a taste of success. But it does come at a cost. First of all, on a short term scale, being able to dig deep means you'll have shot your lot in just a few burns. The low tenacity climber will have way more efforts, as it's the last bit of effort, that all-out-to-the-max, skin-of-the-teeth stuff that causes energy levels to suddenly drop through the floor. On a redpoint I'd rarely get more than two good goes. The second problem for the high tenacity person is entirely connected to the apparent ability to pull harder than they are physically capable. Maybe tenacity is simply a way of bypassing the body's natural defence systems, and as it shouts out 'stop pulling, you are about to rip a tendon' we simply press on with glory burning in our eyes. As a result I've had my fair share of injuries, in fact, more than my fair share. I think I've had them all really. As I leapt into sport climbing I was picking them up as fast as I was shedding them and even though I have this romantic view that my elbow tendonitis simply disappeared, looking back in the diary there is a different story.

> Indoor leading today – awful. I hated it, so unlike real rock. The grades were harder than before too and I did rubbish. Felt injured almost immediately after stopping. Bad elbows, both sides, and bad shoulder. Most pain for over six months. Took five days to get a 90 per cent recovery. Beware indoors.

Despite near permanent tweaks I pushed through, though with at least some degree of restraint, I didn't want another two-year lay-off. Ironically it was indoors during the winter where I'd fall to bits, out on the rock I'd recover and fifteen years on I still have the same problem.

For me it's fortunate to be that way round as my passion is all for the outdoors, but this phenomenon is hard to understand. The indoor world being all nice and cosy with warm-up areas, comfortable holds, well-set routes and a cafe full of recovery food should be soft on the body. The outside is often the complete opposite, freezing cold and damp, with the climbing often beginning by pulling straight into desperate moves on horrendous razor blade edges after having spent an hour standing motionless in an expedition duvet jacket shivering away as we belay a mate. It could be the way in which indoor climbing is so physical, or how moves are uniformly intense, it's also very dynamic, shock-loading joints with almost every move. Whatever the reasons I avoided too much plastic pulling, and with so much to go at I was outside at every available opportunity.

Slowly I started to see my potential. The moves on hard routes began to feel easy and watching top climbers struggle I'd realise I could pull harder than they could. Armed with new strength and skills, my tenacity and through-the-roof motivation, I knew I could push into the big numbers. So what was stopping me? I just had to get on with it. After I climbed *Zeke* I felt good to go with the redpointing lark and in just over a year I'd gone from my first grade 8 to 8c+.

1	Zeke …	8b	31/9/95	1 day
2	Divine	8a+	22/10/95	1 day
3	Masculine …	8a+	12/12/95	2 days
4	Rattle & Hump	8a	22/6/96	1 day
5	Caviar	8a+	4/7/96	1 day
6	Unleashing …	8a	23/7/96	2 days
7	Love amongst …	8a+	28/7/96	1 day
8	Nemesis	8a+	18/9/96	2 days
9	Mecca	8b+	28/9/96	6 days
10	Pump up the Power	8a+	28/9/96	1 day
11	Jehovakill	8b+	30/10/96	2 days
12	Evolution	8c+	8/11/96	6 days

Friday 8 November – Raven Tor
Evolution – 8c/8c+
At last. Amazingly I did it. Conditions not amazing, and I think I had a cold too. Managed on the second redpoint. Felt okay and had plenty left too but very pleasing. First route that I've ever been blown away by. This is proper hard. I feel like I've crossed a threshold here. Where will this lead me? I looked at Hubble too. Much much harder. In fact utterly impossible, I'll never do this.

Evolution was a big milestone for me. It was definitely the hardest route I'd climbed and an undisputed 'hard' route. Whereas routes like *Mecca* at 8b+ had received many ascents, *Evolution* had only a handful of repeats from big name stars. Jerry Moffatt made the first ascent in 1995, followed by Malcolm Smith and Nic Sellars. It felt hard too; the moves were desperate, with no rests or even marginal shakes. An all-out power endurance sprint to the belay, intensely crimpy and conditions dependent, this route was a whole new level. I'd clearly crossed over into a new dimension which was hard to comprehend. Only a year ago I worshipped the top climbers. Now I was in the same league. But there was no way I was a top climber

– surely there was more to being a top climber than just climbing hard routes? I was missing those bits, whatever they were, although gaining them was neither important nor desirable. As I'd worked on *Evolution*, a successful redpoint had been the target with no viewpoint beyond. Though it had pushed me I knew there had been room to move and there was more in the tank – I could climb harder. The door to hard climbing was thrown wide open.

Fear is the single factor holding most climbers back from reaching their potential. Fear will prevent them from climbing even the easiest of moves on a route, moves that, close to the ground, they'd cruise blindfolded wearing roller-skates. In many cases the fear is irrational. The skill is differentiating between rational and irrational fear. Standing on a chair you're obviously not scared; there's absolutely no chance of falling off. Stand on a 50-metre high chair and you'll instantly panic, start wobbling and need to sit down and cling on. To a certain extent this fear is irrational, though there is, of course, still a slight chance that you could simply topple over and fall to your death. This is the realm of mind control, to know that so long as you stay in control and simply stand up you'll be fine, just as you would be on a normal chair close to the ground. The irrational fear is when we're standing there 50 metres up on our chair, but with the total safety of a rope safeguarding us from falling, and still bricking it.

How to go about curing 'the fear'? Sport climbing can make a big difference and be very good for your trad climbing – and almost every trad climber who's got into sport has found their performance on traditional routes went through the roof. Why? Because trad routes aren't very hard in comparison to sport routes, not in relation to how hard you *could* climb. They just feel hard because you're scared, your wires look dodgy, and they took so long to place that you've become utterly pumped. In fact, you've got so pumped that the hardest move you can actually manage is English 2b. But hang on a minute. Perhaps you aren't even that pumped, you just thought you were. Now, after you've scared yourself stupid and turned your arms into concrete, you realise that there's actually a huge ledge right next to you, somehow invisible until you'd stuffed in a load of protection while hanging onto an apparently tiny edge.

There are a lot of strengths a climber needs. Make a list, it's surprising. It isn't just power and endurance. Something fun to do on your rest days on a trip is to make a list and score yourself, relative to your current standard. Then, without letting your mates see the results, get them to score you. This is a good way to see if you have any hidden weaknesses, or if you've just been avoiding the obvious.

Here is my table below, with a mate's score first (out of five, just in case you wondered if it was out of ten). As it turns out there were few surprises, I knew I was weak and feeble and so did everyone else. (Apparently I managed to disguise my shoddy footwork from them.)

Tenacity	4	5
Confidence	4.5	4
Technique	5	5
Fear	5	5
Core	4	4
Finger strength	3	3
Power	2.5	2
Power Endurance	3.5	3
Endurance	3.5	3
Flexibility	3.5	3
Footwork	4	2
Body Position	5	4
Route reading	4	3.5
Pace	4	4
Preparation	3	1.5

What is clear is the huge range of strengths required for performance and also the importance of each. Physical strength, that stuff we spend so long working at in the gym, only accounts for some of our ability on the rock despite it being the only thing that most people ever consider. My ability to move from 8a to 8c+ in just over a year was certainly not due to a physical strength gain alone. In fact, I'd bet it was hardly due to a strength gain at all.

As a pure traditional climber, I thought I was pretty good with the whole 'fear' thing. Being an engineering type of person I could usually separate rational from irrational and know when I should really start looking for my spare underpants. I have a method when traditional climbing where I rate my protection as I place it, giving a score from one to five, five being as good as a bolt, one being body weight only. Less than one means I might as well just take it out again. Having scored my pro I put this number in a secure box in my head where I won't lose it and refer back to it when I'm a few metres out and facing a desperate slap to a nothing edge. Knowing there is a 'five' below me means zero hesitation, if it's a 'one' then I probably wouldn't have got very far above it in the first place and am almost certainly on the wrong route. Basically, if it's as solid as a bolt then I'm good to go. Obviously there are a few other considerations: is the distance between you and the bolt greater than the bolt and the ground? Are you in a horrendous chimney? Is your belayer half asleep? With some degree of awareness there should be no excuses.

Sport climbing is all about solid 'fives', but fear still holds many people back. It held me back for ages. I didn't even realise until it eventually went away. Fear is crippling and if you are truly scared, like you are really aware of it, you won't be able to do anything even remotely harder than climbing the stairs, and even that could be pushing it. At a much more subtle level, when pushing to your max, even the slightest hesitation on a move and you've blown it. If you are trying to climb to your limit there can be no hesitation; think for a second and the move has just become twice as hard.

One of the best ways to reduce fear is through redpointing, leading hard stuff at your limit on a safe sport route where you already know the moves, you know what's coming up. This will solidify commitment and allow you to learn to flow into and through the moves in the most efficient manner without stalling. Why redpointing? Why not just more on-sighting? Just sticking with on-sighting will help, of course, but it's slow. Imagine you want to be a high diver. You start by walking to the top of the highest board, look down, and instantly gibber. Of course, you don't go for it, you have no idea what to do, no idea of what will happen if you get it wrong. So you go straight down to the lowest board and learn how to dive, working your way back up to the top. When you finally get back up there you know all about body position and movement and what happens if you don't land right. You can go for it. Only ever climbing on-sight style is like only ever walking straight to the top board. When faced with a move that looks desperate, where you know there is a chance you'll fall, you never go for it, you can't commit. With redpointing you know what's coming up, you've done the move before, lots of times. It's practised, ingrained in your mind. You know it's safe if you don't make it. You've probably already taken the fall, it's nothing to be afraid of. So you go for it 100 per cent and you need to, because 100 per cent is essential to get through the move. Given time this commitment becomes the norm and it translates back into on-sight climbing fairly quickly. Eventually you'll break free from fear. When you can go for a move with 100 per cent conviction even though you are sure there is only one per cent chance of success, then you are really climbing.

Going back to that question of how to improve as a climber, I mentioned earlier there should be a lot of movement within the comfort zone and a lot of strength-gaining. The third component is to bring in redpointing. This ties everything together. Stick with the comfort zone movement for learning new skills and keeping smooth, but the redpointing will tighten up the strengths and bring in some essential power endurance and in addition will focus the mind and help push fear aside.

Again by accident, as I moved through the grades in my first few years of sport climbing, I was following a training plan many experts would have recommended. With each route I'd notice an extra sliver of focus as I was able to commit more and more. The gains were huge, in part due to the ridiculously feeble level I was starting from. Admittedly I had a half-decent excuse in the form of witnessing some pretty close calls, but for the past few years I'd never pushed my fear envelope any farther than getting a large spider out of the bath. Climbing on the gritstone would involve a long drawn out warm-up while trying to avoid the route I'd come to do, before finally getting on it, gibbering my way to the top and then rushing to the pub before another route could grab my attention. My head never got any better because I so rarely pushed out of my comfort zone, which basically extended no further than three feet above a cluster of bomber wires. In terms of physical improvement, it was hardly surprising my one trad route per week led to negative gains. Those into their sport climbing got better and stronger, while I got worse at double the rate, since boldness is also inversely proportional to age.

As well as getting fitter and stronger, the sport climbers were getting a real taste of proper hard climbing. With the fear removed, they were pushing themselves to the limit and finding out the pumped feeling you get above a dodgy wire often lies only about 10 per cent along the way to the point of actually falling off. By default they were finding out about the huge margin of error introduced by the brain's fear-protection scheme. Pushing hard, they learnt that 80 per cent pumped still leaves enough energy for a fair few more moves and also that feet don't spontaneously slip off ledges and that footholds smaller than 20 millimetres wide do actually exist. Basically, even without any active fear-familiarity plan, they'd just rapidly expanded their trad comfort zone by understanding how the body works. Don't get me wrong, good core trad skills are still essential and this sport-trad continuum only works for the experienced trad climber. Without confidence in protection, even the sport superstar with a complete understanding of their limits will find their head intro-ducing an immediate 100 per cent margin of error the instant the climbing becomes slightly hard, or at a greater height than a set of step ladders.

I passed my final exam on the slate route *The Very Big and the Very Small*. Despite having already ticked 8c+, it wasn't until the following year in the quarries that I finally felt I'd really made it. For the first time I became aware I was completely and totally unaware – if you know what I mean.

Not a hint of fear. Before that I wasn't exactly scared, it wasn't really 'fear' when I was sport climbing, just a marginal awareness of falling. Even that separated me from my own cutting edge. Just that thought, 'I'm clipping now, is my foot perfectly seated on the hold because I don't want to fall?' Too late, you've over-gripped, checked your belayer was watching and readjusted your foot. It only took half a second to do it all, but it was too long, and your cutting edge is blunted.

The Very Big and the Very Small is a sport route. A tad run-out with only three bolts, but a sport route nonetheless. The climbing is very intense, using tiny holds to cross the immense sea of grey that is the beautiful Rainbow Slab. Handholds are millimetres wide and footholds often need a good deal of imagination as well as precision to render them viable. It's a long pitch and demands continuous focus for its whole length – in fact the crux is being able to stay in the zone; stray just a little and you're out of there. Occasionally you feel like you can rest, leaning into the slab once you've stabilised your position on the rare, marginally-decent footholds, but you can't. Your feet are already creeping off the holds; time to go.

On redpoint I fumbled it a few times, aware of the void below and unnerved by a skid down the smooth slab. But nothing happened when I fell. My belayer didn't drop me, the rope didn't snap and my harness didn't fall to bits. I landed perfectly without incident. Next time up at the same spot I pushed a little harder and got a little further. It took three days from start to finish (it could have taken two if the second hadn't ended in a flapper), and when the redpoint finally came I was totally immersed. I was a bubble moving up over the smooth slate, absolutely focused on my movement. There was nothing else. I wasn't even thinking about what was coming up ahead. No space for that. No need for that, because I already knew what was coming up, the mental procedures ready to be accessed when the time was right. It was all about the instant, just my immediate position and whether it was perfect enough to allow movement into the next position. Tiny inaccuracies were instantly adjusted, or calculated to be within tolerance and ignored. Fatigue was monitored by a secondary system, running in the background but only as an information source. Hitting red was just a reference point, like when a driver sees his petrol warning light come on as he passes a sign saying 'Petrol – 20 km'. The driver who knows his car will hardly notice, because he knows he has 30 kilometres left in the tank, at least. Points on the fatigue gauge were placed against positions on the route, logged, plotted and extrapolated to ensure expenditure was on track. The whole route was a continuous string of complex movement patterns operated by a super computer. When I finally exited the programme after all the hard climbing I knew I'd been somewhere pretty special, and I knew what it meant. In terms of my limits, I was scratching the surface.

The Very Big and the Very Small was first climbed by Johnny Dawes in 1990. At the time it was the hardest slab route in the world. He described how he would enter into the meditative state of climbing where there was nothing else but complete immersion and flow. Suddenly I could relate to his thoughts. I'd done a lot of climbing, like really a lot, but this was another level and I wanted more …

19 IT'S ALL DOWN TO MOTIVATION

'It's all down to motivation': Ben Moon's words from the 1996 ITV series *Pennine Rock* which lodged firmly in my mind. A classic quote on a prime time programme from one of the world's best climbers. But it was deeper than a comment; the way he pronounced it struck a chord, it was personal. Highly motivated, Ben had pushed standards to a whole new level. There are many strengths required for sport climbing but motivation is crucial and probably the most important strength of all. Tenacity and controlling fear had taken me a very long way, but motivation was still the key. Motivation is a flexible, bendy little number that's hard to control even on a daily basis. It's up and down and flips directions, following different paths that you never see coming. The key is to go with it and explore it. You can't push your motivation. If it really doesn't fancy playing then you might as well relax. If you haven't seen it for a while it may be somewhere else, waiting for you in a completely different life zone. If you are bored with sport climbing try trad, if you are bored with trad, try sport. If you are bored with climbing, try cycling. If everything bores you, have kids or go and live in a war zone (fairly similar).

I think I'm of the more motivated type in most areas of life and I was particularly motivated during the first few years of my newly-discovered sport climbing. There were so many things pushing me forward and continually a new set of motivators: just being able to climb at all after my broken elbows, the whole movement without fear, the rate of improvement, and even the size of the grades. There was also a scene and, as I gradually worked my way in, I had to pinch myself in the company of my heroes. Were they really talking to me? People noticed as I worked my way through the hard routes. I'd come from nowhere and gained the ridiculous nickname 'Strong Steve', which is clearly laughable. I was never strong, particularly compared to power houses like Moon and Moffatt, who must have pissed themselves when they saw me struggling with a set of ten pull-ups, and pretty soon the name was ditched as it became apparent that I wasn't very strong at all. It's ironic that I ever had that name as I've gone on to become most famous for somehow getting up hard routes despite being incredibly weak. 'Weak Steve' is far more appropriate, though it doesn't have quite the same ring to it. Despite my blatantly incorrect name

I was becoming a scene member. I was a regular at the local crags and invited to parties and included in trip plans. Seb Grieve's parties were infamous in Sheffield. Everybody was there, like really everybody: Johnny, Ben, Jerry, Seb, Bentley, Sellars, Gresham, Jenkins. The parties weren't quite as crazy as I'd expected compared to the North Wales scene, but maybe that was due to the style of the climber. North Wales was a lot about the head, all about RPs, RURPs and heinous mantels above spiky flakes. Sheffield was a combination of head and body, the climbing required you to be physically in shape, with hard sport routes in particular not accessible after too many long nights staggering around on magic mushrooms. There was a lot of beer and a lot of stumbling and a lot of socialising and a lot of planning, with many a trip organised over a few pints and then forgotten after a dangerous mixture of spirits salvaged from the drinks cabinet.

I'm not proud of it, but this acceptance into the scene was addictive. People seemed to want to talk to me. Occasionally I felt a little false, like I was becoming mates with the dudes simply because I'd done a few hard routes, but many of the friendships were real and lasting – it had just taken an entry point. One minute I was nobody in a gloomy bedsit watching TV every night by myself, the next I was out and about with a social life I couldn't keep up with. A hollow description maybe, but at that time it was a little of what I needed, my confidence still shaky after the recent travelling fiasco. We shouldn't need anyone to tell us how well we are doing, but even for the solid of character a dose of compliments never harms and it's probably human nature to enjoy a little flattery. Coming from just about anyone flattery is nice, but when it comes from your peers, people you respect and look up to, well then it definitely has a shine to it. Suddenly my heroes were giving me a pat on the back, the real rock stars from all the magazines, now they were my mates. Of course, there is the totally obvious realisation that top climbers are, in fact, normal people. Of course they are, climbing up a piece of rock with small holds doesn't automatically make anyone into a super hero and it would be fair to say that the majority of well-known climbers are totally ordinary. As in all walks of life, there are plenty of ordinary people who are bordering on dull. I'd probably put myself in the dull bracket, hardly exciting at all with a personality that nowhere near matches my climbing grade, I'm more of an HVS kind of character. The media often paints a false picture; we feel we know a person before we've even met them, and it's almost a bit of a let-down to find your own hero is not particularly interesting as you stare over their shoulder at a party and escape to a more exciting conversation with a bunch of bumblies.

There are, of course, the oddballs, climbing being a sport that attracts such personalities, but that just makes the scene richer, and to be honest I wish we had more colourful characters to corner us at parties. The true stars, the Jerry Moffatts and Leo Houldings, were just cut out to make it big, probably in whatever they did, their looks and personality giving them the edge before they'd even started. We need more of these people too but, as it turns out, the vast majority of fingertip-cranking machines are just like the person sitting opposite you in the office. In my case, one of the cranking machines, Robin Barker, of 8c and much scary gritstone fame, did, in fact, sit pretty close to me at work and from my stunted, 'I don't know what to say to a hero' type conversations we went on to become mates. Rob was one of 'The B Team', my own delegation, alongside Bentley, Welford, Barton, Seb and Heap. All close to the cutting edge on both scary grit and crimpy sport, the B Team was separated from the A mainly by the size of the pedestal I'd placed them upon, with the 'A' reserved for the likes of Moon, Moffatt and Sellars – those that I'd given superhuman status. It's interesting how we elevate perfectly normal people to higher levels, but maybe no bad thing, giving conversations with the stars a certain sparkle. Though I've gone on to become good friends with Ben Moon and Nic Sellars, even now I still feel a little starry-eyed. In my mind they still carry the hero status I'd stamped upon them. They were my inspiration; that doesn't just go away. I'll always remember Ben running after me at a trade show and, having stopped me, asked if I'd think about wearing some of his new Moon range of clothing: 'Could you be an ambassador for my company?' At the time I was tied in with a different clothing brand, but he gave me a few garments anyway: 'Just wear them whenever you fancy.' I knew I'd made it but this massive compliment from Ben was much further down the line than my early sport days. Free kit was a long time coming, and certainly something I'd never have expected. Some upcoming climbers are motivated by sponsorship but for me it was never on the horizon, and didn't even cross my mind. Not that I was going to turn down any help!

Meeting Rob Barker at work had an extra bonus. He had something to do with the organisation of the 5.10 climbing team and as we climbed together on the local limestone he maybe spotted a little potential and managed to wangle me a free pair of 5.10 shoes. I guess, without blowing my own trumpet, that he probably did a good job in bringing me onto the team considering the exposure I've provided for 5.10 over the last eighteen years, but it was a totally relaxed arrangement: 'Just wear them to climb in – no strings attached.' This was the stuff of dreams, the whole climbing thing was gathering more and more momentum and running away with itself. From sad Billy-No-Mates to known sponsored climber – now that's progress.

Confidence counts for a great deal. I'd started to see where I could push my skills but initially struggled to feel worthy of an appearance on hard routes. People would notice, there would be talk. 'Just what was that new kid thinking?' I didn't need the stress, probably couldn't cope with it, there was no way I was risking getting slapped down on an out-of-league route. Being accepted into the scene made a big difference to my overall performance. Encouragement was like a green light for self-belief, it completely opened the door to hard climbing. Of course, as it turned out the scene was not a back-stabbing world but just a collection of friendly individuals doing their own thing.

And so a new chapter opened with ascents of new routes. 'New' as in unclimbed by anyone ever before. New routeing is pretty special and can be different things for different people. For some it's just discovering a new climb or being the first human to conquer a piece of rock, for others it's about climbing something really hard that tests personal limits and it becomes an even bigger animal if it has defeated others in the past; it's about the prize. Not really 'winning' as such, because it becomes your own challenge, but the fact that others couldn't make it elevates the route into a greater contest.

The Peak seemed to be littered with 'projects', routes that had been bolted and cleaned and attempted by the best and then left abandoned for the next generation. Some of these were well-publicised, already graded, their descriptions included in the guidebooks. The 1992 Rockfax *Peak Limestone* guide had a special page devoted to 'projects and eliminates', which was to become a personal hit list.

1998 was my first 'project' year. Raven Tor had become a regular venue and, after ticking pretty much everything (except *Hubble*), unclimbed lines cried out for attention. The first to go down was *Mecca Extension*, the most obvious project at the cliff. Much attempted by Mark Leach, he eventually sacked it and left it open for all. Just about everybody who succeeded on *Mecca* 8b+ came back a few days later for a peek at the extension, but so far no one had bothered to really devote much time and effort. *Mecca* itself is a total classic, one of the best routes of its grade in the country. Maybe not a soaring line but it packs a lot of intricate and powerful moves into its 12 metres. Fiercely crimpy and with tiny footholds, strength alone is not enough. There is even some laybacking and, for those that feel the need, perhaps more than the grade, a kneebar. The route ends at a big flake, an obvious point to finish for sure, but only halfway up the cliff. The extension takes the wall directly above. It's closer to vertical but even more technical and gives nothing away, with hard moves until the very end – 8a+ in its own right. The big flake at the belay of *Mecca* before the extension is a good rest, but not *really* good. The key to climbing *Mecca* and the extension together in one push is to reach the flake with energy to spare, i.e. to find *Mecca* relatively easy, or be incredibly fit and capable of recovering at the flake. The second option sounds feasible, recovering, but imagine how tired you are after a balls-out redpoint attempt that you just managed by the skin of your teeth. A good half-hour sat on the ground is barely enough before you can even untie your shoelaces, so you can appreciate that hanging off a flake for ten minutes, even if it is a massive jug, is still less than adequate. So option one is preferable, finding *Mecca* easy. Easy is the wrong word. My definition of 'easy' is something I can do in my trainers – *Mecca* was and is always hard. But the climbing suited me and with my standard application of trickery and jiggery pokery I found I could hit the flake by the belay with something to spare. The extension was also very accepting to an assortment of weak person techniques, with strength being of relatively minimal use compared to accurate footwork and a good degree of faith that toes would stick on the polished matchstick edges that pretended to be footholds. In the end the extension, cunningly named *Mecca Extension*, took me about six extra days over *Mecca*, with three of them blown when I couldn't get up *Mecca* again due to it being wet. This first new route of my Raven Tor trio was perhaps the best. It's certainly the most repeated. There must be at least fifteen people who have climbed it. Personally I have a soft spot for this route. It's 8c, but is achievable by those operating on 8b power. There are no really hard moves, just lots of quite hard moves, and you can trick it into submission, or just bash your head against it until it gives in. It's really polished, but that doesn't seem to detract from the climbing. You really have to *climb* it: friction won't do you any favours, so you have to understand your body position precisely or you'll scrabble like you're on a sheet of ice. It won't get any more polished now though – it's maxed out. This is partly my fault I admit, with at least a hundred ascents of *Mecca* and over fifty of the extension. Sad, maybe, but it still hasn't lost its appeal and makes both a great training route and a benchmark for my performance.

The second of my trio was not quite so good, straightening out and extending *Make it Funky* (MIF) via a more logical line to an obvious lower-off much further up the cliff. It didn't add a grade, but did add effort, and as such no one has repeated it. Can't blame them really, but my motivation for completing this was different from the effort on *Mecca Extension*.

That had been about the first ascent of a famous line and a brilliant piece of climbing, this was about completing the challenge, taking the route to its natural conclusion. Extending *MIF* was more of a filler-in, a training route, keeping tight for what had become my real target, an extension to *Evolution*.

At 8c+ *Evolution* was the first sport route that really pushed me, the first that felt really hard. It's relentless in its difficulty with super-sustained crimping all the way. The moves are fairly basic, but they hang together to give a surprisingly awesome piece of climbing. The 8c+ grade has wobbled a bit, but so far I think only Nic Sellars ever suggested a definite 8c down-grade, but Nic has no real concept of how good he is. Personally I've lost track. It felt soft for the grade at first, and when I was trying my extension I was lapping it five times in a day, so it felt far from 8c+. But others would weep if a downgrade stuck, including various foreign heroes who have gone home empty-handed suggesting it more than solid at 8c+. UK grades, particularly at Raven Tor, seem to be tough on the ego. After redpointing a 9a in Spain, Ryan Pasquill commented that *Evolution* was harder.

The final move of *Evolution* is a full commitment slap into a blind jug way out left. It's a good place to finish, a big flake in the middle of the blank wall but that's exactly where it is – in the middle of the wall. On my successful redpoint of *Evolution* I was already looking out right to the hold-less expanse for an opportunity to accept the full challenge of the face. I was lucky, like really lucky, there was just enough. Hard though, where *Evolution's* final move springs left, my extension blasted straight up. The very last poor hold of *Evolution*, a two-fingertip edge, is gained with the left hand rather than the right and then the routes split, my extension needing a long stretch for the right hand into a tiny thumb-down flake. To this point it's probably the same difficulty as *Evolution* 8c+, but there is no big jug on which to rest and recover. Instead it's feet up really high with the body position feeling all wrong, and push with the feet and pull hard with the right hand to begin a hideous dynamic cross-over, awkward and unnatural, but incredibly satisfying when it works. It requires 100 per cent commitment and a specific trajectory between body positions. The centre of gravity has to follow an S-shaped path or, for me at least, the move doesn't work. Straight after a rest on the rope this complicated move feels reasonable, but on the link desperate, the combination of timing and force so hard to co-ordinate. When hard moves are all about just pulling you can sometimes muster up something from nowhere, without thinking, but a complex dynamic movement requires solid concentration and, in fact, just pulling harder only screws up the pathway. If the move does somehow work then your left lands a pinch which is sloping but good enough for a quick clip and the right then takes a small undercut. The crux is done but it's far from over. Stretch way up with the left for an extremely disappointing edge, I'm talking poor-foothold standard, and somehow believe that you can pull through on this hold. Body position is essential, bringing your centre of gravity as close to the wall as possible to allow a lightning snatch with the right to another poor-foothold-standard handhold. Now you are on two of the worst handholds you'll ever hang. Without dwelling on this fact, adjust your feet and deadpoint upwards with a precise level of force, just enough to make the distance but not so much as to rip your tips straight off the matchsticks. Your target: a shallow fingertip pocket. On my actual redpoint this final desperate move was so close to the limit that I'm absolutely certain, without any exaggeration, that a gust of wind blew me upwards just enough to hit the pocket. I actually felt it. Going into the move I had total conviction but felt I was going to be just marginally short of the pocket and then, amazingly, I'd just marginally caught it. It shows the power of commitment: to go for a move 100 per cent knowing there is only a 1 per cent chance of success is awesome – but to really go for it knowing you have zero percent and to still pull it off is something pretty special. You need something magical to happen, like the discovery of a slightly new movement pattern en route or catching the target hold in a better and undiscovered way. Relying on a gust of wind would require a monumental leap of faith, not to mention some incredibly accurate timing. It wasn't me just being daft, it was a windy day, and others at the crag spotted the well-timed updraft. Aid maybe? I'll take it thanks very much. Choosing a name around the divine intervention seemed appropriate for a while, but *Mutation* was always going to stick.

The grade was a harder choice and something I'd not tussled with before. Routes like *Mecca Extension* were already a known quantity, graded by many who knew their stuff. *Mutation* was different, no other opinions and no one to blame if I got it wrong. It was a good deal harder than anything else I'd climbed, taking me twenty-one days in total, not including six on *Evolution* and three or four initial days just bolting and cleaning. Plenty of the twenty-one were trying pretty hard, but it hadn't been a sustained effort, the route being a crag 'toy' for two years since I managed *Evolution*, something to play with until moves dropped into place. It took six of the days to just figure out the extension section alone from hideous cross-over to pocket deadpoint, so my final estimation of an 8c+ into an 8a extension was probably rather cautious. And it's easy to forget how the body adapts to climbing movement, ingraining the subtleties to make desperate moves effortless. More importantly, I wanted the extension to be easy to simplify the grade maths. 8c+ added to not much looked like 9a and 9a was a very large number that I didn't feel qualified to use. I didn't dare use it. There weren't many routes of that standard back in 1998. Neil Carson had just made the first ascent of *The Big Bang* in North Wales which he graded 9a, but that was it for the UK, and in the rest of the world there were only around ten others. I studied the hall of fame and pondered if I could justify adding *Mutation*, and also my unknown name, to the list of established celebrities. In fairness I wasn't actually qualified, as my grading was only relative to easier routes, most of which were on the same crag. I'd not even been on any other 9as, and not even many other 8c+s. So grading *Mutation* 9a on the back of it being harder than *Evolution* was dubious, especially with *Evolution*'s grade up for debate but, in the end, it kind of fell out of my hands and before I'd even had chance to try and add 8c+ to something between 8a and 8c the rest of the country, including the press, all graded it 9a for me. I struggled to claw back some kind of cover should some proper wad come and flash it and held onto a pathetic non-committal 'possible 9a' grade, which doesn't mean much really. It's almost certainly 9a and has so far (in 2014) resisted all repeat attempts for over fifteen years.

Orujo	9a+	Malaga, Spain	Bernabé Fernández	1998
Intermezzo	9a	Plom, Austria	Klem Loskot	1997
L'autre Côté de la Ciel	9a	Eaux-Claires, France	Fred Rouhling	1997
The Big Bang	9a	Lower Pen Trwyn, Wales	Neil Carson	1996
Open Air	9a	Schleier, Switzerland	Alex Huber	1996
Akira	9b	Charente, France	Fred Rouhling	1995
Weisse Rose	9a	Schleier, Switzerland	Alex Huber	1994
Bain de Sang	9a	Saint Loup, Switzerland	Fred Nicole	1993
Hugh	9a	Eaux-Claires, France	Fred Rouhling	1993
Om	9a	Triangel, Austria	Alex Huber	1993
Action Directe	9a	Frankenjura, Germany	Wolfgang Güllich	1991

Success on hard routes – that's hard relative to oneself whatever the grade – is more complex than simply pulling on a random bunch of little holds. The most important component, above tenacity, fitness, flexibility and even motivation is the most obvious: simply being able to get to the cliff. Even if you have bags of everything and are the world's best climber, if you only get out on rock once a month your tick-list will be short and you'll soon go rusty. In regards to technique coaching, Neil Gresham famously said for most people their improvement strategy could be written on the back of a postage stamp: 'Get out on rock more.' Motivation may up your chances of getting out by shoving aside other aspects of life but for most people simply getting out more is just not an option. Being a regular climber requires a lot of different ingredients to be mixed in the right way and, to be honest, what's needed is a good dose of luck for the essential components to drop into the right place at the right time.

The biggest problem is, of course, work. We've all got to do it in the end and even the scruffiest dirtbag will need a few pennies to buy his block of chalk. In terms of free time and getting to the cliff I'd really fallen on my feet. My engineering research job had served me very well, fitting exactly into the category of the job I wanted – not a 'real' one. An acceptable level of blagging and some unofficial reorganisation of the contracted working hours led to the perfect platform from which to leap into hard climbing, with one or even two afternoons per week on the local limestone and even enough money to run a wreck of a car. But it was always a ticking clock and with the end of each year a question hung over my future. I somehow managed to stretch it out for around four years. The initial collaboration with Mintex finished pretty quickly but other companies stepped in, largely helped by my boss, it also being in his interest to be supervising a valid research project. With each new project came new responsibilities and greater involvement and I watched my flexibility being slowly chipped away and the desk and computer screen becoming my standard view. Though it was a decent job with many climber perks, it wasn't well-paid, and only really worth having while the flexibility remained intact. Towards the end my motivation was jump-started when Boss-man suggested I wrote up my work for an MPhil (higher degree). This was a fairly simple affair, but didn't inspire me to take it any further and overall was a thoroughly boring experience. I could already see that the nice shiny qualification in material science was unlikely to earn me any life advancement, so when the potential of taking it to PhD level was put on the table I instantly bailed. PhD sounds nice, as well as being known as 'Dr McClure', but everything else had crumbled, investment had ended, my boss retired, and for the PhD I'd have to drop to a bursary of £3,000 per year for fifteen months of desk slogging. It was an easy decision to quit. A few of my Sheffield climbing mates, including Ben Heason and Miles Gibson, were on their way out to Thailand for a four-month trip that coincided with my job ending – I didn't really have to ponder my future in disc brakes.

I was away for the whole winter of 1998-9; two months in Thailand and two more in Australia. Returning to Tonsai on the west coast of Thailand was brilliant. I'd already been back twice since my first travelling experience for short two-week hits, but an extended trip allowed me to become intimate with the environment. It takes a while, but eventually you settle in. You live and breathe the place, sandals and shorts, Thai curry and rice, beer and bongs, climbing and snorkelling. It was paradise, and this time my state of mind was in the right zone to appreciate it. I'm extremely grateful for my timing; the climbing area was developing fast but still maintained an unspoilt feel with only a single bar below *Tidal Wave*, and only rock climber type people populating the entire area. The whole beachfront was still dense jungle as it probably was for thousands of years. It felt really quiet, and within days everyone knew everyone, with perhaps only forty people staying there in total. Since that visit I've been back a further three times, watching in dismay as my paradise was bulldozed over by tourism. In a way it's my fault as much as anyone's and I share some of the guilt. The climbing is still the same, incredible, as is the scenery, but I doubt I'll go back. This particular trip actually ended on a sketchy note, when my knee picked up a nasty infection right on the cap. The whole knee swelled up like a balloon, then slowly the swelling seemed to migrate towards a specific 'spot', resulting in the biggest spot you've ever seen, complete with yellow head the size of a penny. People crowded round to watch as I tried to squeeze it and the amount of pus that came out was utterly revolting. Unsurprisingly my body wasn't handling the whole affair too well and, racked with fevers, I picked up infections in other areas. The lymph glands in my groin swelled to the size of eggs and when they too gained a 'head' from the inside out, and then popped depositing half a litre of yellow gunk inside my shorts, I knew I'd blown it with self-help medication. A much-postponed trip to Krabi Hospital was the only answer, but a thoroughly nerve-jangling affair, their English being equal to my Thai. Sat behind a tattered curtain, a nurse attempted to shove an overgrown cotton bud inside my groin gland through the hole where it had popped. I resisted, and she insisted, but a total whitey on my behalf and a twenty-minute pass-out on the bed ensured the internal part of the treatment was skipped. The knee was apparently fixed by roughly taking a scalpel and chopping it to bits. At the time I assumed they were going in for an amputation, but in retrospect they were just being thorough and removing every bit of infection. A few days later I left Thailand for Australia, hobbling on and off boats like a one-legged pirate. Within about a day of landing into Sydney my knee was totally fixed. Swapping permanent dampness and humidity for the dryness of the outback made all the difference.

Australia was awesome. I lived the campsite life at the Pines, climbing at Arapiles in the week and taking weekend trips to the Grampians. The climbing was brilliant, a perfect mix of traditional and sport, with both styles existing side by side. Some routes are a mix, mainly trad but with a bolt in a dangerous section. This might sound like copping out, but all the different styles make sense. For a route which is mainly well-protected but with one dicey section, a single bolt keeps the character of the route. If the route is generally bold there will be no bolts at all, or perhaps it will be fully bolted. The ethics may be different to those in the UK and may well not work in the UK, but this is Australia, it's their country and we play by their rules. The solid sandstone generally takes gear well or not at all and so for their medium they've got it sorted. Embarking on a hard trad route was exciting rather than petrifying, because I knew there was going to be enough protection all the way, or that if it became dangerous there would be a bolt. There was no fear of getting into a life-threatening fix unless you messed up your kit and no chance of coming across the standard UK *in situ* 'rust' that litters many of our crags and may be anything from bombproof to worthless. Out in Australia I'd be straight in for the on-sight, even up into E6 and E7 terrain, with success being generally about hard-earned protection combined with high performance. It was my perfect style, traditional climbing, but not death.

I covered a lot of ground, a lot of mileage. In terms of the CV there was little to write home about. A flash of *Zorlac the Destroyer* 8b was good for the soul, as was the world's first one-day ascent of *Punks in the Gym* 8b+, but this wasn't a trip about numbers. This was a proper climbing trip about the whole package, unclouded by performance and a desire to hit the big grades. An old-school holiday just like they used to be.

It's what I needed. I'd gotten all mixed up in the world of hard sport, though 'world' only really stretched about as far as the Peak limestone boundary. The four years I'd had driving in sport gear had been an incredible journey, but I'd felt a growing confusion over my direction, not just in climbing but everything. I seemed to be in a state of flux, looking out for the next level and aware of the rest of my social scene striding forward into the normal world. I was still living the life of a dosser, a climbing-student type person while others bought houses and nice cars with salaries from proper jobs. Their path looked bland, but mine was also losing appeal and, more importantly, I didn't know where it led. Life had been easy when it was simple. The ending of the job allowed a rare long trip away, so I legged it without really knowing why I was going.

It hadn't been the plan, but I learned a lot about myself and started unravelling perhaps a little about what I needed from life. Stepping outside of the normal world and shaking things up allowed a different point of view. I tend to live in the moment without ever considering the future, never taking the long view. But I had time to ponder and get all deep and meaningful; right now may be great, but where does it lead? As a trip it was great, but it showed me that the permanent climbing-travelling-bum life was not enough. It was a big lesson, as stuck at home I'd be gagging to escape for as long as possible, assuming I could live in the dirt forever.

My primary goal for the last four years had been to climb all the time, or at least that's how it appeared, with everything else in life demoted or simply chucked away into the 'unnecessary' bin. So it was a surprise to find that I couldn't be a climbing 'lifer'. I need things around climbing to make it special. Climbing is what my life hangs on and without it all the other stuff doesn't fit together properly, like ill-fitting stones in a badly-built wall. Climbing is the glue that holds it all together, the mortar between the stones, perhaps not even the most important ingredient in terms of scale, but essential to avoid collapse. This trip was key to deciphering my priorities, reordering my requirements and maybe even getting a glimpse of how it all fitted together. Still, I hadn't exactly seen the light and figured out the meaning of life, it was more like I'd just hopped over one of my many fences and noted the grass was actually exactly the same colour as it had been in the place I'd just left.

I was desperate to get back to my girlfriend, Vic. For a while after Asia I'd trodden the single path and, to be honest, I was never the most experienced in the relationship department. Perhaps climbing was enough, or more likely I was too selfish to share. There had been a few, but with Vic it felt like the real deal. It was good, really good, our similarities exact and our differences bringing out our best. We were real mates too and we had a good laugh. Our friends were mutual, we had similar interests and we were in it for the long haul; but still I couldn't completely commit, I needed to feel just a little bit free. Selfish perhaps, but that seemed to be the most important thing, to be completely in control and able to steer life in any direction I fancied – though 'direction' was basically anything to do with climbing.

Announcing I was off for a four-month climbing jolly is hardly likely to win the 'romantic gesture of the year' award, but, as supportive as ever, Vic gave me the green light, or at least amber, and I took that to mean green was on its way; in our relationship she was more eager to give and I took. Now, away on the other side of the world, I missed her terribly and without her around my days seemed to lack meaning in the way they had at home. I was part of a team now, it wasn't just about bulldozing over everyone in an attempt to reach my ideal spot.

I'd grasped sport climbing firmly, using it as a tool by which to find myself and then riding along on the back of performance. But it would have been all too easy to lose touch with the real world, side-lining relationships and pastimes in a self-obsessed quest for big numbers, blazing a trail of fire and burning every bridge in the process, allowing my life to spiral inwards towards a glorious pinnacle of self-achievement beyond which nothing else would exist. A stable and potentially 'long term' relationship, previously daunting and tying, now became the foundation on which I could build and move forwards. Shuffling along by myself was uncomplicated and without boundary, but at the end of the day now also seemed rather pointless and lonely. A new 8c+ or 9a might feel amazing for a while, but the euphoria soon wears off, and no one really gives a shit. You soon learn that.

Though Vic was never a 'climber', most importantly she 'got it' – she understood my desire and paid out slack in huge amounts. She did climb, dipping in and out when the right ingredients came together, and was pretty good, 6c on the sport and the odd Extreme here and there. She even survived seconding me up a five-pitch traditional route only to have the bowline knot come undone by itself on the last pitch. Taking the rope in I suddenly came to the end. The memory still fills me with horror. What if she'd asked for a rest moments before … It didn't faze her, but she wasn't destined to be the obsessive who will drop just about anything that stands in the way of a day on the cliff. I couldn't understand it, how could she not be as psyched as me on something obviously so good? And then one day I had a moment of clarity. In the blackest mood ever, having just dropped the last move of an 8a on-sight, I belayed her on some random 6c. She rested a few times on the rope before finally reaching the top, and then lowered to the ground full of enthusiasm, her face a picture of success, thriving on the experience. Maybe I'd lost the plot.

Our differences keep me grounded. Vic isn't impressed by top climbers and hard routes, she's impressed by people and passion – a welcome reality check. Still, she can see the importance of my little sport and how I turn into an idiot without it, and it means everything to me to have her encouragement and support.

I moved into her house straight after Australia. Just one small step on the accommodation ladder but one giant leap into security. Things felt different. I felt like I'd grown up. I was still very much the climbing scruff bag, but rather than just floating around waiting for things to happen I felt rooted and capable of making them happen in a way that I chose. The climbing was just getting better, everywhere I looked there were new and exciting opportunities. At that moment, in the spring of 1999, I didn't seem to be lacking at all, with every one of my life requirements happily balanced. I even had a good-looking job lined up.

I don't think I'm a 'worker', not a conventional worker anyway. That's not to say I shy away from hard work, in fact, I'd probably do well to relax a little. Many people are 'work' people, the type that really need a normal job, they need to go to work to keep stable and their life on track. Without a job they never fill their time meaningfully. These are the kind of people who struggle with working from home, finding the biscuit tin more interesting, or a spot of Hoovering or daytime TV. This is not a fault, it's just a type of person. I'm more the opposite, with a steady job giving me the fear. Given the freedom to do what I want I'll cram every minute with useful activity. If I'm making a phone call I'll also be washing up and cooking lunch at the same time. It almost becomes a curse, with anything less than maximum efficiency deemed a waste of time. I loathe driving unless the car is packed full of mates on the way to work or the crag, in which case I'm effectively sitting in the pub, just without a drink, a far more efficient social period.

A new job had been handed to me on a plate; it's all about who you know. I was to be based at Sheffield University in an engineering department known as the Ibberson Centre, a separate entity working on real industrial projects utilising university facilities. My good friend Tony, who was already employed, got me in and I started straight away, no interview, no meeting, no nothing. It was like I'd always been lined up for the job. Striding straight into normal employment would have given me the fear, but I'd been taken on to run a specific project which ticked all my job description essentials. First things first, my boss, Keith Ridgeway, was from the same family as my last boss, the family of 'as long as the work gets done, I don't mind when you do it' and the project was totally my own show. A bunch of designers had come to the Ibberson Centre with basically no more than an idea and some sketches. Their baby was 'The Autoriser', basically a wheelchair lift, a square flat platform that lifted straight out of the ground and upwards by a half-metre or so. It wasn't a bad idea: disabled access was becoming a standard requirement for all businesses, and in many cases the more typical long ramps were inappropriate. They were hoping to have the right tool at the right time and make a fortune. We accepted the project, agreeing to take it from starting line right up to a finished full-scale working prototype, plus parts list, suppliers, manufacturing details and costings to mass produce their product. The project was daunting but also exciting. I'd be doing everything from CAD drawings and stress analysis on a computer, to making steel components on a milling machine and welding them together. After a whole year of work it came out pretty well and everyone involved was pleased, but I kind of knew deep down, even right from the start, that it was never going to work for mass production. There were too many potential problems and these days all wheelchair lifts are the standard, big, enclosed box style things that are basically an elevator that only goes up a few steps. The Autoriser would have been a far cheaper and considerably smaller solution, but all it would have taken is for one disabled person to fall off the platform or a bunch of pissed yobs to have chucked some bricks underneath and it would have been game over for everyone.

Working at the Ibberson Centre felt like my first 'real' job. I was doing proper stuff that could have an impact on the world, and it had value. I dealt with professionals and had professional meetings where smart clothes had to come out, though fortunately only once a week. The rest of the time it was jeans and T-shirt and scruffing around in the workshop. Very occasionally, Keith would ask how it was going, but mostly I just got on with it and planned carefully around trips to the crag, managing at least one afternoon per week. I felt pretty complete for a while and there didn't seem to be much lacking from my work life, but there was always a nagging question as to where I was going. It all felt very temporary, like a nice transition period between scruffy student and the next stage – though the 'next stage' was far from clear. If anything it was a little confusing, it was obvious now that climbing was the major motivator, but also that I needed some level of stability. Though I craved total freedom, I knew at the same time that freedom would feel empty and hollow. I wanted to go off and just climb, but I now knew that just climbing was not enough.

More work projects came in, and I began to suffer from the classic situation where you do a good job and then get entrusted with more work.

The better you do the more you get. There is a lesson there – find the right balance, make sure you do the correct amount of work. The projects came thick and fast. The toughest one was for British Aerospace Engineering, a set of sketches hitting my desk, this time for a set of scissor lifts to raise aeroplane wings into position prior to bolting onto the aeroplane fuselage. BAE wanted these sketches turned into the actual finished working units, installed on site and good to go. I ran the whole project alone from start to finish including meeting with the suited big boys on a regular basis, designing every component, outsourcing the manufacture, ordering all the hydraulic rams and electrical equipment and overseeing an assembly team. There had been, in my view, an alarming amount of trust placed in my skills and as the massive scissor lifts went into action my brain was overloaded with stress analysis images, margins of safety and safety mechanisms. It all worked well and I've not heard of any industrial disasters so hopefully I've got away with it.

This BAE job, along with other small engineering projects, was incredibly satisfying, but, like in my last research post, I could see my flexibility dissolving away. I resisted by what seemed appropriate amounts but the avoidance tactics became more draining than work itself, it being easier to just work 8 a.m. to 5.30 p.m. than to make excuses for being unavailable. The other staff members were normal workers and relied on me being there when they needed me and that didn't include ten o'clock on a Friday night when I'd be working late to make up for my Tuesday afternoon at Malham Cove. So I slid into normality, the occasional hard-won few hours' escape just about making up for the downsides. Perhaps I could have stayed there forever. Most people probably would. I liked the job and I was pretty good at it. I got paid enough and had six weeks' holiday and some flexibility. What more could I want? And, to be fair, what gave me the right to want more? Most importantly, what were the chances of me realistically achieving a better balance? It looked like I'd really rolled a good number on my life's dice. Maybe even a six. The question was, should I roll it again and risk a lower number?

There is no doubt that I entered the climbing scene at exactly the right moment. On a totally global level, but particularly if focusing specifically on UK sport climbing, all the stars aligned in my favour and allowed me to make a life out of climbing when, if I'd been out by a couple of years, it could have been an entirely different story. Despite being pretty feeble, unfit, and basically totally off the pace when it came to cutting edge sport climbing, I stood out as a performer basically because everyone else gave up. My real lucky break to having any kind of prominence was entirely the result of the UK's need to follow trends. An easily-led nation, headpointing and bouldering blew sport climbing out of the water. Our top performers in both media and on the rock threw away their ropes and invented bouldering mats to save their knees and display their logos in go-large style. Sport climbing had become boring and, to a certain extent, hard work, the two reasons inextricably linked as new lines became difficult to find and even more difficult to redpoint. New styles signalled a return to the grit where a first ascent or relevant magazine-worthy repeat could be made in a number of hours or a couple of days as opposed to an entire season, or worse, of bashing heads against the same piece of bolted white stuff.

Hard Grit, the iconic 1998 film from Slackjaw, paved the way for a headpoint boom. At the same time many of the limestone experts, not really inspired to risk life and limb above a nasty pile of spiky boulders, were taking their strengths to the boulder fields that, despite much attention over previous years, were still yielding many great problems. Possibly the most influential was Ben Moon who, having taken sport to a new level, now looked to bouldering to satisfy an unquenchable thirst for performance. However, after *Hubble* and all his other ground-breaking sport achievements, there was one more gift that Ben was to leave the world, an as yet unrealised gift that I would accept and then use as a foundation on which to build the next fifteen years of my life.

'Ben's Project', as it had become known (and it still often maintains the reference), was perhaps the world's second most famous project at the time, the first being the extension to *Biographie* at Céüse in France which was eventually climbed by Chris Sharma in 2001 to become *Realisation*, the world's first confirmed 9a+. Ben's project predated this by quite a few years, with Ben first getting involved way back in 1992. It quickly gained in reputation, and even without a successful ascent had earned itself the badge of 'hardest route in the world', no doubt partly due to Ben's track record and formidable strength, but perhaps mainly because he was struggling to do it. Three years of effort propelled the route into mythical status, aided by the media who leapt on the story like a nation riding on the back of an Olympic hopeful. It featured in all the magazines, in books and films, and even on national TV. I remember predictions in *OTE* magazine that 1996 would be the big one for Ben and like everyone else I was swept up in the excitement, waiting for the ascent of what would be the UK's first 9a.

But another side of the story was skimmed over, that of frustration and pressure. Poor conditions and injury thwarted Ben year after year and, eventually, with the attraction of bouldering pulling strongly, he finally threw in the towel and threw away his rope leaving the project open. We reeled at this 'failure', a harsh label to a journey that didn't quite work out. In reality Ben had climbed from the second bolt to the top on a practice link, as good as the whole route, only to have the window of opportunity slammed shut as the season yet again closed abruptly for another year. Ben's project slid off the radar, gathered dust and waited for another to do battle.

'You've got to make it count. This is the most important route of your life.' Neil Bentley lectured me, straining round from the front of the car. With five of us packed into the tiny motor we'd made him sit in the front, his shoulders too wide for a back seat position. Today's passenger list read like a who's who of limestone performers, and jammed in the middle between Keith Sharples and Paul Reeve I faced Neil and absorbed his criticism.

'You've got to be professional. You need to eat properly, rest properly, take it seriously. Forget everything else. You're acting like a punter. You won't get up it acting like a punter.' He was right; today's excuses rang hollow, tired arms from mixing three quarters of a tonne of cement the day before. I began to insist the concrete needed to be mixed on a specific day and had been planned in advance, an integral part of my 'Autoriser' base unit with a rapidly approaching deadline, but I could have put it off for a day I guess, maybe even a week, maybe more. But where would it end? Life on hold. There's only so much space on the shelf for the rest of my life.

I'd spent fourteen days at Kilnsey crag that year, always trying the same route, no deviation. A straight line of non-holds direct through the huge blue-grey wall of North Buttress, so steep it's a miracle the whole cliff doesn't fall over. By day seven I was on redpoint and day ten had me within reach of the belay, only to stop short at a tricky sideways slap for a poor two-finger edge. My tactics were rubbish, throwing myself at the route three times a day, only to fail at the same spot as creaking fingers opened before my eyes. I wasn't being professional, I was being a punter. Ben's project had been unfair to Ben. She had tripped him over with awful conditions and pulled the rug from beneath his glory when he was already above it. Now she was giving herself to me on a plate. Under-qualified in terms of fitness and strength, she handed me chance after chance with impeccable conditions week after week. Waiting to die, she'd laid down, handed me the sword and asked for it to be over, but I was crumbling under the pressure and missing the mark. I needed to step back, take a breath, take aim and hit the target.

But I didn't want to step back or take a breath, it felt too close. A few days' refinement could spell the end of the season. It could get too hot, or too cold, or too wet. I could get injured, lose motivation, or more likely, get fired. Too risky a strategy to step back. There were others too: Malcolm Smith had been way up there on redpoint, calling 'take' for no apparent reason. Surely it had to be easy for him? Potentially the strongest climber in the world, all he had to do was show up … And others had been playing, chalk dots and tick marks revealing their presence. Or were they my own? Rumours spread, my paranoia deepened, and my judgement shattered.

Neil tucked into his healthy pasta and the unclicking of Tupperware around me highlighted my lack of preparation. As everyone refuelled and rebuilt on salads and tuna I scoffed a slab of Cadbury's to fend off hunger for the two-hour drive back to Sheffield. Later, somewhere after 11 p.m., I shovelled in a family-sized pizza moments before collapsing into bed with a bifda dessert. I wanted this route badly and yet the only thing I seemed to be doing to aid success was 'wanting'. And 'I want never gets': a childhood lesson. You've got to earn your reward.

The BBC showed a country plastered with yellow suns, 25 degrees and no wind. A bank holiday forecast dream for nearly everybody but me. Panic rose: Kilnsey would be rubbish; no one else would come; no point. I exhausted all my options, adding heavily to the phone bill. Disappointment. Was that it? My shot was over, close but no cigar. Vic dragged me to Langdale and we camped and ate in the O.D.G. and drank and walked and relaxed as I pushed at the string of movements that lingered in my consciousness. A long weekend away did nothing to break the weather, the UK for once scoring points, with a happy 99.999 per cent of the population. Only a miniscule minority longed for the typical unpredictable normality.

Drastic measures were required and the contact list was scanned and re-scanned for back-up potentials.

A whole week dragged by, at least thirty days long it seemed, but at last I was back, the massive bulk of the North Buttress towered over me, scorning me for my absence and yet comforting me with familiarity. Ben Lowe was in tow, a good friend acting above the call of duty. A keen boulderer only, and pulled out as a wild card from the contact list, the carefully-pitched and equally-prioritised trip would give us a guaranteed afternoon's bouldering at the Bridestones after a morning of sport redpointing. My morning of redpointing. To fit in such a day I'd insisted we needed to be at Kilnsey early doors and Ben had taken the bait with my last cast effort at netting decent conditions. Now, at 5 a.m., I sat alone in the mesh inner tent pitched right at the base of the project, so close that the starting holds were within reach. I tapped at the swarm of midges as they battled to find an opening to get at their prey. Relentless, I wondered if they'd been hunting me all night, their early onset in the evening sending us scurrying into our anti-social cocoons only moments after our straight-from-work arrival tactic. It felt like hard work, harder than being at work, which is where I should be four hours from now. I could still make it and no one would even know I'd been here, not have an inkling of my plan to not turn up with no warning whatsoever. But Ben slept on, his stationary bulk just a few lines to my side. This was his day too, though legitimate compared to mine, booked in as holiday. Work colleagues would just assume I was climbing, as always, and mark it down on my growing list of unacceptable absences. Was this worth it? Today I already knew – no. Sun baked the wall, setting it alight in orange-grey; a dusty dryness without a hint of moisture. An unfamiliar sight, the sun would move off the face by 11 a.m., our usual arrival time when driving up from Sheffield, planned to avoid the heat. Today I already knew we'd be well gone by then. The rock heated up and shimmered, spitting its friction away. Ben stirred as I paced up and down, a T-shirt over his face to shade the glare. To him it was a beautiful morning, quite simply spectacular as the intense sunlight poured into the silent valley and the low angle of the light picked up features and corners in the rock, painting the crag as an entirely different picture. Sensing my thoughts he held back his delight, and to break my disappointment suggested a warm-up trad route, a time waster in disguise to pad out the morning before we could satisfactorily depart for a shorter sport where performance and numbers had no relevance. For once the big E2 corner had a place, shaded and something to keep us both 'happy' when in reality we'd both rather be doing something else. Pleasant enough,

I guess, but, mind in other places, I dropped a number 2 cam from the top, watching it drift downwards and thump into the ground. A prized possession, despite its rigid stem and lack of use these days, I'd not leave until I found it.

Now, wading through the long grass, I was losing faith. Ben watched on having helped enough, the old relic and out-of-date bit of kit not worth the time that was draining from his side of the bargain. Sweating, I glanced up again at the bulk of the North Buttress to regain my bearings and recalculate the flight path, already knowing it was hopeless and just wasting time in my refusal to leave. The huge cliff now loomed as the last of the rays caught the wall, a huge black shadow against the pin-sharp blue sky. Around me the reeds stirred as I sifted through them, their movement gradually picking up as they waved in a growing breeze from the north. Was this something? A drop in temperature and better conditions? Unexpected and unlikely but optimism crept in perhaps faster than it should. The cam lost its value as I felt warm, soft fingers begin to harden and invisible forces pulled me towards the cliff for an update; exploring the rock, its black heat lingered, but by now the wind whistled. Again she offered herself against all the odds. Cold fingers bit into warm rock, an inversion of familiar conditions but giving even more, friction stepped up a gear. With flawless moves I absorbed the advantage and tried to ignore the gargoyle on my shoulder who looked down on my positive progress and shouted 'this is it'. The two-finger edge felt like three, and the final hard moves still hard, but the belay was clipped long before I reached it. Hovering on the rope I doubt Ben felt it even go tight as my weightless body rejoiced in freedom. Drifting downwards she played back in reverse, now smiling as she breathed her last. Next stop the Bridestones. I was utterly rubbish, completely useless, spent. My one burn had taken the lot, but I couldn't have cared less.

Northern Lights 9a

22m. The long-standing project up the centre of the wall held out for many years, defeating attempts by some of the UK's best sport climbers. Start below a small roof in the centre of the viciously overhanging blank wall. Attack this with no rest and no real holds to an eventual easing and belay in a groove below the roof.

F.A. Steve McClure, 2000.

'If you want to be a professional climber, take whatever the current cutting edge is in the niche you want to operate in, and better it, convincingly, and understand that you have to do that first, before the sponsorship comes.

'The hard part in gaining sponsorship is looking at it from the cash-strapped marketing manager's point of view. This is where most climbers go wrong. If you think the manager might not already know who you are and lots of things about you, wait until they will have. You need to remind them instantly in words or images why you are exactly what their marketing tactics need to sell more of whatever it is they sell. Did that one pass you by? It does for many young climbers. They think that sponsorship is a reward for climbing hard. It's not. It's about your sponsor being able to sell more product.

'Many frequently overestimate the levels of sponsorship in the climbing world, and view it as a direct result of climbing at a certain level. It comes from a poor understanding of the actual purpose of sponsorship (to sell products) and also forgetting that the level of star climbers right now must be bettered convincingly to stand out from the crowd, both in terms of the climbing level but also the professionalism of the athlete. Some are desperate to get sponsorship to help them on the journey to their climbing goals, but the sponsorship is only likely to come once they get there.'
Dave MacLeod

Fighting the urge to rush I strolled into Smith's newsagents, my eyes fixed on the magazine racks in the far corner. Scanning the sport section I knew exactly what I was looking for. It hadn't been there yesterday, or the day before, despite it being more than due. But today it was. Even from halfway across the shop I could see the unmistakable image on the front cover of *OTE* magazine and my heart began to race. Weaving my way across the shop I was finally in position. I stifled a smile and resisted the desire to grab the mag from its shelf, adopting the air of a regular customer, browsing, just another member of the three-deep crowd all hunting for lunch break entertainment at their desk, or for a free read if they dared stay long enough. Suddenly I felt self-conscious that someone beside me had noticed I was looking at a picture of myself, and quickly rolled the precious magazine and made for the till, half hoping the cashier wouldn't notice my mug on the cover and kind of hoping she would. She didn't and, fumbling my change, I sprinted out of the shop and kept going to a safe distance where, at last, I could pore over the front cover of *OTE* 77, reading and re-reading the news article covering my second ascent of *The Very Big and the Very Small* in the slate quarries.

It was big news, apparently. Or maybe it wasn't, maybe it was over-sensationalised by an editor keen for a scoop. My stomach tightened a little, ashamed by the media attention – but only slightly, more ashamed that I'd ridden on the back of Dawes. Crimping and edging his way up this masterpiece some nine years earlier, he'd created the hardest slab in the world, even though it was only another notch in his unmatchable CV. It barely registered with the British public, blinkered by their beloved British style. A line of bolts (even if there are only three bolts in total), the slab was left to gain its own reputation through time, bolstered by notable failures from notable suitors. That's more the British way, to highlight failure. We love it when foreigners can't do 'our' routes and now, after the route had gained in status, my effort made more headlines than the first ascent. So I kept my head in a vice, avoiding the swell, and when the picture, by Ben Lowe, made the front cover I got my first tiny taste of 'fame'. I'd spent years poring over magazines and to appear in one, never mind on the front cover, was a childhood dream come true.

It wasn't my first magazine picture. A shot of me crimping my way up *Dangerous Brothers* had appeared a month earlier, taking up two-thirds of a page. It was an illustration picture for a destination article written by Keith Sharples. This front cover was a world apart. In the following month's *OTE* a full interview followed, editors keen to follow up and capitalise on this out-of-the-blue nobody. The ball began to roll and pick up speed and I was getting a lot of press, with photographers keen for a shot knowing the magazines would grab it. All the rock stars were busy on the gritstone, scaring themselves stupid and making videos about it, or pulling ridiculously hard on 10-foot high lumps. Everyone had given up on sport climbing and I took all the news. With nothing to lose, I let it happen and floated on the little dream of magazine stardom, a big fish in a tiny little puddle.

Mutation caused a stir, with Ben's pictures again making the headlines. But now I noticed a lack of character in the images. I didn't fit the role, my appearance a scruffy scrag clothed in charity shop tie-dyed pyjamas with a tangle of dreads neglected after too many late-night sessions. Eventually friends persuaded me I should try and acquire some sponsorship or, in other words, blag some free kit. In terms of quality of equipment they did have a point: my jumble of junk found in the bottom of the Verdon Gorge was over thirteen years old and carried an unknown history (at least, unknown other than having been lobbed down a 300-metre cliff). Ropes were sketchy too, spun out for probably a dangerously long time and only ever replaced in a bargain basement sale or when bought from a friend who'd probably got it cheap anyway. It was all looking distinctly shabby next to the matching racks of Mambas professionally displayed by even the most punterish of sport climbers. My cash flow was okay but a new set of 'draws was a big ask, and I figured I could muddle along for quite a while with my current clobber, until I'd just become a laughing stock, or worse, something catastrophically decided it was too old to be safe anymore.

Personally, I doubted my chances, but some 'support' would save me from the inevitable sting. More importantly, I'd have lots of lovely new brightly-coloured kit and, who knew, maybe I could even squeeze out an extra level if I was using the latest technology. My current 'shipping rope', bordering on 20 millimetres, was hardly the lightest on the market and was so fluffy it barely fitted through a karabiner.

But trying to find sponsorship wasn't just about the free stuff, because nothing comes for free, it was about checking out the climbing world to see what it was all about. I never imagined I'd become a climbing professional, or professional climber, or whatever it is that I've ended up becoming.

The Professional. These guys make a living from the sport. This could be through guiding, route-setting, coaching, writing, lectures or various other things. 'Professional climbers' basically have a combination of jobs that happen to be associated with climbing, which is why they don't label themselves as professional route-setters or professional coaches. Most pros struggle with the label, as to the climbing public it seems to imply 'having no work and living off sponsorship'. Which leads on to:

The Sponsored Climber. The sponsored climber gets stuff for free. Or maybe not. They get stuff for doing stuff, not just sitting around. Sponsorship could even be in the form of thousands of pounds a year if you're a hero and accidentally appear in magazines. But this just applies to gods, with 99 per cent of sponsored climbers getting about as much annual free stuff as they could buy with a week's worth of wages stacking shelves at a local corner shop. Sponsorship does not mean you can be a full-time climber by any stretch of the imagination and nearly all 'sponsored climbers' have perfectly normal jobs, which may or may not be associated with climbing.

The Full-Time Climber. The full-timer climbs all the time; they have nothing else to do. A person who works within the climbing industry is not really a full-time climber and, in fact, may be so busy as to barely climb at all. Being full-time is quite attainable by most, but is harder now than twenty-five years ago and is, contrary to popular belief, independent of ability. Years ago, sponsorship was available direct from the dole office, although it did require tolerance of 10 pence beans and sleeping in a woodshed. These days, to be a full-time climber you'll need a van and laptop and hence the easiest way to reach full-time status is to earn plenty and then leave your job. Doing it the other way round, being full-time and then earning plenty, is considerably less likely to work out, with any job prospects you might have once thought you had being totally left in the gutter. Essentially, the full-time climber is a person that can get by with almost no cash. These days, however, surviving on no cash is far from cool, and so full-time status is best achieved through generous parents or lottery wins. It is absolutely not for the homeowner or anyone with any kids.

There is a problem with interpretation and it's easy to get muddled up. It could be said that a 'professional' earns their living from their trade, like a professional plumber, but no one really thinks what a jammy sod a plumber is, being able to go out, day after day, doing exactly what he loves, fixing toilets, unblocking drains and mending taps – and to think people even pay him for doing it.

There are professional climbers and sponsored climbers and full-time climbers, but ideally you want to be a sponsored full-timer with nothing else to do and have enough cash pouring in to pay for essential Wi-Fi for constant scorecard updates and to fuel up your swanky converted Ford Transit. However, it's far more likely you will be a full-timer with no cash at all, or a sponsored climber with a completely normal boring office job who happens to get a few pairs of free shoes.

Becoming a professional climber requires some level of competence at something to do with climbing, though not necessarily a high level of ability in the actual climbing itself. When it works it's great, and is a privileged position, but it's not an easy path. It's a fine balancing act that must strictly adhere to the following well-established equations:

- *Climbing ability + Ego = Sponsorship level*
- *(Sponsorship level + Professional work) ÷ Cash needs = Time to climb*
- *Time to climb α Climbing ability*
  (α is the symbol for proportional, in case you have forgotten from school.)

Basically the dilemma for the professional (though potentially for all climbers) is balancing 'cash *in*' with 'time to climb'. Cash might come from sponsorship or from work, with the relative proportions dependent on whether or not you are a superstar. But being a superstar doesn't make you a superstar – this requires an ability to promote oneself and take flak without flinching. Though climbing ability may be proportional to 'time to climb', you need to climb the right things: routes that are hard and in fashion and you need to tell the world. In fact, being a superstar can be achieved without actually any really hard climbing at all but with a suitable ego. If your climbing ability happens to be awesome but your ego level is poor, you will need to do more work to balance your equation. As a pro the cash needs must be kept to a minimum in order to climb and you should not consider things such as having a real holiday, driving a fast car, buying a house or having a kid. The serious pro should also shun any kind of friendships that may incur costs and refrain from buying a round of drinks in the pub via tactical avoidance procedures. However, one should also consider the following extra equation:

(Full time climbing + nothing else in life) x K = G
Where K is the age of the climber, and G is the level of sad git status.

Sponsorship has changed over the years. So have the requirements and attitudes of the sponsored climber. There are many more companies involved now, and way more disciplines. There are more heroes. The sport is bigger but more diluted. It used to be possible to make a 'decent' amount of cash from sponsorship, but 'decent' had a different definition and meant enough to drive an old banger and camp at Buoux for three years surviving on chucked-away baguettes and wine stolen from the supermarket. You had to be really good too, really good. Photo incentives came along and seemed like a good idea, where logo visibility in the press rewarded the athlete with cash. Amounts per pic were small, but could be clocked up pretty quickly with ground-breaking ascents and an unabashed attitude. It felt awkward though, and Brits generally felt like they were selling out. Unlike Euro punters who sewed logos onto their Decathlon pants, British heroes cut the tags off their spangly free kit and stuck on smaller ones. Then the internet came along and made publicity impossible to monitor and so the photo incentive was generally chucked away. Sponsors changed too, becoming keen to get their athletes involved in their businesses. The few climbers that actually make any money from sponsor-ship now will probably be giving a few lectures and helping with the staff training. Thus we come to the final equation:

Level of sponsored climber α Expectations of climber as a professional

Which basically states that if you want to make any money out of climbing you have to be prepared to work for it.

Glancing in the rear-view mirror of my battered Vauxhall Nova I straightened my hair, or what was left of it – a short crop of spikes in mourning for their once shoulder-length dreadlocks. Ten years in the making, they had been shaved off only months ago. Their time had been up and I needed a change, no matter how painful it was to admit. Still, the freedom felt amazing: no soaking clothes around my neck after every shower and no surprise hairstyles in the morning – in fact, no need to look in the mirror, ever, as it was only exactly the same ugly mug staring back. Handy, but kind of boring. Part of my personality seemed to have vanished with a swift swipe of the clippers. However, I did look more presentable. This was rarely a concern, although, sitting in the car after a three-hour drive from Sheffield and just about to walk into the Lyon Equipment head office, 'presentable' seemed good. Swallowing my pride I'd finally caved into advice and emailed a letter to the 'manager of sponsorship and promotion' asking about the possibility of support. With a few companies to choose from I thought I'd start right at the top and made contact with Lyon Equipment, the Petzl distributor up in the Lake District. Amazingly they'd replied. 'We'd like to invite you to visit our offices to discuss sponsorship. Please arrange an appointment at your earliest convenience.' Shoving engineering meetings and design projects to one side in the usual fashion, my earliest convenience had been very soon indeed and now there I was, feeling rather nervous over what seemed an extremely important job interview.

At least I was well-armed, with a full arsenal of media publicity including two front covers, seven full-page pictures, at least ten other good-sized pics and a printed interview, a guidebook front cover and a calendar appearance. I had England's first 9a (unrepeated), a wedge of notable first ascents and repeats up to 8c+, and a haul of on-sights including a few 8bs – I was the only Brit to have managed that grade. To top it I'd also climbed E9 with *The Big Issue*. All this felt mediocre, but in retrospect my 'CV' was pretty decent and actually considerably superior to many of those hunting support today, despite an apparent rise in climbing standards. Support was a privilege: it was earned, never assumed. That's the way it worked, sponsored climbers were rock stars first. These days many assume sponsorship is a right, deserved for putting in the effort, a reward for trying quite hard, or even getting ready to try. Sponsorship is not a helping hand, it's a job. A company helps you with kit, you help them to sell it. Did that one pass you by? These days kids are looking for multiple free climbing shoes for coming second in a round of the local bouldering league, and if they win it's assumed they won't need to work. Realistically, they are up against the wads. For example, if you are female and think 5.10 might need to have you in their shoes, consider recent team members Shauna Coxsey, Katy Whittaker and Mina Leslie-Wujastyk and see how you fit in.

Frank Bennett of Lyon Equipment made me feel at ease, no selling required from either side. My edge was that I was known, but a shiny CV is only half the battle and, sweaty-palmed, I waited for the expected questioning: 'Well done with all your achievements so far, and thanks for all the advertising, but what are you actually going to do for us, what's next?' This is what it's all about. What have you to offer? The question never came, but I slipped in the answer as a backup: Ben's project was coming along nicely. A slight exaggeration perhaps, considering at that point in time I'd only actually clip-sticked my way up the route, unable to even find most of the handholds. Though I obviously couldn't offer any guarantee whatsoever, it raised an eyelid and seemed to seal the deal. Maybe Frank could see the potential for promotion. I walked out on what seemed my own personal Christmas Day, laden with kit of the highest quality: a full rack of Petzl Spirits; harness; Grigri; helmet; Beal ropes and more.

So I joined the gang, the Bashers and Pollitts and Moons and Vickers that I'd stared at for years in the press. Had they influenced me? Had I bought their stuff? I wasn't sure, and looking at my now-old rack it seemed rather unlikely that I'd been influenced by anything other than not spending any money. Still, everything wears out eventually and the choice of replacement has to come from somewhere. 'Look, Moffatt's wearing Lasers on *Evolution*, I need a pair of them to be as good as him.' The double-edge sword of sponsorship was something I was wielding, yes free kit is all very nice, but the other side of the bargain is the promotion. There are climbers who work at being known – it's their main asset, above performance – but I feared the push, the self-promotion. It turned out that I was lucky, and the sharp side of the competitive promotion world was utterly blunted, barely giving me the slightest discomfort. Ben's project was the tipping point, an avalanche of publicity that swept me away. I watched it happen with no effort on my part whatsoever. Teetering on the edge of comfort, I just turned up, climbed and then viewed the results with a mixture of pride and embarrassment, my personality not quite a match for the exposure and perceived status. I justify it with the excuse that I was simply doing what I'd always been doing. There was no push, no self-promotion, no specifically targeted routes or grade inflation and no overzealous blogs or twitterings about new best bits of kit. I tried to keep it real, to stay the same. There were no sticker logos pasted on my head or glued over every inch of exposed fabric. The public seemed to like that and so did the sponsors, I think …

But I didn't stay the same, not in my outlook. It was nothing to do with hunting out sponsorship or becoming a professional, it was simply that I wanted to climb, hard, a lot. My ascent of Ben's old project became *Northern Lights* and was the pivotal point around which everything moved forward. Suddenly I had to see where I could take my level. The view had opened out and rolling my life's dice became more and more attractive. Normal working life stacked up fairly comfortably but doors opened up at every turn. So I went to see my boss and told him I was out of there, then shook the dice and prepared to roll, knowing I'd not get to see the number for a very long time.

To be fair, my boss made life easy. He gave me a firm pat on the back in a fatherly 'off you go and learn about life' kind of way and insisted my well-worn desk space would be waiting for me, no doubt assuming my legging it away from the real world was just a blip, something to get out of my system. I wasn't so sure I'd fit my office chair in a year's time, or if I'd actually ever fitted it, but the prospect of dropping from an annual wage of around £15,000 to somewhere around £0 was fairly unnerving. I was hardly stepping up the career ladder. But later, after a year of jollying my way around America and Europe on hard-earned savings, I knew my office days were over. I went in to see the old team, just to confirm it, and nothing had changed with the whole office scene. I think they really thought I was coming back, but I was gone before the kettle had even boiled.

Things had changed. Surfing along on the wave of publicity my 'value' picked up. I seemed to be worth something. 5.10 and Petzl threw in the highly exciting, but ultimately dreaded 'photo' incentive deal – not much to look at in terms of pounds per individual picture, but with a flurry of press I was making a few thousand a year, which was probably more than they had expected. Hardly breaking the bank, or actually even enough to pay the mortgage, but enough to convince me that some climber-type employers might like to give me some more and that sitting behind a desk all day was to be avoided at all costs. But cash wasn't going to come from 'sponsorship'. After considering all the previously-listed scientific equations, I figured I was already making my share, so I went direct from rejecting the engineering office to Adobe Photoshop in my bedroom and, using the limits of my skills on a Stone Age desktop, I knocked up the crappest of fliers advertising myself as a route-setter. This was a rather bold move considering my totally limited experience of setting a few routes down at The Foundry for nothing, but I figured I had to start somewhere and if I only charged a small amount the walls wouldn't get too pissed off, even if they had to reset everything all over again. So I highlighted my strong points (basically just climbing a few hard routes) to distract from the lack of experience, emailed the flier to all the climbing walls in the BMC climbing wall directory and waited to see what happened. Most undoubtedly went direct to junk or were deleted, but The Castle in London was the first to bite, way back in 2002, and so armed with an Allen key and a few million moves in my head I stumbled into what was to become my most regular job. From there I just wandered along, watching doors appear along the path and open in front of me, 'A "top climber" are you? Well, of course, you can set routes, but you can also write, and lecture, and coach and design new kit … can't you?' A red carpet was rolled out on the assumption that I'd be able to do the job, every job. So I just lobbed myself in.

So what is my job? Everyone wants or needs to know: insurance, tax, banks, census, new friends, even old friends. Choose from the drop down list online or write it in a box somewhere. I can pick from the list, though choosing I feel like a fraud. How am I a route setter compared to Ian Vickers? Or a writer compared to Andy Cave; a lecturer compared to Andy Kirkpatrick or a coach compared to Neil Gresham? I need to try and lump them all together, but 'climber' sounds pathetic, and 'professional climber' is too serious. I mean, just that word, 'professional', instils an image that I don't see myself fitting into. It's all smart and tidy wearing a tie, organised and planned; an expert. It also implies, to most climbers, that I don't actually do any work at all and am either out climbing, training for climbing, talking about climbing, watching endless dull climbing films or asleep in bed recovering from climbing.

Becoming a professional climber could be described as entering a tunnel – the professional climber tunnel. All qualifications and work experience are left at the entrance and you begin with nothing except maybe a bit of a name, if you've worked hard. Getting further in, the stuff at the entrance becomes more useless and outdated and it gets darker and darker as you grapple for odd jobs. There is a light at the end of the tunnel for some, but not for everyone and plenty of lifers are left scratching at the walls with no way out. I can remember entering my own tunnel, leaving my degree, higher degree and seven years' engineering experience at the door.

I watched as opportunities I'd opened up were closed forever while I took on low paid route-setting and lectured in front of crowds too small to pay my travel costs. It was tough work and not exactly filling my savings account, but it allowed me to be more of what I am, to be free and in control and to get out in the hills for more than just four weeks a year.

On their deathbed, nobody ever wished they'd spent more time in the office.

Pretty quickly my equations balanced out, with enough cash coming in to easily cope with my meagre expenditure and enough free time to climb a fair bit. Although potential cash in was hampered by lack of ego, I was still pulling in some support and the low values were offset by a carefully-planned amount of 'real work'. Then, while typing up an article for *OTE* magazine, I got a call from Fat Face clothing. The voice on the end of the phone introduced itself as the 'Head of marketing and promotion. I'd like to discuss the possibility of entering into a sponsorship agreement, with mutual benefit on both sides, as well as all the great perks that come along with joining a huge multi-national company.' My heart skipped a beat; this was it, this was the big one. Images of tripping over huge wads of cash appeared in front of my eyes. F.F. were massive, they had shops everywhere and everyone had something made by them, even if it was just a pair of socks. Exactly how I'd help them I didn't know, since I was fairly certain they made exactly zero garments that were any good to climb in. Still, that wasn't my concern, and considering I'd been wearing any old cast-offs or rags from the charity shop it was likely that I'd be going up in the world no matter what. I was expecting some dosh here. Fat Face stuff wasn't known for being cheap and nasty – it was expensive and good quality and, at about £50 for a pair of jeans and £20 for a belt, I was hoping for more than a few free T-shirts and a pat on the back. Surprisingly the offer was of kit only, and for not an insignificant amount of work on my part, not to mention the use of my image and name wherever they saw fit. This time I was having none of it and made up an existing sponsor that they'd have to beat. We initially settled on a grand a year, to be reviewed annually. Hardly a fortune, but better than a slap in the face or a bank loan and with the added attraction of extremely decent free Christmas presents for my family and friends.

Fat Face were a great company to be involved with despite the limited range of performance clobber. But that was the whole marketing strategy. They made clothes to look good in *after* you'd done whatever cool sport you happened to be doing and so their stores were plastered with top-end dudes from all the trendy sports. There were skiers and surfers and mountain bikers and paragliders and me – the climber. My more-than-life-size posters were plastered in half the stores in the UK, over fifty of them, and I was regularly met by friends commenting, 'I've just been trying on some clothes at Fat Face and you were in the changing room with me.' A strange marketing plan maybe, but it certainly worked. Joe Normal, who'd never set foot out of the city and spent his whole life in the office or in front of the TV, could pretend he might one day become an adrenaline junkie simply by purchasing a few expensive cotton shirts. They really did make good clothes too and this, along with their associated marketing plan, allowed a bedroom business set up by two penniless skiers and named after a ski slope in Val d'Isere to be sold eventually for a hundred million pounds.

With F.F. I witnessed the way in which companies work, and how there are different budgets and different pots of money and how sponsorship is generally a small thimble of a pot relative to all the others. Having apparently pushed them to the limit with a £1,000 retainer, I found myself invited on a trip to Iceland, a photoshoot for their latest brochure thinly disguised as an expedition across the central glacier. A huge entourage was flown out, including a bunch of models from London on £1,000 per day. I became aware of how it all worked on the meal out on the first night at an extremely posh restaurant. Just looking at the menu made me feel sick and looking for the exit very quickly, even if it meant abandoning my coat, which had been taken from me by the posh cloakroom attendant and hung lovingly amongst the other rather smarter jackets. Even though I wasn't paying, I chose the cheapest thing on the entire menu, unable to bring myself to pick anything else, and avoided any starter, dessert, coffee or even drink, insisting on tap water as 'I was tired from all the travel and didn't want any alcohol.' I was then horrified to see everyone else go for pretty much whatever they fancied and could only assume their menus were missing the price list or that mine had been incorrectly labelled by a factor of ten. As the extortionately-priced alcohol flowed, a number of vintage champagnes were ordered and the price escalated out of control, to eventually finalise at a figure some multiple times my annual retainer. That night, settling into my huge single-occupancy double room in the five-star hotel I was exhausted by the liberal use of cash, which was to continue for the rest of the trip with no expense spared. We drove over the glacier in humongous 4x4 jeeps with 1.5-metre diameter wheels, rode skidoos for fun, were pulled around on dog sleds, had zooming flights with expert paragliders and ate and drank the finest at every chance. It seemed completely over the top. They did get a pretty good brochure out of it though.

This was the first of many 'brochure shoots' and the most lavish by far, probably due to the fact that Tim and Jules, the founders and owners of F.F., were with us. A pair of relatively normal people, they'd seen their business explode by the millions, so were probably entitled to chuck some money around. The following trips were slightly more restrained, but all awesome. There was always a bunch from the sponsored team, varying every time, but rather pleasingly usually including me. Our 'job' was to advise on the pictures and keep things authentic. We'd get the models into position and if they couldn't get into position we'd do it ourselves on the assumption that we were far enough away from the camera for the public to notice our more normal appearance. Having said that, it probably wasn't really an issue for most of the dudes, with the average young skier or mountain biker giving the models a run for their money in the looks department. In my case, being old, small and ugly, getting as far away from the lens as possible seemed the most important tactic. However, I still made it into more than a few of their annual brochures, usually by getting into positions that the cameramen thought would really 'make the shot'. Often I had to draw the line, like when they asked, 'can you just climb up that cliff there and hold a position?' My honest reply, much to their disappointment was, 'not a chance, that's 50 metres of overhanging rubble and there isn't anyone who knows how to belay me, not to mention that it's in a private working quarry.' Generally it was assumed I could do anything associated with being off the ground, and I often had the camera clicking to relatively trivial things like abseiling over a waterfall and jumaring back up, pretty straightforward but viewed as 'totally insane' by the models and crew. My only close call was on a huge barge we were sailing along the fjords of northern Norway. Passing under a massive bridge the team decided it would be awesome if I could abseil off the bridge onto the boat, and so I was dropped off at a local port, ran the few miles back to the rather busy motorway bridge and then proceeded to inconspicuously chuck my ropes over the edge and leap off in the hope that some passing motorist wouldn't raise the alarm and get me banged up in a Norwegian slammer. Sliding down the 45 metres towards the boat in blasting winds I tried to pick my moment and, though I'd absolutely insisted the boat had to be dead still for me to land, it appeared to be moving at a steady pace. Landing squarely on deck in a stunt even James Bond would have been proud of, I tried to hide my panicked face from the applause as I frantically tried to drag the ropes through my abseil device at a rate to match the speed at which we were now moving away from the bridge, the captain having put his foot down in the assumption that the show was over. Pretty quickly the inevitable happened, and as the tangled sea-soaked ropes jammed I was yanked off my feet and dragged across the deck on my back, only managing to right myself and leap over the railings seconds before being smashed into them at a rather rapid speed. Dumped into the freezing Arctic sea with a selection of metalware attached to my harness and a jumble of ropes twisting around my body, I just about managed to stay afloat before the boat circled around and the crew dragged me aboard. Needless to say, the team were less than impressed, and even though it was hardly my fault, the daredevil badge seemed somewhat tainted and this was to be my last trip with Fat Face. However, pretty soon after that the whole company had a massive shake-up. With the credit crunch slapping the high street, F.F. were prime contenders to take the hit. Their first move was to get shot of their sponsored team. I'm sure in retrospect they probably wished they'd done this earlier, as particularly in the case of climbing, it's unlikely that anyone shopping in their stores would have been be influenced by me on the poster. Still, it was a great run with a great company and even though we ended our relationship back in 2009, I still sometimes see myself stuck on their shop walls when I go in and buy some socks for my dad's Christmas present.

Losing a bit of cash was a shame, but I'd seen it coming and most of the Fat Face stuff didn't fit anyway, being designed for rugged macho types as opposed to a short, skinny weakling. Some proper technical outdoor stuff that actually fitted would have been nice. I thought I'd struggle to persuade anyone to hang their clothes off me and so it was very cool to be contacted by the head of marketing from Marmot. I was at last kitted out with gear that really made a difference when the weather turned properly British. It was a shock at times, having never really worn proper outdoor kit due to a combination of being too stingy and not believing it actually worked, and I was blown away when the clothing actually 'performed'. My earlier years of struggling with cast-off macs and charity shop bargains were a bit like struggling with crap and cheap DIY tools. You get what you pay for, and in the case of crap tools that's a crap job that takes ages, looks rubbish, and possibly includes a free smack in the face when the end of your pound-shop hammer flies off. The Marmot stuff was awesome, with fleeces that weighed nothing and waterproofs that were exactly that. I'd assumed all waterproofs leaked. Now, on the odd occasion when the shit really hit the fan, like when I was lost in the middle of nowhere in the middle of the night on the top of a big wall, I was pretty much kept alive by an item of clothing that packed into the size of my sandwich box.

I was lucky with Marmot and with Petzl and 5.10. There's always a dilemma for the sponsored climber: to use and endorse stuff because you are given it (or, for the real heroes, because it pays the most), or to buy the stuff you really want. I just can't work like that. I couldn't stand up for something I didn't believe in. I'd rather be able to say I honestly use the best and this isn't just a blatant plug for my sponsors.

Swapping brands would be for the wrong reasons, for all my kit. Over the years I've been offered shoes from almost every shoe company, and some were decent deals, but there is no way I'd swap from where I'm at because I wouldn't be able to climb as hard. I'm still constantly amazed at how good the 5.10 shoes are and sometimes I feel like I'm cheating. It would have to be one hell of a good deal to drop half a grade, especially considering the amount of time, effort and money I spend trying to add that grade. Basically it would be like just giving up on hard climbing, a complete admission of it being all over and it would be abandoning the primary goal of getting the most out of myself.

By the time I joined Marmot in 2009 sponsorship had changed. For a start, most companies had dumped the dreaded photo incentive. Though it had served me well I had begun to loath it. Scanning hotly-anticipated magazines I'd hunt for the logos, but not being a fan of the stick-on badge or the whole logo placement thing I relied on subtle exposure, using the 'real' logos on equipment and helpful photographers to reveal them. This often didn't work out, with the best picture missing the dollar sign and I could never really influence the choice of shot – this was the photographer's work on display, despite the fact that he was getting paid and I now wasn't. I remember a whole sequence of shots in a bunch of magazines and a collection of front covers all missing the essential logos. I was gutted and that hit me hard – instead of being proud of my efforts and feeling privileged to be included in the press, I was just miserable. A month's pay, maybe even half a year's pay (because I wasn't exactly doing hard new routes every month), had simply vanished.

That said, the photographers I worked with generally knew the score, Tim Glasby and Keith Sharples in particular. It may seem wrong that when a picture hits the press it's the photographer who takes all the cash, but it's a two-way thing, boosting the climber's profile and hopefully helping them in the future. Photoshoots are a double-edged sword: we all need the pictures for inspiration and to keep the scene alive, but often see them as staged and fake, and we hate that. Those shots of Mr Bold on the latest death headpoint – did he really go back and do it again? No, the top rope is going down his sleeve and around the arête. Fortunately I never experienced this. Both Tim and Keith would simply say 'just climb', whether it be an on-sight, a redpoint or a repeat of something I'd already done. I'd not even know they were there, so, in effect, the photos are real, the capture of effort and tenacity and desire is authentic. Tim somehow has the ability to 'get the shot' with a single click of the shutter; he's had no less than ninety-nine front covers around the world, with a whopping twelve displaying my mug. These two good friends have been instrumental to my status and probably my entire career. Keith in particular, my 'other dad', has been a fantastic mentor and an endless source of confidence. At the crag, he's often shared the burden of my efforts and offered advice from his vast pool of knowledge. He was one of the first to look out for me way back at the start and remains a true and solid climbing partner today.

With the ditching of incentives cash was getting harder to come by and as the credit crunch swept the country the outdoor industry held its breath, waiting for the squeeze. Sponsorship morphed into what could perhaps be called 'employment', with many companies using their athletes for specific targeted work in addition to their expected level of exposure. In many ways this was a move in the right direction. 'Work' was typically lectures, staff training or boot demos, gear design and other similar stuff – not easy by any stretch, but massively favouring the 'professional climber' who was probably doing most of it anyway. The move has led to a healthy industry with climbers motivated by their own real desires. Neil Gresham sums it all up perfectly:

> 'I have genuinely never felt the pressure to perform. I'm the first to join in at a friendly local bouldering comp when I'm not on form and do rubbish. To me this is what it's all about. I think it sets a way better example if you are regarded as someone who genuinely loves the sport and is always keen to join in, rather than someone who's image-conscious and only wants to be seen looking good. Besides, if anyone wants to judge me because I can't do the 'blue holds' problem at their local wall, then I'll happily point them in the direction of The Indian Face or Equilibrium. Regarding whether or not I've ever chosen routes because they'd be good for my sponsors – are you kidding? There are better ways to earn a crust than climbing Meshuga. The main thing about climbing hard routes is that they choose you, as opposed to it being the other way round.'

Many climbers still believe there are 'sponsored heroes' out there earning a packet and adding hugely to the cost of a set of shiny new cams. There are a few rock stars on a few bob, but barely enough to count on one hand and the sums they make are only likely to be perceived as sizeable if you are a student living in the 1980s. The vast majority of sponsored heroes work hard for their dollar, and it's likely their results will have more depth and be more real. There is no pressure to perform, no pressure to make the news or be in the news. When you are a top level climber it just happens, because you are climbing at the top level. There's also been a huge change in what 'makes' news. When it was only magazines, which had limited space, they would choose the biggest news of the month – they still do. But now there are websites looking for multiple headlines every day, so the quality of news is watered down. This is kind of good, it means we all get something nice to read over our cornflakes, and if you are sponsored it's way easier to make the headlines doing something that, in reality, would barely have been worth a mention ten years ago. Many climbers struggle with this, keeping ascents to themselves while others roll out the news when they change their underpants from blue to brown. Most sponsored climbers find some kind of middle ground, a comfortable balance, simply letting the exposure take care of itself with the odd photo day, usually at the request of the photographer. The public can see this too; they can see who's grappling for stardom and they can relate much more to the average Joe who's just an average guy, with nothing to separate himself from the rest of the world other than a relatively insignificant ability to pull hard on some small holds.

What seems clear, having spoken to many self-proclaimed 'pros' and others who are nearly pros, even though it appears none of us are actually pros at all, is that it's really a lifestyle thing. Very few have such a huge ego as to think they are superstars. It's about simply choosing a job that fits in with their passion. Public perception is often that 'sponsored climbers' are selling out, but I look at the sponsored climbers of our generation: MacLeod, Bransby, Emmett, Leah Crane, Lucy Creamer and many more, and clearly they are quite normal. They are working with companies and climbing hard. They do stuff we want to read about and be inspired by, and they give depth to our sport. But what about when they get rubbish, or just can't be bothered? Even if they are still awesome at fifty, will anyone really care anyway? Will they be cool anymore? For those who worked at it there will be a natural pathway through the industry … hopefully. Otherwise it will be back to the desk or a nice retirement stacking shelves.

Did I make it through the tunnel? I'm still not sure yet, but at least I can see the light. Maybe I'll only really know when I'm sitting round the fire with the grandkids, which is still a long way off. With no pension plan and around 80 per cent of my work reliant on me being at least 80 per cent fitter than most people, a comfortable old age is hardly guaranteed. But then no work is safe these days and a cast-iron career with lifelong prospects can collapse with zero notice. So with that positive thought in mind I've certainly made it through the tunnel, that is, if making it through the tunnel means having enough work to do.

At the moment it's all a bit busy. I spend on average two days a week route-setting and a day coaching. On top of that I give the odd talk, run boot demos, write for the magazines, keep the blogs up-to-date (badly), attend openings or promotions, help in gear design, work on the BMC ambassador scheme, build the odd bit of climbing wall and run the sponsored Petzl and Beal team for Lyon Equipment. And that's before even starting on the non-climbing work, like bits of labouring here and there. I'm even a landlord, having bought a house for £16,000 in the arse end of Sheffield back in 2001 which nets me a whopping £200 a month for God knows how much hassle. All in all it works out at somewhere around thirty-five to forty hours a week and is a total balancing act trying to fit everything in without becoming too exhausted to climb. That's one of the most rewarding parts, when everything falls into place. There is nothing better than arranging a day's setting, followed by some coaching and then an evening talk all at the same wall.

One of my hardest setting jobs is at the Reebok Gym in London. After the early morning start with obligatory complete soaking on my 15-minute downhill cycle ride to the station, I'll be setting from 10 a.m. 'til 12 p.m., then sleeping at the wall and starting again at 5 a.m. I'll work solidly until 5 p.m., finishing off with a further three hours of coaching before catching the 9 p.m. train home, which will have me sitting on the sofa by 12.30. The last bit, the cycle home, uphill in the rain carrying a rucksack full of setting kit, drills, sleeping bag and mat, computer and other exceptionally heavy stuff, definitely has me wondering if it's all worth it – just as it does when I'm sweeping the dust off the floor in the broom cupboard at the wall before I attempt my four hours of kip. But this is my choice. The cycle ride home saves me a fortune in taxi fares and my doss in the cupboard means I can do a three-day job in two. But quick hits like this pack in the hours and justifies the next day off. Not that I'm fit to do anything with it.

It's all about flexibility. Most of my work is planned well in advance, and I can also plan to *not* work, blocking out whole weeks, every Tuesday for a month, or even a whole month off. I could sack it off for a year if I fancied, though we'd probably be lighting the house with candles and huddling by a fire stoked with skip-found timber. I'm privileged, not just in flexibility, also in that I enjoy much of the work itself.

The main issue I have is quality – I just don't know how good my work is. Life as an engineer is simple: someone has a problem, you fix it. If it works you probably did a good job. With coaching or lecturing I've no idea, and writing is even worse. At school I didn't like English, my punctuation and grammar are appalling, and my spelling so bad that I've already been out-done by my seven-year-old daughter. Route-setting is marginally better: at least I know what a good route feels like, even if it's only my opinion. After a full day's setting I can leave knowing I did a good job, compared to leaving a lecture hall wondering if everyone was bored shitless and annoyed at paying five quid to look at someone's holiday snaps. These concerns aside, it all seems to work out and though I don't exactly earn a fortune it brings in enough dosh for a fairly chilled lifestyle. Okay, so my car is a £700, fourteen-year old Vectra, but it gets from A to B and I think that kind of simplistic attitude helps. More cash would need more effort to just get better versions of the same, and result in less time to climb or enjoy life. If, twenty years ago, I could have looked at myself through a window into the future and seen where I'd ended up I think I'd have been pleased with the view.

25   I'VE MADE IT

Vic woke me with a kiss; 8.45 a.m. Work time, for her at least. Smartly dressed all in black she looked good, professional but carrying a relaxed aura. I watched her glide across the stripped floorboards and past the pine bed frame, the sunlight seeping through the curtains lighting the room in gentle browns and shining in her jet black hair. I turned over and buried my face, hiding from the brightness as my aching muscles reminded me of the previous two weeks' sport climbing in Spain. Vic had slept through as I crept in at one in the morning. Now she breezed away, as fresh as the crisp spring air and full of purpose. Stopping at the door she waved and the clarity of the moment dragged the sleep from my eyes. It would be nice to talk and laugh, to tell her about my trip and the great routes I'd done. But that could wait until later. We often passed like ships in the night these days, with her full time IT job and my all-over-the-place lifestyle, but for once I had a window with nothing arranged: no work, no holidays. I'd planned it, a good chance to catch up – with everything.

Sliding tired legs from under the sheets I sat on the edge of the bed, feet resting on the smooth varnished timber. It felt warm and comforting, with the satisfaction of knowing it was my own work and a job well done. Other DIY jobs rattled in the background – this house from 1870 would always carry a list – but they could be crossed off at my own pace. No need to rush. Today opened up with its lack of agenda, the blue sky suggesting familiar options in the nearby Peak. I wouldn't be climbing today; maybe a bike ride, or a walk, or just nothing. Coming home was easy when you live in a city with so much on the doorstep. Tomorrow I'd climb, maybe.

The phone rang, interrupting my gentle flow. Nine o'clock, Frank Bennett on the phone from Lyon Equipment, 'Petzl have been in touch, they've got one of their Petzl Roc Trips coming up in a week and they'd like you to go. It's in the south of France near Millau. We'd like you to go too, show those Frenchies who's boss.'

I coughed my voice awake, in bed at such a late hour didn't look good, as a professional something or other I should have been up ages ago. Frank was probably at work at 6 a.m.

'Erm, yeah, I'd love to go out … ' the wobble in my voice probably obvious from the knowledge I'd be getting a thorough slapping from the French team.

'Can you go? We need to inform Petzl immediately for their press release.'

I committed, a chance of a lifetime really, of course I'd go. My relaxed morning switched back into holiday mode as I cranked up the Stone Age computer to hunt for the most efficient travel plans, which was kind of strange really, since Petzl would be paying the flight. With various tabs open I checked out flights and matched them alongside potential climbing partners, strategically planning as many ways as possible to stay out in France after the trip to make the most of my free passage. With only a week before the trip my window of catching up had suddenly closed. Vic would be cool with it, because, well, she always was ...

The Roc Trips had been running for a few years now, and I'd already been to one of the first in the Gunks over in America. They'd gained a reputation for being *the* event of the year. It would be a privilege to go, although, in reality, I was surprised to be invited along to another trip, being unable to tick all or, in fact, any of the required athlete boxes:

a. Young
b. Brilliant
c. Cool
d. Handsome

Fortunately I somehow ended up with my name on the list due to one or a number of the following:

a. British
b. A mistake
c. Access to media
d. Because everyone was invited

Quite possibly it could have been d), because this French trip ended up being really big, though in reality it was probably a), there being no other suitable British candidates on the Petzl team. However, it could just as easily have been a mistake – and that's almost certainly what they also assumed, once they saw my performance on the cliff relative to not only all the other invited heroes but just about any French punter who turned up, including multiple schoolboys who'd no doubt chosen climbing as a random add-on to their PE lessons. Most likely I was filling an empty place after someone realised they had a world cup event to win somewhere else. At least on paper I looked okay, as the promotion guys had cunningly fashioned a glossy twenty-page trip booklet profiling all the athletes, to be distributed for everyone to scrutinise. My list of numbers wasn't so bad, just as long as no one figured that most of my routes were on a couple of crappy polished holds at a scruffy excuse of a crag. Doing some new random link at Raven Tor where the four locals are impressed is suddenly put into perspective when absolutely everyone around you on-sights 8b. Most important was that no one attempted to tally my profile with actual performance, though the disparity would be so large anyone would assume I was a different bloke from the UK, with all Brits looking fairly similar in their eyes; pale and scruffy with a distinct lack of finesse.

Taking a cheap Ryanair flight and hitching the rest of the way to save money, I finally made it to the cliff, a huge wave of immaculate limestone peppered with pockets. Just the thought of pulling on them made my fingers ache. An hour of stumbling around at the base of the cliff gaping upwards conjured a confusion of emotions: inspiration, amazement, inferiority and depression, all at the same time.

France, July 2004
Article for *On The Edge* magazine, issue 144

I'm chatting with Christian Brenna when Chris Sharma and Dave Graham walk over. Lynn Hill is climbing just next to me and Said Belhaj is belaying. This is not just another day at the crag. Daniel Dulac swaggers over, complete with Stetson hat, chalk buckets full of testosterone and in situ girls. D. D. is a true climbing dude, but not just a dude, he'd just won the European bouldering championships in Italy four days ago, so he's quite strong. Now he's trying an 8b+, on sight, in the middle of the day, in the full sun, with no warm-up. Phew, he's fallen off, thank God for that, I was about to get seriously depressed but, guess what, he's done it next go without working any of the moves above where he fell.

This Petzl Roc Trip is all about the 'flash contest'. If you fall you are lowered straight down, but you can try again later. Same points for an ascent no matter how many tries you have. So it's more of a yo-yo competition. Ah, just like the old days: fifteen routes for the men and fifteen for the women – a potential fifteen points on the table. For the men there's a token 7c+ and then a collection of pockety horror shows from 8a to 8c, so I'm not expecting to need a very big table for my point collection. Three days to climb when you like, belayed by who you like, so fairly chilled. I like the style: supposedly a competition, but really just a few days out at the crag.

42 Slithering up the crux pitch of *The Quarryman*. One of the best routes on slate.
A childhood dream to try this one! *Photo: Tim Glasby.*

44

43 Teetering across granite slabs in Greenland. *Photo: Nick 'Tufty' Boden.*
44 *Regent Street* (E2 5c), Millstone. One of my favourite routes at my favourite gritstone crag.
   Photo: Tim Glasby.

45 Leading *Ghost Train* (E6 6b) in Stennis Ford, Pembroke. *Photo: Keith Sharples.*
46 Immaculate limestone on *Pleasure Dome* (E3 5c), Pembroke. *Photo: Keith Sharples.*
47 Trying to look cool in front of the cameras at the Petzl Roc Trip in Kalymnos. *Photo: Sam Bié.*

48

49

50

51

48 It's all about seeing the potential rather than the problem!
49 A kiddie carrier is just a tool to allow adults to continue going where they want, regardless of the weather!
50 Cornwall.
51 Vic after the Sheffield half marathon.
52 Amelie at just turned two.
53 Hanging in the south of France. Suddenly climbing was not the main event.

52

53

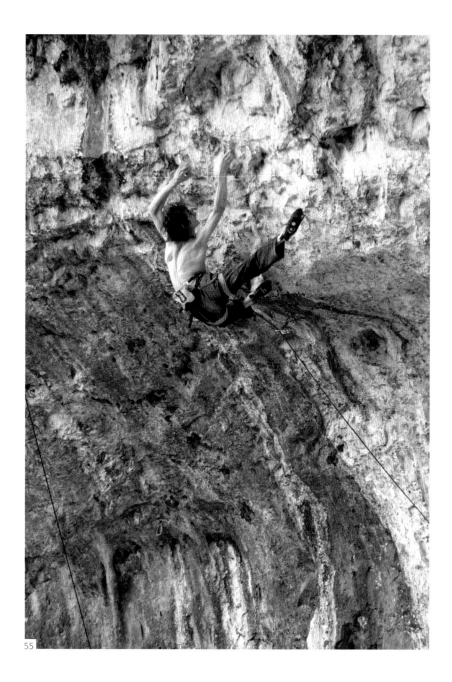

54 A quick run for photos on *Overshadow* a few days after the first ascent.
But it had become impossible due to seepage, my first ascent was just in time! *Photo: Keith Sharples.*
55 Adam Ondra repeats *Overshadow*, but not without a tussle. Phew!
This is a climber on a whole different level. *Photo: Keith Sharples.*

57

58

56 Teaching Amelie the importance of climbing fashion at an early age.
57 *Hubble* – the final exam! *Photo: Ben Pritchard.*
58 Rab Carrington relaxed on our ascent of *Fiesta de los Biceps* (F7a) in Spain.

60

59 Malham Cove. *Photo: Keith Sharples.*
60 The headwall on *Batman* (F9a/+). This section would be F8c+ in its own right. *Photo: Ian Burton.*

61

62

61 Paul Reeve redpointing *Cry Freedom* at Malham – F8c at 50 years old. Paul is one of the most inspiring
   and motivating characters I have ever met: the definition of tenacity! *Photo: Keith Sharples.*
62 Strong company: on stage at the Rock Legends awards in Arco with Alex Megos and Adam Ondra.
   Ondra won … of course! *Photo: Petr Piechowicz.*
63 *Total Brutal* (F8b+) Zillertal, Austria. *Photo: Tim Glasby.*
64 The majestic Verdon Gorge. *Photo: Tim Glasby.*

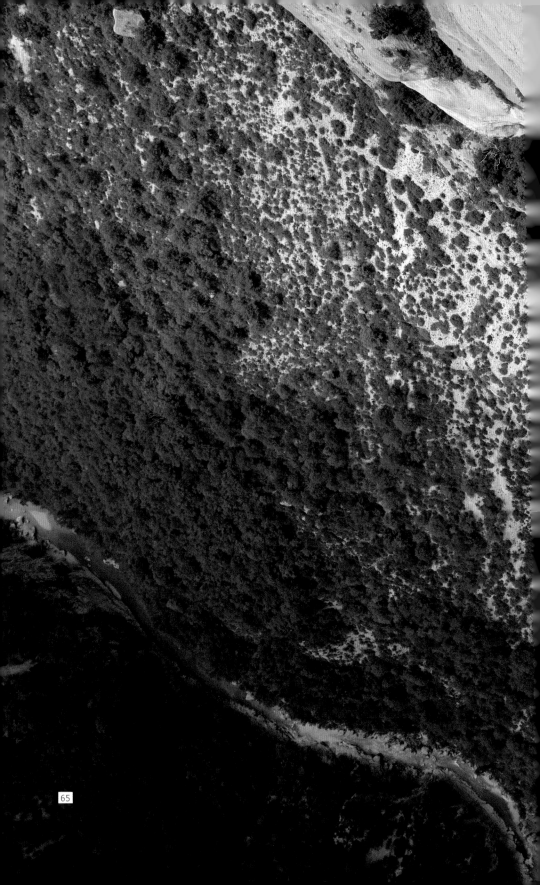

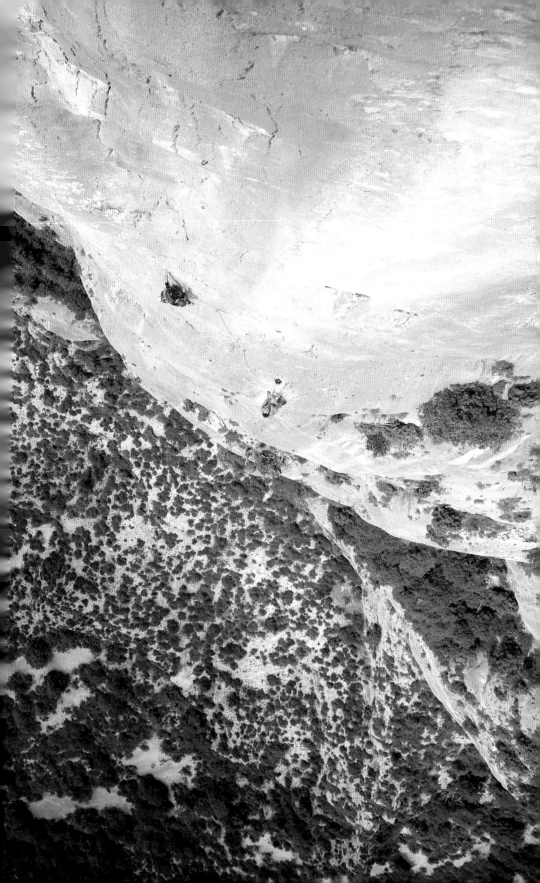

66

67

65 *L'Ange en Décomposition* (F7a), Verdon. One of the very best routes in the gorge. It's hard to imagine
 a route more perfect. Natural route setting at its very best *Photo: Rich Heap*.
66 Harry at Scugdale in the North York Moors. Perhaps the perfect school for climbing.
67 Amelie and Harry chilling at The Orange House.
68 Neil Mawson leading *Surveiller et Punir* (F7a+), one of the finest routes in the Verdon Gorge. *Photo: Tim Glasby*.

69 The last hard move on the *Great Arch*, Pabbay – a lunge for a good hold on the lip of the roof. I got the hold, then promptly fell off, having climbed all of the route up to that point on sight! *Photo: Tim Glasby.*
70 Focused on the flash of *Tom et Je Ris* (F8b+), Verdon. *Photo: Tim Glasby.*
71 Sorting gear on Pabbay with Lucy Creamer. *Photo: Tim Glasby.*
72 *Strawberries.* On sight. A stand-out moment in my life. Not the hardest route but one of the most important and most satisfying. Filling my field of view from when I was seventeen years old it took twenty-seven years for me to take on the challenge. *Photo: Tim Glasby.*

The 8c looks evil, so evil no one dares try it. Still a project, most of the holds are like shoving your hands in a dog's mouth. Massive spans between tiny holds to a dyno to a broken bottle jug. The crux is obvious: a couple of edges six feet apart on a 45-degree overhanging wall with one lonely little mono in between. Lovely. My favourite. No one tries it until the Yanks arrive. Sharma is taking it easy, having only on-sighted three grade 8s today, so he potters off to cruise some other easy routes, seemingly unaware of the mass of followers scrabbling along behind him. Dave Graham arrives looking like a few pains au chocolate would go down well, but that would double his weight and by the way he's pulling on the holds he appears to have no weight. That mono must be massive, surely, the move looked easy. He sends the route first redpoint after thirty seconds' rest, declaring it might be only hard 8b+. The crowd of hundreds go wild, enlightened by their god. I'm in the queue for my attempt, but leapfrog backwards at a faster rate than people are climbing in the hope that I fall off the end of the line and no one knows I'm even here.

Daniel Andrada and Pedro Pons turn up late, but it doesn't matter because the routes are only about 20 metres long. That's half a route when you have their stamina so they can do twice as many as everyone else. Between easy ramblings they hang around in the sun with flocks of beautiful girls. Dani is the ultimate macho man: massive muscles, grating deep voice, deep brown skin and the ability to grow a full beard in two hours. I hang around by myself in the shade feeling exhausted and sunburnt with some bum-fluff on my chin. Tony Lamiche appears blaring French/English/Spanish/Italian at the same time and then Sharma cruises back from an afternoon interlude and warms up by flashing through the crux of the 8c to the last move, inspiring me to get some muscles as I slope off to get my protein intake in the form of two kilos of cheese on top of a pizza. At last the day is over and I realise I'd done a really fantastic job, but only in avoiding any kind of humiliation whatsoever by trying the easy routes or the occasional hard one when no one was looking. This was a fairly simple task of co-ordinating my attempt with just about anyone else starting to climb, the real stars undoubtedly offering a far greater display on a far harder route, as well as looking like rock stars as opposed to appearing like an ill, white person just let out of the scruff bag hospital.

At last the climbing is over for today; my fingers gave up ages ago and I've just spent the last two hours pretending to be waiting. Now it's time to party, and Petzl have yet again come up with the goods. It's like a mini Glastonbury, live bands with crazy light shows, fire swirlers, *excessive alcohol and loads of stalls selling the usual: food, karabiners, rock boots ... I'm chatting with Graham about some crazy project ... actually I'm not saying anything, he's frantically explaining the radical moves like a kid with a new toy, his mouth on overdrive between puffs on his rollie. Then the masses spot him and I get trampled over in the rush for autographs. Two hours later I see him putting on a brave and bored face for a hundred young adoring kids. Being famous would be nice, but not that nice.*

Next day is the last competition day, it's even hotter and my hangover seems quite bad. No one else has a hangover though. That's strange as everyone seemed to be really drunk, at least that's how they looked to me after I'd glugged through the free wine. One of the 8as I did before I became completely shagged was really hard apparently, 40 metres long with some small crimps; the only route with my name on it. No one else has got up it yet so an extra point is awarded. For an excited moment my score lifted from the bottom of the pile, but then Brenna finds a secret way and, of course, everyone else then wanders up the route as a warm down.

Climbing over, everyone gathers in a big field below the cliff for a truly French buffet of salad, bread, cheese and wine. It's free, and so my plate is actually three plates. Looking around no one else has such a mound. This is the world of the beautiful people, young, brown, jolly and thin. The only fat in sight is the half kilo of Roquefort spilling off the edge of my tray. Perhaps I don't really need all that. In true Brit style I roll it up in a napkin and save it for later. The winners are announced and some prizes given out, but it's not the winning that counts at all, it's the taking part, especially when there was absolutely no chance of winning.

I think I came somewhere in the middle, a pretty pleasing and surprising result and could only assume it was thanks to the rubbish maths from the person who totted up the scores. However, my track record at the Roc Trips over the years was to become rather good.

I'd gotten off to a great start the previous year in the Gunks where they had set up an informal competition for all the Petzl 'athletes'. A really chilled affair it was points for routes or boulders ascended, with points converted into cash and donated to the Access Fund – so I couldn't skive off without looking like a bad sport, and, after quickly assessing I'd not be able to manage any of the problems, I opted for routes. Unfortunately no one else was interested, routes being far too boring, anti-social and old school. So I packed off with the only mate I could find, good old Mr Shunt, and proceeded to have a rather lovely day cruising a whole raft of Gunks' classics. The Yanks thought I was totally crazy and insisted on me handing in my score card even though I explained I hadn't really done the routes at all and that the grade of the routes was completely irrelevant when effectively climbing on top rope. However, they weren't having it, and were all suitably impressed with my huge tally, amassing a stack of points which blew everyone else out of the water. Feeling rather fraudulent to say the least I was glad my dollars went to a worthy cause rather than direct into my pocket.

This opportunistic, and perhaps undeserved, win was to set the scene for many of the Roc Trips and is probably mirrored by most of my climbing life. The trip to Red River was a similar affair, a single-day competition at the Motherlode, the definition of a long, steep crag. A monumental 45-degree overhanging, 35-metre wall covered in crimps. Fitness was the word – 8a would probably be around E7 5c; no really hard moves but rather a lot of quite hard moves for a really long way. Competition rules were simple: lots of routes were set aside at grades from 7a to 8c, each worth 1,000 points, and the points were divided by the number of people climbing any one route. The winning strategy appeared to be to tick a hard route no one else could do. I got close, falling off the last move of an 8b+ and in the process used up all my energy for exactly no points. Everyone else had the same plan, skipping the easy numbers to score the big tick. Thoroughly exhausted, I watched from a distance as I struggled up the warm-up routes, noting with surprise that I was getting a full thousand points for each of the easiest routes in the comp simply because no one else had bothered. An easy win, though with a rather feeble tally of low 7s I was again glad of my haul of points being donated to the Access Fund. Up on stage, however, I was presented with a huge bottle of champagne and spraying it over the 500-strong crowd was a cool experience – although unlike a racing driver I stopped short, because I wanted to drink it.

At the next Roc Trip to Squamish in Canada real cash prizes were on offer, with big potential for a fat wallet. Same 1,000 points rule, divided up by the number who succeeded. A two-day comp, routes on day one, boulders on day two. Obviously I opted for routes, and while nearly everyone rested up for the big bouldering day I fluked my way up an 8b+ no one else managed, as well as an 8a that everyone managed, thus giving a score of just over a thousand. The boulders comp consisted of five unbelievably hard projects and one existing Font 8a that so far only Sharma had climbed, and clearly the organisers were a tad optimistic to assume any of these projects would go in a day when they had resisted attempts from some of the world's best boulderers over many years of effort. They had also unfortunately forgotten to book in some good weather and as the clag settled down no one could do anything. Battered and sore from my half day of routes I dragged myself around in a Gore-Tex watching strong youths trying to shelter from the drizzle under a beanie. In the end the only person to climb anything was Sharma who repeated his existing problem, thus scoring a thousand points, which was marginally below my 1,050. Rather excitedly I accepted my cheque with my score converted into dollars, though with the organisers expecting such high point tallies they'd used the equation of 'points x 0.058 = UK pounds' and I walked away with a monumental £65, roughly enough to keep me stocked up with chocolate biscuits for the remainder of my two-week stay.

And so I gained a reputation, though I'm not entirely sure what the reputation was. Best not think about it. At least I managed to redeem myself in Kalymnos with a true win, even though it was a joint first position. Having been to Kalymnos plenty of times and thoroughly in love with the place, I was pretty excited when the venue was announced. Long routes on tufas requiring hands like shovels are not really my style, but cramming myself into ridiculous rests, hanging by my toes and generally cheating my way around the hard bits is what I'm good at. For a change I was confident that I would at least not come last – despite most of the best climbers in the world turning up, all also no doubt even more confident they'd not come last.

For the athletes on this trip it was all about the 'Ultimate Routes', though the title of 'athlete' may be stretching things having seen some doubtful states at the various parties over the years. There was one route for the men and one for the women, both at least 50 metres long and permanently in upside-down-world, battling with the stalactites dripping from the vast Sikati Cave. Anyone who got up was a winner. Each person had just one hour to work the route followed by a redpoint attempt some days later. The men's route was 8c (and destined to become *Jaws*) so I laid my British excuse cards early, and they were good ones. I was drawn to climb right at the start which meant getting up at 6.30 a.m. after only one hour's sleep following my sixteen-hour overnight journey. Everybody else had been on the island for ages and had had far too much sleep for their own good. Everybody after me would have a line of chalk to follow and all the sequences worked out. In true Brit style I tried to on-sight the route with no warm up. This ensured that when I eventually fell off I was too tired to work the rest of the route and also had no idea how I'd managed to fluke my way up the bottom bit. Thus I spent the last fifty minutes of my hour failing to make a massive span across a roof at half-height before lowering off declaring it impossible for the short. Being first out also meant that, due to the laws of fair play, I'd be attempting my redpoint last, and as there were sixteen men on the route I'd not get to try for a full five days. Thus by the time my turn came round my only recollection was of a really hard bit in the middle that I couldn't do. So it was hardly a professional redpoint effort, more of an anti-flash, with no positive information whatsoever, the only prior knowledge being that I'd certainly fail. At least I wouldn't come last in the competition as most people were falling off at the roof span and, having already got there on the flash, I would be equal to them without even leaving the floor. Climbing last gave me the chance to watch both Chris and Dani get the route on their second redpoint attempt. Nobody else managed it, so at least it was confirmed as hard, and my fear of being the old, traditional, moaning Brit who only got halfway up was removed.

Breathing hard at a rest point before the span I tried to recover some energy and flush the lactic from my arms, having just flashed the 8a lower section for the second time. Peering up I tried to ignore the clutch of photographers and filmmakers hanging from a complex web of ropes above. They were bored, they'd been there for days and days, legs numb from uncomfortable harnesses. They'd had enough, and the winners were already confirmed, the correct names and faces fitting nicely to the headlines and full page spreads already designed and laid out and waiting to be printed. No need to bother with this no-hoper. As the light began to fade I glanced out to the deserted scene below and the few stragglers making their way to the last waiting boat back into town. Pumped arms insisted more rest, but it was time to go. Maybe I was having a tall day but somehow I ended up past the roof, my brain suddenly confused in unfamiliar terrain. A torrent of conflicting information I'd overheard but ignored, assuming it was surplus to requirements, helped slightly with the coming moves, but mostly it became an on-sight battle with an extra chunk of motivation from knowing I'd never get through the span move again, or try the route, or even be back at this cliff. Somehow it came together, a strange mix of pressure and total relaxation knowing no one was watching or cared – and what a buzz. The ultimate route had gone from a damp, reachy, disappointing pain in the ass to the best route ever, with topping out of this vast hole in the ground, untying and dropping the rope into the darkness below being the icing on the cake.

But no one really cared, because there was no winning really. The Roc Trips were a way of getting a bunch of climbers into one place at the same time, with a rough selection of rules jotted down on the back of a fag packet as a thinly disguised reason for being there. The atmosphere was distinctly non-competitive, often with the front runners not bothering to 'compete' because they'd seen a better looking line around the corner or were knackered from trying a new 9b ten minutes earlier. It didn't matter, because everyone was there, all climbing. This chilled style was probably why I enjoyed them so much, with 'real' competitions giving me the fear. Being invited along and then hanging out with the stars and climbing on the same routes was really special. Heroes I'd only read about became friends on an equal level, with performance becoming irrelevant, as it only does with a true friend. I felt like I'd really made it in the climbing world, surpassing every expectation. I'd climb multi-pitch routes with Lynn Hill, chill in the evening with Sharma and then dance madly to techno till 4 a.m. with Dave Graham.

These guys are massive global rock stars and hanging back on a belay, shoulder to shoulder with Lynn, I'd have to pinch myself to check that it was really happening. But the real gift wasn't the chance to share chalk with the stars, it was to see how they work, become real friends and take motivation from their individual skills. Though they are, of course, normal people, they all have an edge, something that sets them apart. Not simply the fingers to crimp really hard, but an inner strength and personality and drive and the ability to focus or find that quiet spot before the most important ascent of their life. Lynn always made me feel relaxed, like climbing with a best mate. She carried nothing of an overblown star's personality, but what inner strength she has. There is something within, like she's made of titanium. She just won't break and won't give up. At just over five-foot she's tiny, massively disadvantaged, but has often put the strong boys to shame doing 'impossible for the short' moves when there were simply no holds to pull on. Spending time with Lynn makes me want to get out and have adventures. She makes it all look so easy. She oozes the climbing lifestyle and is absolutely at one with nature. She's chilled, relaxed and seems at peace.

Dave could not be more different. Though in some ways he's exactly the same, with a competitive edge so blunt as to make everyone feel at ease. He'd try routes in the public eye knowing he'd fail, and genuinely encourage and help others to do better. His position and ranking didn't matter, it's all about giving his best – a solid lesson for me, as I'd roll out the excuses for not doing very well even before I'd turned up at the crag. Dave had something extra, a hidden genius running alongside his apparent madness. Similar to Johnny Dawes, his mind seems to operate on another level, difficult to engage with, but once connected to, a thoroughly enlightening look into the world of the obsessed rock-climber. Both Johnny and Dave are intelligent beyond measure, with a depth of understanding of their relationship with nature and their sport deeper and more colourful than I can even imagine. Occasionally, when I get to grips with their ramblings, bits of my life open up and are laid bare, casting aside complexities and confusions. It's obvious they should have excelled so much in climbing, they have a unique ability to visualise movement between body positions and a complete understanding of the holds, the friction and their own personal strengths. They make climbing sound so much fun – as long as you don't get cornered for the whole evening ...

No chance of that with Chris, almost the opposite of Dave, he keeps himself to himself, simply rolling with the limelight like he doesn't even notice. It seems to just happen around him. The absolute golden boy of rock climbing, he has everything a rock star has to have – except the way-out personality and lifestyle. This on its own is enlightening, that someone so famous and talented can be just so normal. But Chris is far from normal, with an internal strength and desire to get the most out of himself that simply pours from him for all to see. This is what sets him apart, and climbing with him and the other guys makes me want to raise my game. Not simply to crank harder, because that isn't the point, but to want more, to give more and to take more, to purify the whole experience of rock climbing and take this through into the rest of my life.

And I have to mention the Swedish climber, Said Belhaj. From the very first comp I latched onto him, singling him out as an appropriate match for my climbing level and personality. We made an excellent team, at the same climbing standard but with zero competition, a rare combination. But Said is so much more than a climber. Fluent in five languages and highly proficient in playing just about every musical instrument invented, he appears to be the perfect human being. Friendly, funny and good-looking, the girls flock to him with his multiple-9a ability almost an irrelevant add-on. I quickly realised I'd overestimated my personality with the specu-lation of an ideal match, but it never showed, he's honest and supportive and behind me every step of the way. That kind of stuff means a lot.

Hanging with the stars definitely had an influence. Although, just as in school, I adopted my position in the class, aware of my status in both performance and personality, I was welcomed wholeheartedly onto the level playing field they spread out before me. I felt like I'd made it, and though there may have been a few more rungs on the ladder I didn't need to climb them. I'd found my spot, that place where at last I was comfortable with myself. But hanging with the stars was only a part of the big picture. I'd woven myself around climbing and it took me into places I could never have dreamed, with doors opening in front of me at every turn. There were trips of a lifetime on a regular basis, great work opportunities and a shopping list of hard projects stretching ahead. Climbing surrounded me, with the rest of my life slotting in perfectly to form what was apparently a perfect balance. My home life was stable with a great set of mates and a solid relationship with a loving and supportive partner. I couldn't have asked for anything more, at least in that moment. I crammed my life full of things with barely a moment to breathe. I was bulldozing my way through, pushing anything aside that stood in my path and dragging everything behind in my wake. Completely blinkered, I was without any consideration for the future or anyone else in my life.

Vic woke me up, 8.45, work time, for her at least. She looked tired. I watched as she made her way across the room in the darkness of a late autumn morning, the trees having long since shed their leaves. The sound of rain battered the windows. They needed painting, the old coats peeling and the wood beginning to rot, another job pushed aside that should have been done years ago. Stumbling in at two in the morning, wide awake but jetlag-knackered from an Atlantic crossing, I'd woken her up, full of enthusiasm from a great Roc Trip. The trip had been to Squamish, a whole year since the last Roc Trip to France. I explained how much fun I'd had, but maybe all my trips sounded the same. I also explained that I'd be off abroad again in a few days on yet another flight out from Manchester Airport: a great job had come up I couldn't refuse, some route-setting, lectures and poster signings and since the travel would be paid I could stay on afterwards, just for a while … She hadn't been particularly impressed, but not particularly surprised. At the bedroom door she smiled and waved goodbye as I flopped back against the pillow, creaking fingers and dodgy elbows reminding me that after a few weeks' intensive climbing, maybe I could do with a rest. Though to be fair the few weeks away *had* been a rest, relatively, with lots of on-sighting, some trad climbing and even some hill walking.

I was climbing a lot these days, all the time in fact, day on day off or more, with route-setting thrown in as my main job, hoping it might double as some kind of active recovery. Progress had stalled a while back. Training didn't seem to work and just holding the level seemed like an effort. There was something missing, a sliver of motivation. Or perhaps I was asking too much, a continual push for gains from a body that couldn't give any more?

I dragged my legs from the bed, feet resting on the smooth varnished timber. It felt cold, and maybe in need of another coat. There seemed a dampness in the air and my mood felt heavy, the depression of an oncoming winter. Arriving back in Sheffield after such a great time was tough, at least at first, but once I was in the swing of it I'd be back on track, motivated again. At the computer I scoffed dry muesli and planned. Work abroad had to be squeezed in between now and another two-week trip to Spain in December. This part of life was fun, the planning, like a crossword diary. I crammed things in, aiming for the highest efficiency. There's something satisfying about combining a few days' route-setting in London with an evening's coaching and a lecture, not to mention the five hours of computer work on the train. Seven in the morning until ten at night, non-stop for two days in a row. Then I'd take a day off to climb, or even two, a great balance. I always seemed to have something planned, but this didn't give me much chance to catch up – with anything.

Brain turning to mush from the long haul flight, I abandoned the admin in favour of training: a split session indoors, first half power, second half endurance. Despite feeling like I could sleep for a week I needed to up my game, the last few weeks in Canada had done nothing for my performance other than tire me out, and with another chunk of work coming up I'd be losing my edge. I'd probably already well and truly lost it.

The phone rang, interrupting my packing as I shoved boots and chalk into a bag, keen for an early start down at The Foundry. Simon on the phone: 'we're off to Malham tomorrow, three of us in the car, do you want to come?' I glanced at my worn tips and momentarily considered my day's training plans. Of course I'd go, I had a project beckoning that needed a lot of investment. There'd already been a lot of investment. I'd be off the pace for sure on the route, but any time on it was money in the familiarity bank. It would mean a late return to Sheffield the day before heading back out to work. Vic would be cool with it, probably, though I pondered how I'd break the news, doubtful she'd be entirely enthusiastic.

The following morning greeted me from a restless sleep, mind still hung-over from a different time zone. Raining again, a gentle mizzle drifting from a heavy grey sky that seemed to paint droplets in every direction. Cobwebs outside the windows hung heavy under their watery load, gently swaying in a chill breeze. Malham was off for the team, rightly abandoned considering the likely conditions but I still went up, alone, the two-hour drive dragging, missing the banter of a quality car team. Soaking roads and muddy roadside puddles dampened my enthusiasm. There's a glimpsing view of the crag as you drive through the moorland villages, enough to know what's in store, today black stripes marked the seepage as wintry rains followed predetermined paths across the cliff. It didn't look great, more black than white. I kept going, because that's what you have to do, you have to keep turning up, you have to put in the effort. No one else at the crag, not surprising. Icy winds lifted damp leaves, throwing them upwards through the flat half-light in spiralling gusts. I self-belayed my way up *Consenting* 7a, then clipsticked up *Overnite* 8a+ and ran laps on a Shunt. The unclimbed extension section to *Overnite* was soaked anyway, the project over for the year. To be honest it was hardly unexpected, and even if it had been dry I'd never have managed it, the essential slick refinement lost on a different rock type in a different country. At an expected 9a+ I needed all the cards stacked in my favour, a perfect hand. Though I'd been close already it was over for this year, but yet I still turned up, because that's what I did, turn up. Though I had to ask myself – why? What exactly did I gain, a useful day on the project, or a lonely day out in the hills simply because, well, I couldn't think of anything else to do?

Next morning I was broken, more mentally than physically. My one-man trip to Malham had used up the whole day, pushing everything else into a panicked night of packing and admin before another week away. Now, slumped on the train to Manchester Airport, I scribbled in the climbing diary, not that there was much to add. Last entry:

> *Terrible conditions, freezing and seeping. Overnite felt desperate. Performance in reverse from too much route-setting and messing around on easy stuff abroad. The project was drenched anyway, out for this year.*

Flicking back through the pages my year played out in reverse. It seemed one-directional, like something was missing. A list of numbers alongside meaningless foreign names, numbers that were no longer exciting, too low to register on a world scale and showing no progression of my own. More recently, the latest project seemed to occupy a lot of pages in the diary. Maybe this would raise the bar, maybe it would fill the gap, or perhaps it was making it. I needed some progress. This was year three on the project, and though years one and two had been more of a dabble, this was a long-term affair by any stretch. A tick in the box would be nice, though any box would do, my climbing recently having been distilled into the desperate. Performance had taken over somewhere along the line. Slowly there'd been a shift in focus until a day felt empty unless I'd pushed myself to the limit. Easier routes lost their appeal and if I wasn't battered and broken I'd let myself down, certain I'd be losing my edge. I'd entered the Performance Tunnel without even realising it.

The Performance Tunnel. This is not something from a training book, it's just a term I made up a while ago to describe a place I was in. It's a path that many end up following, a shadowy place where climbing hard is more important than climbing happy. They enter without realising, not even knowing until they can't get out. For some the tunnel is long, maybe without end, and dark and lonely. For others there are doors and windows along the way to catch a view and step out for a while. Is it a good or a bad place? Well, that all depends.

Somehow I'd slipped in. Maybe I had perceived it as a shallow cave I'd quickly step back out of. I crossed the threshold deciding I was going to get better. Or maybe it was about not getting worse, a paranoia that hard-earned gains were about to be lost, slowly piling up in an unstable heap about to avalanche off out of existence. (Actually that is a problem, training and improving is like building a wall, with each brick a tiny gain in performance. Unfortunately most of us are cowboy builders who have sacked off the foundations and not bothered with a spirit level: the wall goes up quickly but looks a bit shoddy and soon falls down and leaves a mess. If it doesn't fall down we spend our lives patching it up and never get the chance to make it any higher.) I *needed* to crank, to get better, and, above all, to not get worse. But at the same time I'd set the bar pretty low as to just how much I was prepared to do to hold equilibrium. I knew I could climb harder if I tried harder, but I'd have to try a lot harder to get a little better. The point is, we set our own bar and then work around it, and we know when we are under it and are happy when we are above it. It's all about being realistic and not becoming jealous of those stick insects who train six hours a day and still seem keen enough to watch the latest dose of videos on YouTube in the evening.

There's a big difference between wanting and actually deciding to improve. Apparently the hardest part of training is actually deciding you are going to do something. I can see the logic: once a plan is formed and a solid promise made the rest is easy: you just do it. It's a bit like giving up smoking, after a whole life on twenty a day the hard part is saying that enough is enough. Then after that it's easy and you can spend a smoke-free life moaning about fag breaks and the drain on the NHS. Yeah right, it's that easy. I told myself I'd go for a run every other evening, a solid promise.

I even wrote it down somewhere. Unfortunately I still couldn't be arsed and my plan lasted only three days. It didn't matter how solid my promise was, I never started running, or gave up chocolate or my second breakfast, or began my well-planned fingerboard session. I ended up with three fingerboards around the house and a pretty good 40-degree wall in the garage, but the fingerboards would have made better spice racks and the garage wall's only purpose was to have piles of junk chucked behind it.

Blinking my eyes I adjusted to new light levels. The train carriage had suddenly become brighter as it emerged from one of the long tunnels under the Peak District, en route to the airport for my week of work. It was far from bright outside, with a damp clag hanging on the moors, the top of the hills disappearing into the mist. I was glad to be off, even if it was for work, glad to be away from the end of the British season. If I was home I'd be clutching at straws as cold winter mornings jostled good conditions with oncoming seepage – but I'd be getting nowhere. I didn't feel like I was slacking. I was putting in real effort in a quest for acceptable performance, with the bar being reset marginally higher the moment it came into reach. However, my effort lacked focus; 'effort' on my part could be translated as 'shoving everything else out of the way', as opposed to a carefully calculated approach to performance increments. I was barging through without knowing where I was going or making any real effort to get there.

Shifting uncomfortably in the train seat I flipped open the climbing diary for some answers but there was little to gain, with minimal write-ups and even the occasional blank page under a date and venue telling clearly of my lack of enthusiasm. That alone suggested something. I used to write up everything the second I came home, squeezing in detailed observations, plans and excitement. I'd maybe even write a precursor to the next expected day. I was energised and psyched. Now each entry was backdated forever, half made up, half what I partially remembered, the most likely observation being that I was feeling weak and needed to train. Whole weeks and even months displayed negative single line comments and a to-do list that would never be done.

Still, a recent trip to Pembroke stood out proudly in the climbing diary, pages crammed with words, the letters neat and small to fit in the detail. Familiar cliff names evoked deep memories from my youth, far further back than my recent summer visit just a few months ago. Routes and their attached grades in familiar format comforted me with feelings of fun and adventure – not just hard climbing. I'd returned to Pembroke with the same goal as in my youth: to immerse myself in fantastic movement and the whole package that is traditional climbing. I'd needed an escape from performance. Sitting at the top in the sun with friends after some awesome routes it seemed clear why climbing is so good and the memories of early days sitting beside us confirmed these reasons.

But despite everything being so perfect, there was also something missing. I realised I'd just stepped out of the tunnel for a while – and now it was time to get back in. Or maybe I'd not even been out of it, but had just glimpsed an alternate view from a window, familiar from my youth. So I ended up on something hard, a job by most descriptions: a hard headpoint, and I don't even really understand headpointing. Physically hard and mentally draining, it needed practice and re-practice, top-roping and shunting, preparing the gear and making sure I knew exactly how it went in. Falling off was possible, and falls would be big, maybe dangerous. The route entered my head and filled it, occupying any free space and making its own by pushing out nearly everything else. It was stressful, the thought of setting off harrowing, like stepping out to deliver a lecture to a 500-strong crowd, but with dire consequences should I forget my lines. Why would I want to do this – why not cruise up easy-but-awesome routes in the sun and then sit relaxing on the top? Or push just a little bit harder and revel in a battle with pumping arms and well-placed gear, happy in the knowledge that I would most likely win? In the end I didn't do the headpoint route, didn't even try, with conditions getting the better of me and thus writing off the second half of the trip.

Most climbers don't end up in the tunnel. It takes a certain sort of person to find the entrance. If there are any windows along the way or even a light at the end, then the tunnel can be a great place to be. The desire to perform can be a natural progression, and once the honeymoon period of the climbing love affair is over, this combines with an inbuilt desire to explore physical and mental limits. Some people, most people, don't need that extra effort, staying happily married to climbing without ever asking too much, just enjoying its company. For others, that new element – performance – prevents things from going stale. You can choose your own definition of performance relative to how much you want to dedicate, with a 'maximum performance' that understands and fits in around other things in life like relaxing and work and other perceived immovable necessities. Wherever you draw the line, it's there to stop you from slacking off, reminding you that you can't rest until you've raised your game.

Outside the tunnel, before I fell in, I didn't need to improve. The concept was nice, but I could live without it. Days off climbing were taken without a second's thought, in fact, they weren't 'days off climbing', they were days doing something equally valid. There was no fear of any physical decline. Then I entered the tunnel and everything changed. It opened up a whole new world that I never knew existed, blocking out the light of everything else. Now nothing was as valid.

It was a bright world, at least at first, the single-path nature of the tunnel driving me, and thousands of like-minded people, to previously-undreamed levels of performance and allowing a different side of climbing to be embraced. I needed more than just pottering along ticking fine lines and the exploration of physical and mental limits gave me a whole new sport that seemed open ended.

Without being trapped in the tunnel I won't dedicate myself, as there are too many things to do, and if I don't dedicate myself then I won't get where I want to be, which I guess is the end of the tunnel. But what exactly is at the end? A dead end, a solid dark wall with no escape and a lonely tumble down from a never-achieved pinnacle, or an emergence into the light, bursting through the other end having reached more than you dreamed and now ready to put all the experiences you learned to use on another journey?

9 a.m., December. I sat up in bed rubbing tired eyes. Vic had already gone to work, leaving while I slept. Winter sun poured through unpainted windows lighting up the room in gentle pine and oaks. I watched the light track slowly across the floor as finger skin throbbed from the previous days' setting abroad. My right elbow didn't fancy straightening, and the shoulder felt all out of place, repetitive strain from too many holds pushed against a plywood panel.

Dragging tired legs from under the sheets I settled my feet on the scruffy rug that covered and hid the worn floorboards. It felt rough and full of bits, scratching at my soles. Flexing my fingers they felt stiff, like my skin was coated in resin, or perhaps the joints were simply shagged. At the kitchen table I shuffled a week of mail into 'junk' and 'important', with a climbing magazine sitting somewhere in between. Still wrapped in plastic my own picture stared out, yet another front cover, though it barely registered. I'd take a look when I got time, maybe. The answering machine blinked and I pressed play, Ste Smith, asking what I was up to, I'd not seen him for ages. Then next Paul, aargh, shit, missed his birthday, again. Then Dad, just wondering where I was these days. Last message from Dave asking about the upcoming sport climbing trip to Spain next week, had I sorted the car hire? Not yet, I'd do it later.

On the sofa I crunched through the usual breakfast mixture; muesli, branflakes and cornflakes. No milk, it turns it all soggy – I like to eat it slowly. Sunbeams cut through the air, tiny dust particles drifted gently, sparkling in the light, and surrounding me in a comforting smell of timber from the warming floor. A deep blue sky niggled. I should be out today bouldering at Stanage or Burbage. Or even on a bike ride. I should have been, but I wasn't, I just couldn't be bothered, disappointed at the fine weather that fuelled my guilt. A light swaying of the trees outside allowed me to cultivate my excuses: it would be windy out there, too cold. I wished it would rain, rain made life easy. I could train at the indoor wall, telling the locals how, 'I'd tried to go out but it was awful', just to make sure they knew I was still keen, pretending to myself I was still a real climber.

The 'glass is half full' person would switch it round, admit they had gone off the boil outdoors and run with a new motivation. Winter could be a window of opportunity to raise my game, a chance for a structured plan to work on weaknesses and hit the ground running when the crags came into condition in the spring. But already I'd crumbled, with a string of half-arsed sessions starting late and finishing early with no purpose and no goal. I was struggling to turn up and then looking for an excuse to leave, with the lack of effort painfully obvious. Muscles were beginning to relax and joints and tendons probably rejoicing with new demands, or lack of. Work was more appealing. I stuffed in as much route-setting as I could, and so the tendons never got their rest. When there was nothing in the diary I turned up at the climbing wall, simply because, as a climber, the type of climber I'd become, that's what I did, that's what I had to do. I didn't really want to be there, I needed an excuse, something real that would pass. Being lazy wouldn't cut it, particularly with myself. What about an injury? That would do it, a solid reason to simply not bother. I half wished I could just pop a tendon and be done with it.

Spain offered a ray of hope, but it didn't shine brightly like in the past. Bruixes again near Terradets, my fourth visit. I'd done every route bar two 8c+s. These would be my target, I guess, a tough challenge and certainly not a given. I'd have a job on my hands to come back with any ticks in the bank and that was the deal – it felt like a job. I cast forward to Christmas, which shone brightly, all tinsel-covered and lit up with fairy lights. I like Christmas, lounging around in front of crap TV eating Quality Street, popping them into a totally stuffed belly at exactly the rate the last one is digested. I'd started to like it more and more: the eating, the drinking, hanging with friends, celebrations with family, time off climbing … No climbing, that was the key, the best bit. This year I'd take a month off, that would be great, something to really look forward to. I pondered this for a while, relaxing back into the sofa and feeling the warmth of the sun on my feet. I drifted with the sparkling dust particles that glittered in the sun and time gently rolled by. I couldn't get myself together, didn't know what I wanted to do. I annoyed myself with the lack of drive. I felt like I'd lost it, completely.

Memories of boundless enthusiasm seemed distant. Looking back, I realised I'd been sliding downwards now for some time. Climbing had lost its sparkle. It needed a kick up the backside with a new focus and direction. I was stuck. Maybe my whole life needed a new direction, something different. Now, sitting back in the sofa, things were different anyway. Very different, and as I travelled to Spain in a week's time I'd be carrying a lot more baggage than would fit in any rucksack. I had news, big news and scary, though with a strange glimmer of unknown excitement. Things were about to change forever. This news was bigger than climbing, and I had absolutely no idea how things were going to pan out, the path before me completely unknown.

It started ever so quietly, almost imperceptibly, unnoticeable above the background noise of life. Or maybe I chose not to hear it, and as it became obvious I pretended it wasn't relevant and hoped it would go away: the gentle reminder of Vic's natural clock running towards the alarm and due to go off in the near future. There had been talk of kids many times, but I'd assumed, hoped … These rapidly cut short, one-sided conversations were about other people. Kids didn't fit with my schedule, they'd never been in my plan and, basically, up until recently, I'd assumed they were a major complication for normal people with plenty of spare time on their hands. Conversely they'd always been on the horizon for Vic, an inbuilt and growing knowledge of something she wanted to do, but which was always pushed back by my flat refusal to even come close to a discussion. Conversations about friends who'd taken the plunge increased in frequency, Vic noting all the happy bits while I observed the horrors of baby world and an instant drop out of the scene – every scene. My conclusion was that babies were not only a total epic, which I knew anyway, but that they absorbed all your known life. Not only that, but when new parents visited they had changed beyond all recognition, wearing boring, smart and undoubtedly sick-covered clothes. Offensive stains were displayed with pride, especially by the blokes as a kind of 'look at me I'm a proper dad' badge. They also seemed to be gaining a stack of weight and a certain roundness and had absolutely nothing to talk about whatsoever other than how little Johnny managed his first poo last week or how his other little friends at nursery all had chicken pox.

It made me cringe and run to the hills, almost literally … Some people actually would have done, being of a certain type and more likely to leg it. Climbers, in particular, are often way more scared of family life than of falling onto a marginal RP above a death landing on a pile of spiky boulders. Gradually I became aware the issue wasn't going to disappear. At thirty, kids had been someone else's problem. At thirty-four they were looking like mine. The reality had become too thick for me to push out of the way. I was speeding towards a three-choice junction and the decision which I'd been fobbing off for ages had to be made. I could run away to the hills, leaving Vic behind along with most of my life, and hope that rock climbing was enough to keep me happy in my retirement. Not ideal, far from fair on Vic, and probably way more of a loss than my projected losses due to most of my free time falling into a child vacuum. I could have kids, hopefully not too many, do the decent thing and make everyone happy while praying that the kids would be super-fast learners and capable of looking after themselves entirely by the age of three and of belaying by five. Or I could refuse point blank to have kids, chopping off my willy if necessary. I could build a wall against all the nasty partner comments, deal with the fall-out with parents and parents-in-law and get by knowing that, once again, I got my own way and Vic had put up with it. Though being selfish was one of my key skills, this choice seemed to be pushing it a bit fine, and even then there was the potential for Vic to chuck in the towel and head off to find a more suitable candidate, which to be fair when I looked at myself, wouldn't have been exactly difficult.

In the end I took the route I'd always known I would take – I didn't take any at all, instead stalling at the junction and waiting for something to happen. Decision making just isn't my bag. I'll spend twenty minutes in a bakery deciding between a chocolate brownie, a cookie or an almond slice, dismayed at how others can simply walk in and know instantly, like there was no decision to make. My problem is that I'm too worried about getting it wrong, stressed that the brownie won't be up to scratch, though to be fair, choosing between kids and no kids is hardly comparable to the quality of a bakery counter selection. By doing nothing at all I could pretend my life would continue as normal without upsetting anyone too much.

Eventually the inevitable happened. One evening after training I came in and Vic looked at me; there was no need for words. It would have been nice to have mirrored all the Hollywood films, where an elated husband showers their partner in happiness and tells them how it's the happiest day of their life. I thought I might at least put on a brave face but, as it turned out, I even disappointed myself with my total lack of encouragement, instantly going into a huff and making it quite clear that I'd very definitely not got my own way. Considering this apparent bombshell had actually been more of a guaranteed outcome, I should have made more of an effort even if it was for display purposes only. The fact was, it was now fact, and as one of my friends kindly pointed out, 'in nine months' time your life will change beyond all recognition.'

It's impossible to comprehend how children will change your life, so I was told, and I adopted this wise advice and didn't try to comprehend it at all, finding it far easier to vacuum pack the whole issue and hide it away in a dusty corner of my mind. Perhaps this was possible because Vic clearly was on it with the organising, allowing me to completely ditch any responsibility. After all, there didn't seem the need for both of us to know everything, and it was beyond making sense anyway. It felt like a complete beginner reading a book on how to drive and then suddenly finding themselves in the driving seat on the outside lane of a busy M1 at night doing 80 miles per hour. I went into normal mode, pretending nothing was going on as Vic's body displayed the reality, and I slapped my sour face as excited friends and relatives clucked over microscopic clothing in painfully cute colours. No one seemed to get my feelings, with everyone apparently so happy and pleased for me. Obviously they had no idea of the panic building on a daily basis. But a few thoughtful comments really stuck. Neil Pearsons, *OTE* editor, father of two and very keen climber, told me in a completely soothing and honest voice, 'this is the best thing that will ever happen to you,' and Aid Baxter, with a genuine smile, encouraged, 'you'll make a really great dad, you're going to love it.' This particularly seemed like a bit of a guess at best, as I'd already put myself down in the 'useless dad' category by being utterly hopeless even before I started. However these comments, among others, sparked a tiny flame and I warmed to the concept. There was even some pride; I was doing something grown up. Along with that was a level of purpose. I was very definitely going somewhere. Suddenly I had direction.

Having a baby is apparently the most important and happiest moment of your life, with grown men busting into tears, peeing their pants or collapsing on the floor with joy. I'd have been quite accepting to any elated loss of function, but as expected I didn't find myself crying tears of happiness into the midwife's lap. It was, however, pretty cool to say the least, the whole birth thing being fairly off the scale, and when the little bundle was handed over I couldn't help but feel an instant bond that I'd never have seen coming. Looking into Amelie's eyes I didn't see stress and exhaustion, I saw something amazing, something new and exciting.

Having her home didn't seem too tricky at first, with Vic taking on the bulk of the work. After all, there isn't much dads can really do for a one-day-old person. There was very definitely a difference in the vibe around the house, and no amount of carrying on as normal was ever going to cut it, but nature, combined with Vic being a perfect mum, made the early months relatively easy, with a reasonable chunk of my life staying exactly the same, even if it was operated in a slightly sleep-deprived state. It's a bit like acquiring a third leg – sitting at a desk, or slobbed out in front of the TV you don't notice it, but as soon as you stand up you tumble over in a heap, tripping over the new appendage and finding yourself unable to get anything together, with the knowledge that things will never be the same again. Half an hour into the latest episode of *Lost* and you've allowed yourself to become absorbed by the entertainment – a carefully chosen hour-long slot you chose in the knowledge that you'd never get through a full-length film due to either interruption or exhaustion or both – and there is a cry from the baby monitor in the corner. It can't be ignored despite the fact that Lock from *Lost* needs to decide whether or not to press the button, it needs to be dealt with, and dealt with now. All requests need to be fixed and sorted immediately. Though a newborn can't do much, they all come ready fitted with a well-developed and thoroughly intolerable screaming procedure.

It amazes me that anyone is allowed to have kids. There are no exams to pass or forms to fill out or sensibility questionnaires. You can't even have a dog without some kind of licence. I was fairly sure I'd be a low scorer at best on any parental examination, more likely an all-out fail. But, as it appears, most humans have some kind of in-built ability to know what to do with a helpless bundle of skin and bone. Either that or it's actually extremely easy and you just imagine it's going to be hard. In fact, it must be easy, considering that most people manage just fine and they manage it when half asleep. Previously, any baby that came near me instantly yelled, and though this gave me a slight complex about my appearance, it at least meant I didn't have to endure the utter discomfort of holding someone else's pride and joy which was clearly about to be sick on my shoulder. Other than knowing it all looked grim, my baby experience was zero, and yet now that I had my own I was finding it all rather easy, enjoying it even, including the bits that should be all-out awful. Even nappy changes are no big deal, with the contents often sparking a whole afternoon's conversation. I'd look with interest to see what I'd find, amazed at how fast sweetcorn can make its way from mouth to bum and how raisins come out so blatantly unchewed that, if you were really saving the pennies, you could simply give them a quick wash and pop them back in the little cardboard box and no one would know the difference. Provided the box remained healthy you could make a pack last at least a few weeks.

There aren't many people that you'd give up your life for, having only known them for half a second, but that's the way it is with children. From the moment they are born you know they are the most important thing in your life. Mums probably know even before they are born. You don't realise it, but everything that was essential to your existence has now been pushed into second place, including climbing. A close second obviously, with first and second interchangeable depending on which mode the baby happens to be in. It's possible to continue as if nothing happened, but only for a very small part of your new life, with huge chunks of what you took for granted suddenly collapsing out of existence, like deciding to watch a nice film, going out for a meal, having a lie in, or perhaps most importantly, popping out whenever you fancy for a quick clamber. Structure becomes your most important skill, along with negotiation, or in some instances, stubbornness and unreasonableness when it comes to organising your own time. Those afternoon sessions at the wall have now become a few hours, and deciding to bomb over to North Wales on a good forecast becomes a distant memory. It's a difficult transition and you can push against it and fail, or roll with it and refocus. The Scottish winter climber will suffer, and the weekend warrior may become the monthly warrior, but it doesn't have to be all nappies and cleaning up slop – it can be a chance to make a difference.

For me it was a chance to train. I'd been telling myself for years to put in a bit of effort and knew fine well that days of bumbling on easy trad routes, or just doing the same ten routes down at The Foundry was never going to get me up anything hard. Well now those bumbling days were gone. In a way the lack of time made climbing simpler. There was no frustration over where to climb or what style, as most of the options instantly vanished, leaving a single, clear-cut option that needed to be seized with both hands. Indoor training was transformed, with all-day plodding replaced by a two-hour blast that left me exhausted. I even thought about what I was doing – a revelation. Efficiency went up and intensity with it, driven by the desire to make every minute count. With the next session remaining unplanned, or perhaps planned but knowing it could easily be abandoned, I'd climb like I was about to have a week off, because I probably was.

They say you can't have your cake and eat it, and in terms of climbing and getting my own way I'd clearly been eating rather a lot for a rather long time: a huge chocolate-covered, cream-filled, family size monster that I'd shovel down before pushing the empty plate away in disgust, not even enjoying most of what I'd taken. Now the portions were small, each slice barely enough, but each taste as sweet as ever. And with each mouthful I was left desperate for more.

Positive attitude, experts tell us, goes a long way. American climbers are masters of the positive: before climbing they're bouncing around full of energy shouting how 'this is it', how the route's going to be easy and how awesome they feel. Everyone's fired up, the climber's about to explode, the belayer psyched and the crowd expecting a great effort. Brits seem to have a different approach, the opposite, the more excuses the better. Before setting off everyone is informed of tiredness, illness, injury and bad conditions, putting a downer on the whole situation. Reverse psychology? We don't like expectations, we don't want everyone watching and expecting a dazzling display of power. In good old British style we'd rather no one was bothered or cared. If nobody expects anything and then nothing happens, no one is disappointed.

I guess the problem is when all the negative vibes result in negative performance. The key is to keep positive, at least in your own mind, no matter how the cards are stacked against you.

I've been accused of working with a dose of reverse psychology, with my string of complaints about general physical condition probably getting rather tiresome. If you're at the crag hearing all about how weak I am, yet again, it must get really annoying if, having made all my excuses, I promptly flash your project and declare it not that bad after all, or warm-up on your twenty-five-day redpoint effort. Perhaps it's a fault. Some would see it that way, but it seems better than shouting 'I'm the greatest' and, in a way, it is honest. My natural tendency is to want the best from myself, and I see the best in others, comparing myself to those traits. So in terms of physical 'strengths' I really am off the pace, and I'd invite anyone to compare my fitness to Neil Bentley's, my finger strength to Shauna Coxsey's or my endurance to Ed Hamer's. There really is no comparison, but it's the comparisons I make that drive me to get better. They stand out and remind me of what I need to do, that there is work to be done. There's no point in settling back and relaxing with what I'm already good at. For outdoor sport I do well, leaning on tenacity and technique, but it's from the masters at the other disciplines of climbing that I draw my motivation: Ben Heason and his bold head; James McHaffie and his control under pressure;

Moon and his power; Johnny and his dynamic movement; Paul Reeve with his unending ability to just keep on going. From people like this I have much to learn. It's important to be grounded and remain humble, to not just focus on what you are good at. Climbing a chunk of rock is such an irrelevant activity anyway, life requires a great deal of skills, and no matter how good you are at something, it's pretty likely there are a lot more people far better at something far more important.

Still, at the crag the amount of excuses we come up with can be outrageous. The excuse cards people lay on the table vary from the obvious and acceptable to obscure and vague. Some of us are master card players, always with a good hand and always with a trump card beating anything. This ensures no matter how badly they climb their excuse will be the best on show. Some of the real hustlers can be found around the limestone of the Peak and Dales and I've witnessed some awesome displays. I learnt a lot, playing a few cautious hands and even doing quite well. Eventually I became a master, up with the best of them. It's all about knowing what cards to play and when, and about keeping a cool head when bluffing.

A typical suit from the standard climbers' pack:

2. Have brought the wrong climbing clothes.
3. Have brought wrong boots (though two lefts/two rights is worth a 10).
4. Conditions not very good.
5. Stress at home or work (better card for redundancy/house move).
6. Still sore from training yesterday.
7. Flapper in finger.
8. Injury (but since you're climbing it can't be bad – use carefully).
9. DIY epic yesterday: digging/cementing/bricklaying etc.
10. Just returned from a twelve-hour flight this morning.
Jack. Illness, must be visible in form of cough/vomit/sneezing/turning green.
Queen. Route is soaking wet and probably unclimbable.
King. Have young baby and been on marginal sleep forever.
Ace. Last night was at all-night party obviously getting no kip whatsoever.

Malham Cove is a great arena for playing cards, only slightly behind Raven Tor, the crucible of card playing and the number one venue, where the finest hustlers will be found. It was at Malham when I found I had a truly great hand, having an eight, nine, Jack, Queen and King. There was clearly no chance of getting up my route, or apparently even any point being there. As it was, prior knowledge of already having a Queen led me to collect the nine which unfortunately led to acquiring a Jack. Basically, the route I was trying had got wet, so expecting no success I spent twelve hours the previous day mixing and carrying two tonnes of concrete, leading to exhaustion and easy entry for the cold that had been niggling for a while. With the added complications of a nine-month old baby who seemed to be operating in the New Zealand time zone, attempting to redpoint my hardest route ever was rather ambitious to say the least. Obviously I laid down my amazing hand just before attempting a redpoint where I promptly fell off the very last move, a high point by a long way after nearly forty days of effort. Pressure off or cheating at cards? But this wasn't a case of reverse psychology, I didn't feel like a gladiator inside, my hand wasn't a bluff. I think the route was simply ready to give in, and there's a lot to be said for being relaxed.

After forty days on the same route most climbers would only need to play one card: 'I'm flipping sick of this route and I'm not trying anymore.' The vast majority of climbers have never redpointed anything, and fail to see any attraction in it at all, and those that have redpointed will play the 'sick of it' card long before they even reach day ten. I kind of feel the same, but what happens when you've either on-sighted or fallen off everything local? You've got three choices: move to another country, climb the route again (in other words, redpoint them), or just give up.

Personally, the latter option never appealed, and though the first option was interesting, the family addition meant that it had been well and truly crossed off the list. Thus I found myself in redpoint land, which left me more often than not on the same collection of rubbish holds for quite some time. Like being stuck in the Performance Tunnel, this has been a gift, taking me in a direction I'd probably not have chosen. On-sight I love, and quick redpoints are great, but the hard projects are something else, the really hard ones, the ones that in all honesty are probably too hard, these are the real test, forcing you to question your motivation, raise your game, and taking you to places you'd have never imagined.

My first ever trip to Malham Cove was interesting. At first glance everything looked easy. My next glance was at the reflection of myself in the polished holds as I sat on the rope after a very short-lived on-sight attempt at *Raindogs*. Despite clearly being one of the most amazing cliffs in the world, I didn't like it, and quickly legged it back to the Peak. The problem with Malham is that most of the holds are upside down, which explains why everything looks so easy as you peer up at an apparently hold-covered wall. It also explains why I didn't like it, having arms like a piece of string and no ability to pull on undercuts whatsoever. Slowly it grew on me, how could it not? Okay, it's polished in places but the routes are brilliant and the concentration of hard routes is about as good as anywhere in the world. Combine that with amazing Yorkshire Dales scenery and basically you've got the UK's best sport cliff.

In 2003 I got stuck into a hard project above *Raindogs*. It was one of the hardest and most amazing climbs I'd ever been on and when I finally clipped the belay after about seventeen days of climbing effort I was well and truly in love with the place. I guessed this ascent of *Rainshadow, 9a*, would be my personal high point, but the good thing about climbing, or bad thing depending on which way you're looking at it, is that the challenges just never end, and as I lowered off, basking in my personal glory, I was already glancing sideways at a huge chunk of unclimbed rock. And that is exactly where I found myself a few years later.

The original concept of *Overnite Sensation* was bolted by Paul Ingham in the eighties. The first part was climbed to the point where it turns considerably harder and a belay was placed to give the classic and very popular – though incomplete – *Overnite Sensation* at 8a+. This route begins with a nasty Font 7B boulder problem straight off the floor, snatching between crimps before moving into slightly easier yarding-up-to-the-redpoint crux and the tricky clip of the middle-of-nowhere belay. However, this belay is actually well-placed for most climbers, as immediately afterwards all the holds get tiny and have apparently been put on upside down. This is where the project began, the project I'd adopted, and with barely chance to chalk up it's straight into the business. Ten hard moves lead into the new crux sequence, the old crux feeling like a walk in the park. Bad crimps for the hands and a tenuous drop knee allow, sometimes, a big slap to an undercut edge. Cunning use of feet and a few hopeful slaps with the left hand finally land you on a thin pinch grip. Good enough to clip off, panic, then press on into some steep UK 6b pulls to a tufa hold. Another clip (having already missed a few out) and a final section of complicated desperateness that must be at least 8a+. When I first looked at this extension I couldn't even find the holds on the crux, with the rest of the moves utterly brutal. On my fifth day of effort my climbing book said:

All the moves done except the middle that I can hardly imagine doing even in isolation. Note to self, if I ever do this I'll be psyched, way harder than anything I've ever been on, must be 9a+ or worse, it's going to be a long haul.

The line was so awesome that there had to be a way, so I ignored the crux and spent time on the upper bit in the hope that if that went free the tough bit in-between might grow some handholds over the projected lifetime the route was obviously going to take. In the end it took about six days to do the crux, once, and more than twenty visits to make the link I wanted: to climb from the original *Overnite* belay to the top. Theoretically that made just the link quite hard since it took way less time to climb *Northern Lights* at 9a. It felt like a major achievement, almost like I'd done a new route, which I guess I had in a two-pitch kind of way.

Redpointing can be a tough business. It's certainly one of the hardest disciplines in climbing. Some assume it's easy since if you fall off you can just have another go at your leisure – but that's the problem. Falling from an on-sight marks the end, one chance only. Disappointing maybe, but game over. The redpoint isn't ever over till it's over. That's fine if you're on something easily within reach, but the real game is up there at your limit. That's the beauty, finding the limit, exploring it, stepping right up to it and then pushing it further. The climbing news pages are crammed full of redpoint ascents, pictures of happy climbers captioned with 'so happy, my hardest route ever, a real challenge'. Onlookers would believe it was just a matter of time and no challenge, but the real rewards are to the few who can look back and know success was definitely in the balance. Maybe the balance was even against them – it wasn't a matter of just turning up. For every success story in this area of uncertainty there are many failures. We just don't hear of them, the years on a single route, only to end up empty-handed. Looking back, in reality, only two of my climbs took me to the edge, and these are the most rewarding. Though having succeeded on them both was I really at the edge?

At first the *Overnite* extension wasn't stressing me. In fact, I'd barely considered it a route, just a project, and perhaps a project for someone else, a collection of hard moves that I tried every now and again. The end goal was barely visible, replaced by a series of more attainable targets: climb the top bit in one, the crux in isolation, *Overnite* belay to crux, route in three sections … I first looked at the line in 2004, spending just a few days on it, looking and replacing the odd rusty bolt. In 2005 I was there for eight days and in the following year I put in about ten. By then I knew it would go, for someone at least, but was I capable of it? It was a way off. I had to train, but more than training I had to be cunning and I had to be cunning with my training.

The best hold on the route is probably after the crux, a round hole like the inside of a mini football, flat and smooth but with a razor edge at the lip. Making a great bird's nest, it had been used as a home for the past 10,000 years, polishing the inside to a sheen as the starlings flapped their way in and out. A potential shake-out, but unfortunately with a UK 6c move to get to it and with no footholds at all, it was basically a desperate hang from one arm. Strangely, it was easier to flick both toes into the hole and drop down into an awesome bat hang position. Still, it was a killer on the feet, feeling like a thousand sit-ups crammed into twenty seconds, and was UK 6c to get out of. It was only after twelve days that I even considered it, but then it became essential. Some short bits of webbing between the tongue and the laces of my boots helped with the foot pain on the sharp edge, but a winter of hanging by my toes from a bar was the only way to make the 'rest' into a rest.

Rich Simpson was known for his impossible climbing strength and he gave me some advice. 'You're weak! You need to get stronger. You don't need to get any better technically. If you want to climb harder you need to train. Don't bother climbing outside for half a year, get to the gym and put some effort in.' I knew this already, but hearing it so bluntly made me think twice. I'm an outdoor climber you see, with the primary goal of just getting outside overwhelming the importance of grades. But the winter of 2006–7 was a chance to get involved – it was my first year with a youngster. Suddenly I was mad for it with motivation flying through the roof. In the past I'd lost focus but now the frustrating confusion of many climbing options was lifted. All the options simply vanished. I didn't need to beat myself up about missing a nice day on the grit, or about how I'd not placed a wire for six months, or how I should be out on the limestone but ended up indoors. The simplicity was enlightening. I knew where I was going. For the first time ever I trained. Sure it wasn't like the first time I'd been to a climbing wall, but I gave it some thought rather than just doing what I fancied. It felt like training, it had structure, and though I expected it to be totally boring I found I was actually getting into it. It was something new and it was working. From zero one-arm pull-ups I went to three and that's proper ones: straight-arm two-second hang in-between, not exactly impressive by a strong person's standards but an infinite improvement in my own. Finger strength went up and I could front lever for ten seconds. The Malham project remained at the core, but I was training because I wanted to train. I was enjoying the process, watching the gains and feeling better in myself. Would it help on the rock? Hard to say for sure, but I hoped so.

As the winter of 2007 retreated into spring it revealed the depth of my focus on the Malham project. Stripped of other options I'd poured everything in one direction, the huge spectrum of rock climbing distilling down into a single route. It was what I needed and with my renewed vigour the awesome bulk of Malham Cove couldn't dry fast enough. On the first day I went from the *Overnite* belay to the top. It was the link I wanted. The training had worked. The project was suddenly on, but with this burst of excitement everything instantly changed. No longer was it my mate who I shared a nice time with, no longer was it a collection of hard sections to be linked in the future, instead it became possible – now. When I positioned myself on the starting line I was playing for real. No more fun and games. Success tantalised me, it was within reach; my pinnacle of achievement.

The early link spurred me on and I threw myself into redpoint mode. But I'd rushed it and I wasn't quite ready. Each effort took me into the crux, only moves away from easier ground, but spat me off, leaving me confused. Should I be trying? Was I actually ready? Should I be still getting stronger or fitter? I was certain I was good enough, and I was, but there was no slack in the system. I needed everything to come together at once, with all the cards in my favour, and in the game of sport climbing this is rare, almost never. The route became an enemy, it seemed to cheat and deceive me in every game. It handed out the excuse cards every visit, real ones, 'too hot today sir', 'too wet today sir', 'nesting birds today sir', 'too many people trying *Overnite*'. Days and days were spent sitting around waiting for the temperature to drop, only to find they didn't and the crag radiated heat late into the evening, baked from a full day in the sun. I turned up and banged my head against the wall making negative progress in the hope all the groundwork would pay off. I was on the redpoint now, three times per day, zooming up *Overnite* to a microscopic shake by the belay then blasting into the crux only to fall where, to be honest, I expected to fall. Drive to Malham, warm up, three goes, fall from the same move every time, drive home, repeat. It seemed my life was becoming this saga in the vague hope that someday I'd get through this desperate move, but even then I had no idea what would happen next, with a ton of hard climbing above at somewhere around 8a+ and only a pathetic upside down rest, it could all end in the realisation that getting through the crux was still, in fact, miles away. I knew this, but didn't want to face it, thinking positively that if I made it to the bat hang I'd surely get enough back to get high. Long links on the route may have been the professional approach, third bolt to top, second bolt to top, or maybe a retreat to specific training, but I was way past that now. To drop out of redpoint mode would have felt like I'd failed, even if it was the only way to succeed.

Twenty days in year four, nearly six weeks. Barely no other climbing. Halfway through, mates were ready for a change as Malham heated up and other crags came into condition. Frustrated, I spent hours collecting the phone numbers of potential belayers. I began to pour myself in. Ironically,

I'd willingly put so much of my climbing to one side with dad responsibilities, but now clawed back time in even greater measures, all focused on one route. Days were long, 10 a.m. until 11 p.m., three days a week, with some training the next day. Everything was dropped and casualties fell by the wayside as I blinkered myself, friends, family, work … I'd put off every job to make sure I had as many days free as possible, but things were stretching out and I was skint. Climbing trips were cancelled, even in the autumn, because I'd probably already blown it for the spring season. A snapped hold made things even harder. It was hot, but then it also got wet, a week of rain had turned the line into a river. A good thing really, as my body was collapsing; tweaks from specific holds, a finger ligament from the crux crimp, a busted shoulder from a weird upside down edge move and a bad knee from knee-dropping. Every night was spent with ice packs rotating around various knackered bits. I needed to rest, but I couldn't rest until I'd done it … and I couldn't do it until I rested …

The route seemed to be slipping away. My family were pissed off with me turning up at 11 p.m., and pissed off with me being constantly pissed off. I wanted time with Amelie, only ten months old and changing every minute. I was missing them, the best days of her life, the best days of *our* life, in my ridiculous quest up a random lump of rock with numerous easier possibilities only metres to either side. DIY on our building site of a house had been utterly sidelined. One of the floors in particular was still damp bare soil and one day Amelie opened the door and fell in, tumbling down the drop to lie crumpled on the earth amongst hammers and drills and timber joists. What was I playing at? I cranked up the mixer, chucked in a few tonnes of ingredients and laid down the concrete floor. Next visit to the crag I was staring at the last hold. It wasn't the top, but it was the breakthrough I needed. If I could get through the crux after a bunch of physical work then surely I was ready.

But still the route twisted and turned and pushed me beyond where I thought I could go. The line dried out in spring sunshine, nearly, but progress reversed with increasing obstacles as the window of opportunity swung against me. Two weeks later, having run out of free time and on my final opportunity, I laid out my excuse cards: pretty much a full pack, along with the withheld 'no point being there card', which I preferred to keep to myself along with the 'mentally given up' card that was due from the printers any time soon. There was even the 'letting the team down' card, with good friends Keith Sharples and Rab Carrington regularly holding my rope. The connection with these guys as I climbed was much greater than a piece of string. They willed me and energised me in

all the right ways, assessing what I needed and how to pitch encouragement and then shared the burden with each failed attempt.

Preparations were monotonous: warming up, traversing, a quick jog,
some recruitment … but somehow the fire still burned and I fought against
the odds, hunting for any bit of cunning to give me the edge. 'Racking up'
took on a whole new meaning as I tied into a brand new shoelace of a rope,
wrapped a cycle inner tube round my leg for a painful knee-bar, stuffed
tape into my shoes and rubbed half a block of chalk into my T-shirt ready
for a 'super rapid chalking' to combat damp holds where getting a hand
into the chalk bag was not an option. This was to be a valuable lesson in
relaxation and as I pulled through the desperate starting moves the
finishing line didn't figure as the target. It was simply to climb as perfectly
as I could. Johnny Dawes once said you could climb for a whole year to
find that one perfect climbing moment, where you become nothing but
complete climbing movement, mind and body utterly focused. I don't
think I get as few as one per year, but they're not many, probably they're
countable on one hand, experiences so powerful as to never be forgotten.
This was one of those moments, the ascent everything it should be,
completely absorbed, aware only of the moves. At the same time energy
levels were monitored, adjusting position and force even mid-move to
give the optimum chance. Though redpointing is a practised art, the real
skill is in the micro-on-sight. Nothing is ever exactly the same and being
able to make tiny adjustments and wing it on the go is key: a little finger
not quite seated on the crimp means more force on the left toe and in turn
a twist of the heel to avoid blowing off the poor smear; a supercomputer
processing at top speed. Eyeing the slap move, 100 per cent commitment
was required and provided, fingers nestling on the flat hold at the end of
the hardest climbing. A small chance for a breather before the final UK 6b
moves, with the rest period quickly calculated, recovery plotted against
time considering current fatigue and conditions, desire removed from the
equation – it had to be, to rush is to fail. The finishing line came into view
but I looked away, instead allowing myself to pull focus from hand and
footholds and momentarily view the surroundings. But, like glimpsing an
irrelevant TV programme in a shop window, they barely registered, just
an essential rest for the mind alongside the body. Then back in, the final
hard moves executed perfectly and the first of the finishing holds reached,
a small but incut hold on vertical ground. To fall here is impossible,
so long as the eyes remain on the feet, 5.10s edging in with nature's gift.
Then the rope is going in, and like a prisoner wrongly imprisoned and at
last released after a lengthy appeal, the doors are swung open revealing the

world outside: brighter and more colourful than ever remembered and, as the rope took my weight, I stepped over the threshold into freedom.

Drifting downwards just one task remained, the ribbon on the gift passed first to me and then to the world: a name and a grade. Grading was easy, throw moves and sequences into the random number generator and out comes 9a+. Confirmed by Ondra and 'nearly 9b'. Now that would have been nice. The name is more difficult, though not by much, *Overshadow*, representing the struggle, overshadowing all my other efforts on every other route so far. The route had pushed me, she'd taken me to the edge. Success was on a plate long ago, but that would have been too easy. She knew the challenge I needed. Instead she waited until the very last chance, until I was almost out of time – the route became soaking wet and completely unclimbable the very next day. Looking back I wouldn't have changed a thing, learning vast amounts not only about my climbing, but the inner workings of myself as a person. Ironically, afterwards, there still seemed room to move, to take difficulty even further, but this route marked a change in my climbing. No longer had I anything to prove to myself. I'd reached my top, I didn't need to go there again and though I'd try, and possibly even surpass this level, the conquering of the desire opened up a space in the process to enjoy and see climbing again for all that it should be.

31 WORTH THE RISK?

The first drops of rain drifted down from a dull-grey sky, icy cold as they brushed against hands and face. Heavy clouds hung low, windless and silent, the vast walls above vanishing into mist. Fifteen pitches into *Hoka Hey*, a thousand-metre, twenty-one-pitch E5 on the massive Norwegian cliff of Kjerag, things had potential to go distinctly pear-shaped. I stole a glance across the emerald green fjord far below that sliced a deep trench all the way in from the North Sea. The opposite cliffs stood barely a mile from my delicate stance on a six-inch-wide ledge 700 vertical metres above the scree. The weather had turned and a thick wall of water faded my view as much as it focused the fear. Internet forecasts had insisted fair, but clearly there'd been at least a small miscalculation which had, in turn, led to our own miscalculation in climbing 'fast and light' and sacking off most of our gear, in particular waterproofs and warm clothing. If the rains were to hit I wasn't exactly sure of our next move and, obviously, they were going to hit.

Far below, Neil appeared, struggling with the weight of the rucksack and the steepness of the cliff. Tethered together by what seemed like an inadequate strand of rope our eyes made momentary contact, the single glance releasing my isolation but confirming similar concerns. At E5 the climbing above would be way too difficult if soaked and retreat would be complicated down the weaving line, not to mention expensive, having to leave at least two bits of gear at every abseil. Thus retreat was immediately ruled out of the equation, replaced with hope that somehow the encroaching downpour would either miss us or simply run out of water. Miraculously it struck just a glancing blow, gifting us with damper pants than holds and a chance to reflect on the seriousness of our situation. Though we were hardly stuck on the south face of Annapurna, we were still way up there on a big wall with barely enough stuff for a sunny afternoon's outing to Stanage Edge. In a country notorious for bad weather and for getting seriously cold at any time of year, we were beginning to feel unprepared and under pressure.

After an early four o'clock start and fourteen hours of continuous climbing, we were both feeling beaten up. Six more pitches to go and we were running low on light, food, water, energy, everything. I led upwards through a scrappy corner described as 'lost' on the topo, which we didn't understand and guessed was something to do with protection – some type of peg maybe?

It actually meant 'loose', which should have been apparent, it being the only distinguishing feature of the pitch other than scary and fairly tricky. A poor stance arrived with gear that felt like a runner rather than a belay: a single piece above a foot-wide sloping ledge. Stopping there didn't appeal and I saw the chance to run two pitches together, saving time. There was also another motive: a deviation off-route onto an A2 variation pitch, to date unclimbed without aid apparently. I'd spotted it in the guide, a flicker of interest that might later be investigated. Now, as I balanced on the ledge at the junction, the chance of an extra gold star shone brighter than a standard repeat of a twenty-one-pitch wander. I saw the challenge being rolled out and noted the reward at the end: just a story to tell the lads and perhaps a single-line mention in the next Norwegian guidebook. More importantly by far, it looked like it would satisfy a desire to push myself to the max, to quench my thirst for exploring my limits. It looked hard, vertical or maybe just over, but the normal route was soaked anyway and I looked down on my inner voices arguing as I set off into the unknown, the decision already made.

Sketchy moves surprised me and, hesitating, I glanced back at the gear, a fairly decent Rock 6. Decent enough? I tried to remember, I'd only just placed it but already couldn't be sure. What protection was before that? The loose corner below curved away devoid of any gear whatsoever. There was something perhaps 10 metres below – ah yes, the cam 2. That was pretty good … or had it walked out of value now, rattling in the back of a rotten crack? Above me, a tiny overlap with a thin seam in the back. Just a few metres until I could reach it. It looked reasonable, and surely must take some good pro, so I committed, high steps on small flakes taking me to my short range target. Reaching slowly upwards, creeping my fingers up the wall I fingered the crack, sloping, not good enough. Piano left and right, searching for something positive. Nothing, and wet in most spots, but no going back. I chalked, searched again, found a tiny dish for my right, noted this as a last chance option and searched again, nothing. Back to the dish, quick chalk again, and a launch up on poor feet, not quite knowing what kind of move I was making but improvising as I went along. The sloping dish instantly became useless and my left hand beside it was doing nothing either and suddenly I was throwing my left into the crack, but underneath in an undercut position, and then flicking the right to join it. In this position the crack was good, but level with my waist, a powerful position and out of view completely. Wires fumbled in and slid out, nothing would bite. Half size cams didn't fit, wires again, dragging them sideways, twisting and feeling until something stuck, rattling maybe, but it wouldn't come out. I tried to view it, twisting my neck down to check the position but couldn't get a line of sight. Doubts were creeping in now. The Rock 6 looked a very long way below, but the next hold up looked decent and above that was some kind of flake system. I tugged at the wire again and then moved upwards, kind of impressed with myself. This was a proper trad experience and I was fully involved. The next edge was small, but incut. It needed to be, as the reach from it was huge, the move a touch dynamic but for another good edge, flat and maybe 15 millimetres deep; wide enough for three fingertips, like the smallest side of a small matchbox. But this one felt slippery, and as I moved up I noticed a trickle of water running onto it as the chalk on my fingers turned to paste. With no space to share I felt a rising panic. I had to move fast or for sure I would ping off backwards. My free hand searched frantically for something, anything, just a wafer to release my sliding fingers. The only hold was above me, another move upwards, away from the protection and into the unknown. Inner voices suddenly made themselves heard. They'd been there all the time, making sense from the start but I chose not to listen. 'Just what the fuck are you doing, this is absolutely totally not a good idea.' I did a quick bit of rational thinking: assuming the wire below was rubbish, there was now one wire about 7 metres below separating me from life and death if I fell off, or at least a proper injury, as I'd be going an incredibly long way if it popped. That didn't stack up so well – even if it had been a glue-in 12 millimetre stainless, bombproof bolt I'd still be having a wobble. If the wire just below was okay, then maybe I could take the risk. Perhaps it was okay? Stalemate. I found a wafer for my free hand that allowed a super quick chalk and the wet edge now felt a tad better. Glory and reward didn't look so shiny now and I felt I'd already reached the limit of exploring my limits …

Images of Ste's Pembroke accident flashed before me, not actual images of the event, but notes of consequence, the fragility of the body. The edge of my comfort zone stood before me. Many years ago, after the accident, I'd let traditional climbing take a back seat, but more recently I'd fallen for it again, forming a new relationship with a better understanding of my needs. I played within my comfort zone without shame – I'd found my place, with no desire to prove myself amongst the traditional masters. Gradually my zone had expanded with greater knowledge of my physical limits. I'd managed E8 on sight and E11 headpoint; not a bad effort, but on carefully chosen routes to fit my ability and, more importantly, to fit in with my definition of acceptable risk.

The risk is the danger, but now there was another, different, risk. Something else was nagging, something I'd heard about but never really experienced, something that a few years ago I could never have imagined and probably even thought a bit wet and feeble. I saw Amelie, a couple of years old now, I guess I didn't actually see her, maybe I did, it was more the thought of her, the time we'd have together in the future and what she'd do if I didn't make it out of there, her life without a father. Risk took on a whole new level. It's different with wives and girlfriends and partners. Somehow you know they'll get by, or at least you can blinker yourself to the pain you will cause, offsetting it through desire and selfishness, but kids change perspective completely. They deserve way more than everything being messed up by a simple fix of difficult climbing.

Still, I pushed that to the side, slightly. It wasn't so bad yet. It wasn't totally out of control and I explored the puzzle above me at the same rate as my feelings tried to hold me back. Somehow ego won out and I found myself spanning upwards into a long reach off the wet edge to a vertical flake. This needed speedy movement as the position was powerful, and then a poor intermediate handhold to stabilise my position and move my feet. A toe was carefully placed on the wet edge and with another big span I hit my target, a flake of rock standing proud amongst the surrounding blankness. Its size hit me like the disappointment of a kid opening a Christmas present that was absolutely not what they wanted at all: rubbish, sloping, wet. Absolutely not enough, and absolutely nothing else on offer. Instantly the level of risk totally outweighed any kind of pitiful reward, pouring down on it like an avalanche, like I'd been holding back the risk with a dam that had suddenly broken to reveal the true size of the torrent which now overwhelmed me with its scale. Pumping badly I went immediately into reverse, no questions asked, elbows rising and feet skating. On the limit, I reached for the undercut crack but by now I was gone, I was off and screaming, 'Take!' I felt the ridiculously thin bit of string, our lifeline, go tighter and tighter while Neil rapidly took in the slack until I could sag onto the wire I'd snagged in the seam. Now, as it came into view, every bit of my attention focused on the placement. Staring in I realised with horror that it was totally rubbish, balancing on two corners, a miracle it could even support the weight of a quickdraw. My heart missed a beat and breathing stopped as I scanned for options. Fortunately, experience was on my side and I spotted a new placement straight off and knew exactly where I'd find the DMM 3 on my harness. It slipped in without complaint, totally bomber, impossible to come out. I'd have pushed a lot harder with this in place but it was game over now. For a start I was sat on the rope, but my confidence and drive were totally smashed. I lowered off, leaving behind the gear as a monument to my efforts. There was no way I was going to down climb without protection above.

Belaying Neil up I had time to reflect. I was shattered, physically and mentally. I felt like I'd really been somewhere, like on some kind of intensive course on risk and ego management, all crammed into a few minutes. I guess I passed, passed in that I got away with it, but definitions of risk and reward threw stones at each other as I scalded myself for even considering such a ridiculous idea.

And I'd burned time. Neil led through into the dusk, a soaking corner double its grade, and then a protectionless slab with holds of grass and soil funnelled us into the final thrutchy chimney. On top was the relief of the horizontal, but also the acture awareness that reaching the summit is only half the journey. We set off immediately, thankful of the long Norwegian days, but knowing full well the light was fading. Mist surrounded us, blown on an icy wind. Marching, almost at a jog, we followed half-forgotten advice taken lightly and without concern whilst sitting in the sun in the meadow far below. 'Just stick to the edge of the cliff on the left and you should hit the road in two and a half hours.' Our descent plan now seemed somewhat lacking detail. On a bright summer's evening maybe we'd have fluked it, but as we zigzagged and tracked in and out avoiding bottom-less zawns our bearings were shattered. Without conversation we ploughed on, the word 'lost' on both of our lips, but neither of us daring to speak it. We were absolutely in the middle of nowhere with only a thousand-metre cliff now far behind in an unknown direction. To admit being lost meant giving up; there wouldn't be any point carrying on because we didn't know where we were going and the penalty for error was heading off randomly into a vast plateau of no towns, houses, or even roads for at least a few tens of miles. Simply stopping in our tracks in the pitch black dampness was far from appealing and so we kept moving, our target only as far as the beam of a torch as it cut through the mist. We were freezing, wearing everything we had, and hungry, but we'd eaten everything. We'd been on the go for twenty-two hours. We weren't going to die, but it was going to be rubbish.

At the point of no more going forward, Neil noticed a vague familiarity. We'd been here before. More exploration revealed we were back exactly at the top of the cliff, at the very spot we'd summitted. The relief was incredible, for both of us, which is strange really as we were now nowhere nearer getting down than we'd been two hours earlier, were utterly exhausted and knew for sure that we didn't know how to get down. Energised by the illusion of knowing where we were we set off again, this time taking more care, backtracking the instant we became unsure. Eventually there was a cairn, and a path, and a gradual realisation that we were at last on the right track. A good night's sleep and a lovely comfy sleeping bag, previously lost in the misty despair, slipped back into view and became an overpowering target injecting imaginary energy into pushing one foot in front of the other.

Minds wandered as at last our stress drained away. Conversation dried to nothing, the patch of white light on the vague path our here and now. This was supposed to be fun, a holiday. I'd chosen Norway, this crag, and even this route as a break from the norm, an escape. After *Overshadow* and too many sport climbing trips with no focus other than the belay chains, I needed something different, or perhaps something the same as my youth, something I could relate to and feel comfortable with. But comfortable was pretty far from what I was feeling as freezing water squeezed from my shoes with every step. It would be worth it, of course, sitting in the soft grass in the morning, baked by the sun with a celebratory pastry selection. It's always worth it, afterwards. There had been some great climbing, the layback pitch had been truly fantastic, as had the finger crack. There'd been a lot of stress, and potential in a few places for our worth-it-in-the-morning experience to have turned into an all-out epic, although assuming we survived, didn't get injured and it didn't cost too much, even a proper epic would have ended up being worth it, eventually.

Surrounded by blackness, I drifted back into the route and my botched effort on the unclimbed pitch. The experience agitated me, prodded me and wouldn't leave me alone. Why did I even set off, what was I hoping to gain? Did I consider what I had to lose, what others had to lose? It haunted me, like when you know you've made a really bad mistake and are about to pay for it big time, leaving a sickening feeling in the pit of your stomach. I'd gotten away with it, another reminder and refresher course in what I really want from climbing, but the experience added to an already confused state of mind. These days I didn't know what I wanted, like I'd fallen into a premature mid-life crisis but without the need for sports cars and fast driving. Amelie had been the catalyst, opening my eyes to a different world, but at the same time blurring a once-clear direction of where I was going.

Just a week ago, at the doorstep, wet-cheeked Amelie had sobbed. Clinging to Vic's leg she waved mournfully whilst pleading, 'Don't go Daddy, I don't want you to go.' I'd forced my steps down the garden path, having moments earlier prised her tiny body from mine, arms grasping. Did she deserve this? Did I want this? I didn't know what I wanted anymore. Slipping out of view the pain hit like a knife to the heart, real, physical. Later I flew over Sheffield at 20,000 feet on a crystal clear day. In another time this view would have been savoured, a special bird's eye view of the Peak and my home city. Not today. I could see her school, the playground, maybe I could even see her, running with her friends, having fun, or maybe not, missing me? This fantastic flightpath was a cruel reminder of my selfishness.

Selfish? Maybe, in fact, of course, to some extent, but there was a deeper issue and confusion as to where I wanted to be and what I wanted to do. At home I'd be itching to get away on a trip, desperate for new rock and my fix of movement. Always the instigator, I'd be gathering the team and pushing the venue. Then, having fixed a plan, I'd chip away at the dates knowing how desperately I'd miss Amelie, delaying the departure and bringing forward the return, shrinking the trip into a period I could handle and annoying my trip mates. Then with flights booked I'd look forward with dread and once, finally, I was away, I'd count the hours until return, only to find that, once home, I was planning new rock and new places within days. 'Selfishness' was a smokescreen, I hid behind it and used it as a reason for my confusion but, in reality, as I drowned myself in my own self-pity, I knew there was more to it. Through Amelie I'd been given a new side of life, my blinkered eyes opened to the world around me. Suddenly climbing wasn't everything; a marked departure from all I thought I knew. The foundations on which I had lived pretty much my entire life now seemed irrelevant. Pulled from both sides, I could no longer grasp who I was as I tried to cling onto a familiar way of life and drag an out-dated personality into a family where it didn't fit. It wasn't even that I'd lost anything – I'd only gained, bar a few hours' sleep and a bit of inconvenience here and there. I'd gained on so many levels, but I struggled with how new and old fitted together. I was failing to relax and to enjoy them both.

I'd never have seen it coming, the depth of bond between father and child. If you're a dad you will know what I mean. If you're not, you quite probably won't, especially if you're young and of the psyched climber variety. Let's be under no illusions, having kids is no walk in the park or gentle Diff-grade warm-up. You will be more tired than you've ever been. You'll be skint, work more, argue with your partner, see your friends less, and have less time to climb, in fact, less time to do anything. Sometimes it seems impossible to see anything positive in the experience at all. You'll want to strangle them as they ditch a carefully-prepared pasta bake down the back of the sofa or lob your new iPhone into the sink (yes, this did happen). You won't strangle them, because you'd let nothing harm them, nothing. They are the most precious thing in your life, by a large margin, nothing comes close. Even after a whole day of child hell with a standard assortment of tantrums, mess and exhaustion all it takes is a moment, a smile or a word or a cuddle, and you're reminded instantly of how much better your life has become. I found it overwhelming and it caught me by surprise. I didn't know I had it in me to have feelings so strong. It was like discovering an inner self. It wasn't only about me anymore.

In fact pre-kid life seemed completely empty. As she grew I'd marvel at her learning, from first words to the alphabet to the stars and the moon. She'd want the answers to everything and it was my job to come back with a solution. Can you imagine knowing nothing? Looking up into the world from her eyes we'd laugh hysterically for hours, a laughter purer than any drug had ever invoked. It made me realise I didn't laugh that much before. Her life was so simple, her outlook so innocent, that it made me view my own problems in a different light. It put everything in perspective.

Definitions began to change, an evening sitting watching Peppa Pig was more fun than training at The Foundry, a walk around Burbage better than a session on the boulders, and a beach holiday building sandcastles way more appealing than a week in Spain, breaking my fingers on a line of crimps only to get pissed off because I didn't reach the top. I felt I was becoming 'normal' and I wanted to do what normal people did. Inside there was a completely normal, non-climbing type person who'd just been sidetracked by a pointless desire to push himself to the max and climb the hardest way up a random lump of rock with numerous easier ways and even a path round the back.

That's how it felt, sometimes. But I hadn't been sidetracked by a pointless desire and as I ventured forward on my incredible parental journey my need to climb didn't diminish – it burned as strongly as ever before. If anything, having kids had shown just how precious climbing is to me. The problem was that I'd found something at least its equal and didn't know how to fit them together.

So I went round in circles, pondering the situation. The solution was as obvious as it was necessary: compromise, unfortunately, one of my greatest failings. I felt I was already compromising, I'd willingly changed my path and, looking inwardly, viewed the individual components of my life with joy and fulfilment. I'd moved on. It wasn't just about hard climbing and reaching my own cutting edge on a rock face. Through Amelie I'd found a life beyond limits, but I spent too much time looking outwards to what I didn't have and what I'd apparently lost rather than what I'd gained. I'd always been like this, searching for a different balance, not content with the beauty surrounding me. Becoming a parent boosted motivation and took me to whole new levels but I still woefully missed the weekend trips to Wales and Spanish sport hits that I'd actually lost interest in anyway. I was looking frustratedly back at the person I used to be and not happily at what I'd become. If I could only just be content with the compromise, to relax and enjoy the moment, and then flow with a constantly changing balance of life, to roll with it rather than push against it. As usual, I just stumbled on in my usual style, waiting for things to sort themselves out, just as I stumbled on into the blackness of the Norwegian night-time, waiting for it all to turn out okay.

A faint red light in the distance caught my eye, bringing me out of my half-sleep daydream. Through the mist it was barely visible, not moving, but then another appeared, and another, evenly spaced – roadside markers. Suddenly the road sailed into view from the thick air, feet silent on complete flatness, the body relaxing into the regularity, almost tripping over, and the mind sighing with relief, which was premature to say the least, it being still about 10 miles back to the tent with exactly no chance of any cars passing us in the middle of the night. We would still be on for a nightmare even if this was our starting point. However, we'd already thought ahead on this one, and resorted to the classic solution to any great problem: if in doubt, phone a friend. When venturing into the outdoors the rule is, get yourself out of any mess you get yourself into; no bail-out. So it took much soul-searching before we resorted to the wonders of modern technology, a complete cop-out, but in reality taking only moments to come to a unanimous decision to phone Charlie. He'd be sleeping comfortably in his tent and the last thing he'd want is to crawl out at five in the morning to come and collect two stray idiots. However, Charlie was a good mate, and if things were reversed we'd definitely come and sort him out, and this thought was enough to swing any decision as we tentatively pressed the send button on the text messenger, figuring a few beeps at this time in the morning would be less distressing and less likely to immediately put him off than a loud annoying ring tone followed by an urgent request for rescue.

As the headlights swung into view we at last relaxed and, sinking into the hire car seats, eagerly described the day – all positive and full of humour. With the campsite around the corner it was worth it, all of it, of course it was. Everything had turned out well.

Footnote

After making it back at 5 a.m. from our ascent the weather turned Norwegian and we were totally washed out. Retreating back to Stavanger we stayed with my good friend Stein Ivar for a few days, a Norwegian legend known for many hard routes across the country. We discussed my experience. He could totally relate to it, having just had a daughter the year before. In early 2012 Stein set out with his climbing partner on a winter ascent of a route on Kjerag and they were both killed. My very deepest thoughts go out to his wife and daughter.

A July sun hung high in the cloudless sky, heating my tin box of a car. Bouncing along the arrow-straight road slicing its way through the high tops of Blacka Moor, the air above the tarmac shimmered and in the heat of summer even the surrounding bleak heathland felt soft and forgiving. To the left and right familiar landmarks stood proudly like old friends. On first name terms I felt at home and Stanage, Froggatt and Burbage waved as I passed through. These days we rarely spent time together, but when we did and a sunny winter's day coincided with a day off work, we'd pick up where we'd left off, sharing friction and skin like years gone by. Like true old friends we didn't need to keep in touch.

Sheffield filled the rear view mirror, amazing for a city to border such remoteness. In front, the limestone dales spread out, green and lush, winding valleys offering a chance of shade, essential for today. I reached for the window winder to let in some cool, and stuck out a hand into the 70-mile-per-hour air flow for a conditions report, not great, same temperature out as in. It wouldn't be a top performance day, it would be all about sweating fingers sliding on polished crimps. Raven Tor was my destination and she gives little away. I knew from experience exactly what to expect. How much experience? Maybe a thousand visits? Surely not, but probably more than 500. I roughly calculated to fill a solo driver's headspace, coming to the conclusion that whatever the tally it was a ridiculous number and probably shouldn't be publicised or even dwelt upon. There would be many more visits to come, this relatively small and slightly unstable lump giving me more climbing than pretty much anywhere else in the world. There'd been some ups and downs – no one can be psyched all the time – but today, despite the warmth and humidity, I was as keen as ever. I'd made a new friend, *Hubble*, a route I'd chatted to in the past but never beyond the small talk. Lately, I'd made an effort to break through the unforgiving exterior to find something interesting and far deeper than initial appearances would suggest. Hard going at first, but we'd entered into a relationship quite different to any other I'd forged. Keen to progress, I took every chance to get to know *Hubble* better. Today, I already knew there would be little new ground, no deep and meaningful conversations, more of a quick chat, becoming comfortable together. But just spending time with a route like *Hubble*, a route with such status, is a privilege, especially when the relationship is really going places …

Hubble was first climbed by Ben Moon. Prior to this, the world watched as he demolished famous test pieces and established new hardest lines. His credentials could not be doubted and his level of power was legendary. He was one of the best climbers in the world. Then came *Hubble*, the world's first 8c+, one small set of moves for man, but one giant leap for mankind. The route is pure power, it's a boulder problem, though 12 metres long, which isn't even that long really, the hard climbing is over after 4 metres. It would be a Font 8B+ boulder problem if it had a flat grassy landing. Seven hand moves, nine if you're short.

To the average climber these details would serve to demean the route of its quality, the expectation being that a breakthrough in difficulty, the hardest route in the world, would be a soaring line – visually spectacular. However, what the route lacks in stature it more than makes up for in status, the diminutive scale glossed over by the colossal grade. On its way to glory it dragged the crag with it, also lacking in scale but leading in difficulty, both route and cliff were projected out to the rest of the world, gaining a fierce reputation that is still upheld today.

Ben's ascent was in 1990, slapping his way into history a mere 18 miles from my student house. No doubt stumbling around in a wasted daze, I had no idea just how close I was to the cutting edge as it sliced forward in a scene that might as well have been on a different planet. Of course, I'd learn about the ascent much later as it filled the press, moving from headline news eventually into adverts, 'Ben Moon and Mammut versus the mighty *Hubble* – no contest'. The timing was perfect, the route somehow injecting motivation into my own climbing despite being about as achievable as a personal lunar landing. Somehow *Hubble* was special and the images and news stories stayed with me like major childhood memories, ranking higher than learning to ride a bike or moving to big school.

Later, I began to understand what real difficulty was all about. Maybe when I'd on-sighted 8a+ and redpointed 8c I could just about comprehend the difficulty of *Hubble*. Prior to this there was no idea. But the better I got, the more the route seemed to move away from me, its reputation growing on a daily basis as the wads tried and failed. It did have repeats, but only by the real powerhouses. Malcolm Smith built a replica in his bedroom and lived on a diet of broccoli before his ascent, and John Gaskins trained on his own specific 'Hubble board' and spent many visits to the crag to snag the redpoint, driving all the way from the Lakes to arrive at 6 a.m. for the best conditions. Many others tried as well. Some could do a few of the moves, but putting it together was a different world. A comment by John Welford summed it up. He'd just climbed *The Bastard* at Rubicon, an 8c+ in the same style: short and bouldery. I asked if *Hubble* was next. 'No way, *Hubble* is just in a totally different league from *The Bastard*, it's in a different league from everything.' This became apparent as I moved through the grades, *Mecca* 8b+, *Make it Funky* 8c, *Evolution* 8c+, *Kaabah* 8c+, *Mutation* 9a. Along the way I tried *Hubble*, once or twice per year, and every time made zero impression. The great leveller, the true test. Plenty doubted my credentials, grading *Mutation* 9a and *Northern Lights* 9a when I still hadn't done *Hubble* seemed a step above my status. I shrugged this off with a cover story that the route just wasn't for me. Sometimes they aren't, they don't fit your body or your strengths. *Hubble* is brutally bouldery, requires serious bicep strength and has moves that are considerably easier if you are tall – all my weaknesses combined! But I always knew it would call out to me, standing in the way of my own path to a self-defined completeness: the final exam.

Hubble begins with a pull off the ground from a small but decent side pull, hands matched on it and high feet on small edges. Then the first hard move, a massive span out left to 'the block' – a hard move for those of average stature but gaining exponentially in difficulty for every missing inch of reach. There is no way around it and I guess there is a cut-off point where it's simply impossible. At 5' 6" height with zero ape index I could take a poor intermediate and then swing to the block, catching the very base at the maximum of my stretch. Placing a heel-toe with my right foot and concentrating hard on it, I could move my right hand to a poor intermediate and then, at last, bump my left hand into the block proper. It's not a good hold, maybe three cassette boxes glued together in size but tapering out the wrong way and more slippery than plastic. From here the difficulty really starts. Hauling on the heel-toe, the right hand spans to a very poor undercut pinch, each finger position critical on its miniscule size, the thumb pressing hard to make it even barely possible to use. So to the crux, the famous UK 7b move, a left hand movement of a mere half a metre. Feet over the roof, pasting on ultra-polished smears, haul the body up on the block and the pinch, max out the bicep and snatch into a pocket for the left hand. Under the roof it's hard to see, accuracy and timing are everything. Good enough for two fingers but only just. If you've got this far the next few moves are easy, maybe only UK 6c, but if you didn't get the last few moves quite right, if those fingers are slightly misaligned, if your tips are marginally sweating or your feet creeping, then these next moves will be the living end. A slap with the right hand, at last leaving that awful pinch in favour of a pathetic crimp the size of a twenty-pence piece but sloping at 45 degrees and polished beyond measure. Crimped on by so many, cared for and brushed, polished up like some antique hold in the climbing museum. It used to have friction apparently, oh how that must have been nice. Bear down hard on this and the feet go into action, legs uncurling and moving together, robot-like to find their new contorted position, left toe hooking marginally behind the block, right foot smearing on a tiny polished bump, trying to get something out of the toe hook as best it can. Without the left toe, the polished crimp is nothing, unholdable. Squeezing hard with the legs, the left hand finds its new position on an undercut edge just by the polished crimp. Another undercut. Concentrate hard on this and the feet move again – the route is all in the feet, as all climbing is apparently, and as the instructor will shout to the beginner dithering up an easy-angled slab – but here they're critical: left foot on a tiny corner the size of a baked bean, right foot on a marginal smear, or for the short, a sloping shelf just 50 centimetres below your hands. Either way, the redpoint crux follows with a violent slap with the right hand to a dimply crimp. It's a rubbish hold, but by far the best thing for a long time. Maintain body tension and keep the feet in order, stepping up onto an edge two matchsticks wide and slapping with the left hand to a good hold, a proper hold, a place where you know you should be in now, to clip a bolt and begin to smile. But don't relax yet – the upper section is no path, maybe 7c/7c+ and certainly harder for the short. It's been dropped from before, the disappointed climbers lowering off with their premature excitement shattered in a moment's loss of concentration, devastated in the knowledge that for success everything has to come together in one place and time – and that that one place and time may have just been passed. Keep it together and the moves will flow, a tenuous move left and at last you reach the junction with *Revelations*. More awkward moves lie on the scary slab above, but now it's all in the mind, stay focused and the belay will arrive; *Hubble* conquered.

To be fair, I wasn't giving myself the best chance. The odd day each year was never going to be enough with the specific nature of the moves and holds. Everybody had trained for it specifically, even building replicas on indoor walls. I was nowhere, an amateur, hoping to trick it into submission like I do with so many other hard routes, finding cunning sequences, holds and body positions no one else has seen. But *Hubble* cannot be tricked. There are no easy ways round it and I hated it for this fact, so cruelly exposing my weaknesses but, at the same time, drawing me in. It was the ultimate test, a pass guaranteeing a place in the hall of power.

Eventually it was time to become involved. It wasn't planned, it kind of sneaked up on me, kidnapping me away from other options. But having done everything at the crag, there weren't many other options and *Hubble* cried coward as I searched for alternatives or slipped into training days on well-known routes. 2009 was a strange year in terms of weather, again, and wet rock at other venues drew me back repeatedly to the Tor. There was no escape and no excuse. I made a pact with *Hubble*. I'd go on it every visit, no matter how hot it was, how humid or how tired I was, even if it was for just ten minutes. That way I would become familiar with the moves and become friends with the holds. I wasn't ready to train yet, to go indoors on a specific model or gain recruitment on tinfoil moulded replicas, so this was a good compromise. On a route so short, motivation is key. I expected a struggle but this was a new experience, a venture into the world of the short. I began to revel in it, to be operating right at the limit on every move. I was exploring that top 1 percent of power only found when everything comes together at the same time – and I needed everything. It may be the ultimate in power routes but it may also be the most delicate, with feet and body position absolutely critical. It may be untrickable, but every day I was finding some new trick, the slightest twist of a toe or pressing of a thumb at a different angle. As my power levels on each hold increased it opened up new options to use my body in slightly different ways, this, in turn, opening up even more possibilities, all tiny but all so relevant.

On a cold but damp day in the middle of June I tied on to look at the moves again. Conditions were poor but I'd made the pact. First go up and I was through the crux, my left hand snatching into the undercut, fingers slotting neatly into the slot. Startled but composed, I moved swiftly onwards. I'd been there before, just once, but not with the upper moves so dialled. To reach this point meant there was a chance, but reaching into the final undercut and setting up for that last slap I already knew it wasn't the day. It didn't matter, this was real progress, this was close, this meant I might really be able to do it. How can that be? Was I even worthy? For so long this one route has been such a source of inspiration, representing the top of the game. Driving home I had little flashbacks, little risings of excitement … I nearly did *Hubble*.

A few days later we returned, but the weather had flipped, a cold summer had become standard issue, hot and sweaty. Stepping from the car it was obvious, white limestone now a dull brown and the polished holds black. Condensation was thick and the crag soaked. Straight back in the car and home to The Foundry; indoors in the middle of summer. I'd made the pact, but sometimes it really had to be broken. That was okay, it was late June,

September would be cooler. In fact, a break was an opportunity, I would train, build a replica with specific holds, just like the experts. It was all part of the process – but for something so short, for just one route? My motivation surprised me as I threw myself in and standing back I viewed it in a different light. *Hubble* was what I needed at a moment in time, the right route at the right place. Low on time demands and high on desirability it fitted neatly into the slot of the climber I needed to be. The rest fell away, all the other parts I'd clung so desperately onto: the Lakeland climber; the Snowdonian climber; the Spanish sport climber; the Pembroke trad climber. For now I couldn't be them all. I was juggling with too many balls and making a half-arsed job of everything. Three balls was okay, I could manage to juggle three indefinitely: work, family and climbing. But with the weight of work gaining daily, the size of the family ball increasing exponentially when I became a parent, and having a spiky and awkward DIY ball chucked in for good measure, I was now really struggling. I couldn't juggle with four. Climbing was the easiest to drop. Years ago work would be slashed and DIY abandoned; climbing would have been the very last to go. But now, somehow, it found itself at the front of the queue. Work was essential, the house barely habitable, and as early years flew by with Amelie there was a rising panic I would miss out on something I'd never get back. Time spent with your kids is the most precious in your life, not apparent at first, but becoming increasingly obvious as the rest of life's essentials suddenly seem rather trivial. Climbing could wait, it had to wait, but at the same time I could only juggle everything else with climbing at the core. More than ever I realised how central it was to my entire existence. Five o'clock starts for a morning hit, fingerboarding whilst making dinner and pull-up sets on the park climbing frame between goes down the slide showed the strength of my desire, but I simply couldn't be the climber I was before. Becoming a parent had changed everything. I had to let it go, at least for now. *Hubble* stepped in, a route big enough and valid enough to be all of my climbing, at least for a while. I allowed it to take over, relieving me of the duty to be the climber I felt I needed to be. The relief was incredible; at last I was looking inwards and aware of the beauty of my life. Of course, it would be temporary, I knew that, but there seemed a little space to think for a change rather than always chasing something just out of reach.

But *Hubble* remained just out of reach. I wanted it as badly as ever; I was back in the zone on familiar ground in redpoint world. *Mutation, Northern Lights* and *Overshadow* all came into view, the effort, the tenacity, the theft of my life by a simple set of holds … but there was a difference, there was no pressure to perform. Though in effect my approach was exactly the same,

I felt free of the need for success. I felt lighter and wiser, it didn't really matter if I climbed this little lump of rock. Perhaps it was kids throwing perspective into a new brighter light and giving the process more clarity, but really it was about reaching a peace with my performance. I'd reached the end of the line with *Overshadow*, the line I set out for myself. I'd known before I'd even committed to *Overshadow* and knew as soon as I'd succeeded. It was a huge sigh of relief. I'd passed every test I set, pushed myself to the limit and beyond, and there was nothing left to prove. If it all ended right then I'd be content.

But there was still one final test…

On a boiling sunny morning Al Austin phoned, he was keen for the Tor. I didn't want to go, to drive all the way there alone only to drive back, or perhaps slither around desperately on easy routes as an obligation to Al. *Hubble* would be an enemy and even though I'd made the pact it would be a backwards step, an undoing of progress. I had things to do: DIY on the house, writing for the magazines and essential training to edge me forward. But Al was keen and I caved in; I owed him many a belay. Crossing Blacka Moor the car thermometer indicated 21.5 degrees at 10.40 a.m., hardly the 'Gaskins' start. Surprisingly, conditions were reasonable, though more importantly I actually felt strong, a rare feeling for me. It was worth going on the route again, if only to stay familiar. I was on redpoint, but not really. I set off on an attempt, but wasn't really trying. It was too hot and too sweaty, but in that moment everything was right, like I'd used my own 'subtle knife' to cut my way into another world where conditions were different – barely discernible but slightly cooler and fresher and with slightly lower gravity. Moving in this other world everything worked correctly. My fingers dropped perfectly into the pocket where previously they had never quite sat. My toe held fast where it usually started to creep. Every position felt solid. It felt slow and there was time to think. It was not supposed to be like this; everything was going too well. Don't get me wrong, it was a fight, a fight to the death, but snagging the first of the good holds after the hard climbing, I had the slightest feeling the route had given up. It had been just that bit too easy. It was my time for success, *Hubble* knew it and at last it had admitted defeat, laid down and died. The top section was smooth, even placing the 'draws as I went (so sure I would not succeed I hadn't even put them in for the redpoint) then it was over. Of all the routes I'll ever repeat this one will be the most satisfying. This was the big one – the final exam.

33 FULL CIRCLE

'If you're not trying something where you could fail then it isn't hard. And I almost know in my mind if I'm sure I can do whatever I'm trying, then it probably isn't hard enough to be really important.'
Dave MacLeod

Redpointing. It's all about the journey. It's only a game.

It might only be a game, but are we just playing with it, or is it playing with us?

If it's only a game then it doesn't matter who wins or loses. It's just about the taking part.

Maybe.

I was thinking that, until it got close.

Then it was more than a game. It's always more than a game.

If I list the ten most important events of my entire life, probably half will be redpoint ascents. My motivation and drive has come from projects, my entire career based on successful redpoints. This is no game.

The very first time I visited Malham Cove I stood underneath *Raindogs* and stared up beyond the finishing chains at the future. The extension was a line of immeasurable difficulty, right in the centre of the cove, which soared directly towards the finishing ledge 40 metres above me. It crossed the most difficult terrain and the blankest rock, impossible to comprehend. Fifteen years later I tied in ready for an attempt on this line. Fifteen years of experience, training, blood, sweat and tears all led up to this moment. It would be the hardest route of my life, by far, should I succeed.

But I didn't and I knew I wouldn't. This route was, and is, beyond me for now. I was trying the route, but knew my place in its ranking. I'd fallen into the process, accepting failure as part of the deal. If you can afford to let a few get away then it's likely climbing will be a richer and more rounded experience. Failure does not have to take on its dictionary definition, failure brings on motivation, a desire to improve and overcome. Failure is the only sure way of finding your limits. Failure is a good thing, it's essential; failure leads to success.

Malham Cove has held my attention for many years with some of my most memorable climbing experiences on my hardest and finest routes, *Rainshadow* and *Overshadow* both pushing me and forcing me to be my best. It's the greatest sport cliff in the UK and still has new lines to offer. Way back in 2010 I bolted a new line, *the* line, between *Rainshadow* and *Bat Route*. Like a football dream team it had all of the best; it was the perfect route. It was obviously hard, another level, and I didn't even dare get involved. The route was simply a toy that I played with and put back on the shelf at the end of the session. But as moves fell into place it nagged at me to make it mine, to commit, to take it home. But I didn't want it. It was too big a job to take on. I wasn't qualified, I wasn't worthy. Without commitment there could be no failure, so I continued playing, not wanting to accept the challenge and at the same time kidding myself …

This line is an incredible find, taking in fantastic movement over immaculate rock in a mind-blowing position and, similar to *Hubble*, it has meaning, encircling a huge portion of my climbing life from the initial excited youthful imagination of futuristic potential right through to my final attempts. Really, deep down, I knew it was too hard. An ageing body, expanding family and ever-growing work commitments were drawing me away from the level it demanded, a level that was probably above me even when at my best. But I invested some time anyway – it was good training if nothing else. In 2013 I found myself at Malham again. I was on the route, after a year's gap due to injury and terrible weather. My own words felt more relevant than ever: 'It's all about the journey.' Too true, I would learn from this route, get fit, get strong, have fun days out in one of the most beautiful places in the world. I didn't have to actually complete it. I played at a level beyond my limit and as my friend Rab Carrington said, 'What else are you going to do?' With pretty much every other route completed I knew he was right. He was steering me towards it, he knew it would bring out the best in me. Having the support of Rab spurred me on. More than twenty years my elder he remains one of my greatest sources of inspiration. An absolute glass half full person, even when it's obviously nearly empty, he's always positive, always eager to get out and about. To climb with Rab is to be part of a team as he willingly donates energy from vast reserves.

The project is an extension with a huge amount of new climbing, eventually joining the final section of *Bat Route* for a fitting end on the huge ledge with a sit-down belay clip and a comfortable view of the breathtaking Yorkshire scenery. The new climbing is incredibly continuous, tiny edges and poor footholds. There's barely any possibility to clip, never mind chalk; I skipped two clips in a row on lead taking regular 10-metre falls. All the moves are now ingrained, burnt into memory for a lifetime.

The new section is 8c+ in its own right, beginning with a tricky traverse and a snatch into a wide pinch and a burly clip at the steepest part of the bulge. Small undercuts and a deep kneedrop just about allow a span onto a tiny edge, 5 millimetres wide, and barely qualifying as a foothold. It only works as the kneedrop deepens, pushing my centre of gravity into the wall and taking a few pounds of weight off my fingertips. Another couple of long reaches from poor edges lead to an undercut and yet another burly clip – the last one I'll make, the next two abandoned. This point is a halfway marker in the extension, the ten hand movements to this point being desperate, but not as hard as the fourteen to come. The next series of holds are all terrible, only the coarse nature of the rock, combined with incredibly accurate footwork, giving any chance of use. Each hand movement requires multiple, precise foot placements. How I'd pored over the options, felt for the potential. Hanging on the rope I'd studied the sequences into submission, applying detailed mathematics to solve the puzzle of forces, vectors, angles and friction, all constrained by strength. Like deciphering a maze I'd follow how one hold insisted on a particular movement to the next, only to reach a dead end and have to backtrack. Some holds were abandoned, giving nothing, others, initially discounted, were re-established as essential.

From the final clip an unlikely pinch leads to a pencil tufa and a snatch to an edge, a wide reach into a crozzly undercut and complex footwork before the set up for a long slap to 'the razor blade' – a miserable edge just a few millimetres wide and only holdable due to its sharp nature. Completely conditions dependant, any sweat on my tips makes this useless and any more than four or five attempts takes skin close to its limit. A tiny undercut crimp is then held, and knuckled into, to generate enough force to span upwards for a small pocket. More crack than pocket, it can only be held from below with a marginal finger lock on my little finger, the next two stacking on top, and my first finger splayed out on a small divot. Each component is essential, like the four legs on a chair, take one away and it crashes immediately to the ground. Pushing the body up on smears, a tiny spike for the other hand allows the pocket to be switched to a side pull, little finger now redundant, first and second fingers better placed for the coming move. The use of this spike was to unlock the entire route. A hold initially not even noticed due to size and position, it allowed the rapid shift of fingers in the pocket to make possible the final desperate crux move. This is the 'heartbreaker move' – an all-out slap for a distant sloping edge, the size of the smallest side of a cigarette packet but too sloping to hang on, only usable with a miraculous thumb catch in a perfect position.

This move on its own is incredible, for me impossible static, and requiring a subtle balance of power and timing and a very specific trajectory of my centre of gravity, with fingers and thumb meeting their exact target at exactly the same moment. Close to the ground it would be awesome, but 25 metres up, after all that climbing …

It's an incredible find for me, it's absolutely exactly what I was looking for. Even a half decent hold would change it completely, but there isn't one. Somehow there is just enough.

There are two options for the start, before the extension, either up *Rainshadow* 9a or *Bat Route* 8c. In terms of actual line it makes little difference, both are equally as good, but starting through *Rainshadow* is harder. This was my initial concept and the dream line, working title the '*Easy Easy Project*'. I played with this and took it as far as I could in 2013 on redpoint, knowing I'd not succeed. Sometimes you really just know, you can't just trick it or bang your head against it. It's time to go away and get better. My high point redpointing from the floor was to the razor blade, just six tough moves to go – a good link. From that point in time I knew it was game on but I also knew I wouldn't do it before summer closed the window, a massive confidence boost but at the same time frustrating. Knowing my improvement curve would miss the mark dampened enthusiasm. I'd reached the end of the line, proving to myself I was capable but running out of time. To continue seemed fruitless but I was happy with the progress.

When I redpointed *Rainshadow* in 2004 it felt my hardest route and I was sure I'd never climb any harder. *Rainshadow* climbs *Raindogs* to its belay, but without the legendary chain-grab finish, 8a+ to there. Then a poor rest on side pulls hopefully gives enough recovery for the Font 7C+ crux through the bulge. This fourteen-move section has everything from pinches to footlocks and leads to a crozzly edge and a quick clip. It's 8c+ to that point, and then *Rainshadow* breaks hard left with the upper wall, boosting the grade into 9a. The *Easy Easy* steps right. When I climbed *Rainshadow* I made it through the crux bulge just twice in over twenty-one days of effort, falling near the top once, and reaching the chains the second time. Now, nine years later, I was climbing through the bulge and well beyond two or three times a day, twice a week. Maybe I'd not 'succeeded' on this new project, but I'd certainly got better. That has to be success, on some level at least.

But it had not come without effort and cost. Just how hard could I push? As each winter began to bite it felt harder and harder to squeeze out that final pull-up when training, knowing I'd probably not touch rock for another four months. This is what it takes to climb at your limit, sets of press-ups between chopping the veg, fingerboard hangs whilst listening to homework and stretching aching muscles on the train. There'd be sessions at 11 p.m., double hits when already broken and sneaky trips to The Foundry when Vic thought I was somewhere else. I pushed to my max and my body agreed. Fingers, elbows, shoulders and back ached from too much abuse. I was getting old – most people my age had stopped climbing ages ago. Was it worth it? And now, is it worth the constant torrent of abuse to probably never go beyond where I've already been? Will I pay for it all later? Speaking to an ex-Spanish star recently he made a comment that made me think deeply: 'I didn't realise I had to pay. I thought it was free, all my fun, my climbing and my training but suddenly I was handed the bill. It was not free and now it was time to pay, and I'll be paying for the rest of my life.' Twisted with injury, for him climbing had slid well off the agenda a while back. In his mid-forties, I asked if it was worth it. I expected he'd say, 'Yes, of course it was, every moment, the highlight of my life.' It's kind of what I wanted him to say, to justify my own blatant disregard of the warning signs but he didn't, he just quietly said, 'No' and then stared off into the distance and remained silent.

The *Bat Route* start was never on the agenda, not even considered. Why, I'm not sure, perhaps simply because it wasn't the hardest. Someone suggested it as obvious and like a flicked switch my energy instantly diverted into a new circuit. I almost felt foolish to have missed it, a punter error, blatantly obvious. If anything this link would have made a far better build-up into the *Easy Easy Project*. More importantly, at that moment my eyes lit up as success came into focus, playing was fun and the journey is all very nice, but like rounding the final corner on a race track, there's nothing like a view of the finishing line for picking up the pace and giving that little bit extra.

So I moved straight into the *Bat Route* project, incredible in its own right and equally valid as an independent route – and with careful labelling as training for the main event I could pretend there was no pressure. I wasn't the gold medal I was after, but the silver would do.

No pressure was my ideal, but as glory came into view I found myself tumbling into project mode, I could see it washing over me, all too familiar from years gone by. It started slowly, gnawing away, then consumed me, absorbing my every thought, my existence planned around it. Work, leisure, training, family, all now fitted in around the project. Even sleep was altered and I'd go to bed early just to think about the moves, to wire them in, maybe think out an easier method.

The race was my ability versus the length of season. An improvement curve can be plotted versus time, rising sharply at first and gradually flattening to eventually become horizontal. For a successful ascent this curve must cross the required level at some point, if the route is too hard the curve flattens below the level. With this project I knew there *should* be an intersection, but it was deep into the time axis with little margin for error. It weighed on me as I watched my improvement tail off, flattening to run almost parallel to, but just under, where I needed to be. Cards were stacked against me; I needed a perfect hand before even setting off, conditions, rest and confidence at 100 per cent in order for the full amount of my ability to only just tickle the underside of the success level.

Slowly I inched higher and then suddenly the project toppled into possible with an exciting high point, my fingers in the pocket just a few moves below the final hard heartbreaker lunge …

I'd played this game before, with *Overshadow*. I'd mastered the strategy and now I was there again. On the same cliff, only metres apart, a similar length of climbing, similar grade, similar style. My life followed the same path with numerous visits taking me closer and closer. Again I let it take over, work postponed, holidays abandoned, family engagements avoided. I was skint, in need of a break and in the bad books. Climbing partners moved away, having completed their projects or in need of a change of scene. I planned and schemed and pondered, the level of immersion again taking me by surprise. But there was a big difference, a huge one, and a factor now standing out as the most important of all – motivation. This time it was different, perhaps a subtle difference to an observer, but a huge one to me. I didn't have to do this route. *Overshadow* had been essential, not that I'd have admitted it, I needed it, it was my test to myself, I had to pass. Now qualified, a master of my own course, I had nothing to prove.

I drew parallels with *Hubble*, but this was in a different league altogether. *Hubble* had helped me escape from an outdated outlook and find peace in the moment. This new project above *Bat Route* was my entrance back in to playing at my limit. But I played on a higher level and on this project part of me didn't actually want to succeed. I was drawing so much from myself, so much positive energy, pushing myself to be absolutely the best I could possibly be. I was climbing for the love of it, loving the whole process, the stress, the movement, the progress, the crag banter and the privilege of being at one with an element of nature. As I became more involved I realised my climbing had turned a corner, or perhaps made the final curve of a full circle, taking me back to a type of climber long forgotten. Motives had changed, I was trying this route simply because I was enjoying it.

So climbing became what it used to be, all about the climbing, the movement, the outdoors, the whole package, reaching the top was not the only goal. I didn't want it to end but at the same time so desperately wanted closure, an exquisite paradox of the finest nature.

I rested up and hit the crag good to go, but the perfect conditions of spring disappeared and drizzle poured in, blown by a wrong-direction wind. Twice I hit the sloper and twice I pinged off it, damp with moisture. The window was closing, with bad weather forecast. A team was heading up next day but I turned down the offer tired from my efforts and needing more rest. A painful decision – maybe it would have still been possible, maybe I did have enough in the tank. Was that my last chance? The rain poured and I slept badly.

At last there was another chance and I returned to a soaking crag streaked with water. But my line was just dry, although only just and conditions were poor. But I wanted it badly. Being filmed for the first time by expert cameraman Rich Heap maybe brought even more incentive as he released himself from the quickdraws as I moved upwards. I shut him out and each move felt perfect and suddenly I was set for the heartbreaker. It went in dream-like fashion as only it can on that perfect final redpoint effort. Sloper in hand, thumb on its miraculous catch, I held it together, kept my feet precise on the micro edges as I stretched out right on marginally easing moves before the very last stretch into the good holds on *Bat Route*. It was all perfect. I'd done it. I'd already started celebrating. The jug was in my hand …

But it wasn't, my fingers tickled it but something was pulling me down, pulling hard. I pulled against it, still some energy on the small handholds, but the force wouldn't give. Confused I looked down. My heart skipped a beat as I computed the situation, somehow the karabiner of the final quickdraw that I don't clip on lead had buried itself within my figure of eight knot. The final lunge to the jug had jammed it solid, reversing back into hard moves I couldn't free it and with the 'draw mallioned into the bolt I couldn't unclip it. Panicking, I tried to figure a quick fix but there was none to be had and then suddenly I was sat on the quickdraw, a 100 per cent reverse in my feelings. Total euphoria to utter disappointment. Instantly I knew what had happened, the krab was sticky, the gate stiff – it had stayed open having been beaten by weather for a few months. Normally it didn't matter, I knew I didn't clip it on lead and I always made sure it was clipped shut, but Rich hadn't, he didn't know and as he'd released himself, this offending piece of equipment had turned itself into the perfect hook. Screaming my frustrations at him he hid behind the lens, capturing my child-like outburst for all to see. Embarrassed I tried to calm down, but the disappointment surrounded me. I couldn't shake it. How could this happen?

Next go I didn't get so far, the sloper just out of reach, and on the third go I held the sloper for a second before my other hand blew out, damp from poor conditions, cartwheeling me backwards into the 10-metre fall and awkward slam into the wall. Last go up I went to the top of the crag just to re-familiarise myself with the moves on the final section of *Bat Route*. With horror I realised this relatively easy 10-metre section was now wet, unclimbable. The rain had come through. At least this helped forgive Rich; if I'd made it into *Bat Route* I'd have fallen anyway, and maybe that would have been more disappointing. At least I had a slightly funny story. But that was it. That was my window. It had opened wide to show me I was good enough, but now closed to test my integrity as a climber. 'If you only climb to get the top you should seriously question why you climb.' Timeless words from John Redhead. They sat uneasily in my stomach as I tried to settle into a personal success.

> *Climbing is about the process. Take a long look at your definition of success: is it only about rattling a chain? If you can afford to let a few get away then it's likely your climbing will be a richer and more rounded experience.*

My own words seemed to have a hollow ring to them, previously unnoticed. Could I afford to let this one get away? Against all the stress and anxiety I was revelling in the tension. I was in my own film, on the edge of my seat, not knowing how the ending would turn out. The quest for the biggest rewards flirts with the highest chance of failure. 'How far is too far?' is the question, and the answer, once so elusive, now stood out painfully with the definitive line of 'too far' scored right in front of me. I pushed at it and sidestepped it but eventually I'd step over and fail, or if I was really lucky, step right on it and succeed. I was going to be right on the edge ...

I returned to Malham on a bad forecast, carrying a deflated ambition. I'd done it but I hadn't. I *could* have done it. Would I ever have the drive to push through again and was the window closed anyway? At least the bad forecast was bad in a different way: blazing sun. I picked out my route through the glare, seepage lines dotting the way and signalling impossibility – a double disaster, wet and hot. But closer inspection showed the power of the sun as dampness tracked back up the wall. The window cracked open again, but today the gap would be marginal. The rock, warm to the touch, would gradually cool in the shade and then the dampness would return in the evening. When to try? I waited like a pro, and then threw myself in at a calculated moment.

A good friend asked how I dealt with redpoint pressure and I replied by saying I never thought of any effort as a final go, that there would always be another chance. For once I didn't believe myself. The crag was falling out of condition and my diary insisted it was the end of the road. I'd pushed family and work too far and commitments had been made. As summer loomed I could count potential visits on less than half of one hand. Today had to count.

Conditions surprised me after such a sunny day: warm, but with no humidity – a marked change to previous cold days. Warm fingers found new texture, previously stiff and wooden, they now conformed to the intricacies of the holds. Suddenly I was facing the heartbreaker. Concentrating 100 per cent I hit the sloper perfectly, then took on the complex final sequence into *Bat Route*, the stretch to good holds this time unhindered by a vicious hook. Then at last I could relax a little and take stock and keep a lid on my building euphoria. But the end was far from near. I'd expected the final wall of *Bat Route* to be hard but a relative formality. Now it loomed, my fatigue levels way higher than I'd anticipated. This took me by surprise and I desperately shook out in a state of panic – whilst practising the coming section I'd fallen off many times when considerably less tired.

The final wall is about 8a, the moves pumpy and technical: no giveaway. Most fall from this upper section whilst attempting *Bat Route*. Blinkering this thought, I focused on the moves and recovery; I had to choose exactly the right moment to go. Waiting patiently I tried to spot where the recovery curve peaked. I needed it all, a mistake would be disastrous. Monitoring it carefully the peak appeared; there was just the slightest sign I was tiring and that recovery was falling into reverse. It was time to go – now. I closely watched my petrol gauge through a third eye, already in red and dropping fast it would bottom out as I hit the finishing jug. More haste, less speed. Efficiency was crucial, too fast and I'd burn excess fuel, too slow and I'd run out. There was no margin for error.

I topped the route with nothing to spare, my physical ability dropping at exactly the same rate as the difficulty of the moves, even down to the final UK 4a mantel. Then safety. Turning back the view hit me, the beautiful Yorkshire Dales stretching out into a sun-soaked spring evening. I had a bit of a moment and let it sink in.

It's only a game. Maybe …

The name came easily, with a bat hang rest before the new section and this project moving out of and back into *Bat Route*, as well as the amount of time I adopt toe hangs to compensate for feeble arms; *Batman* was the obvious choice. It's an essential technique; fifteen years ago Miles Gibson and I figured the future of climbing was all in the toes, with incredible toe strength it would be possible to rest in numerous places, even on the smallest of edges. Strangely no one seems interested.

Batman   9a/9a+

Start as for *Bat Route*, climbing as far as the knee-bar rest. Milk this for all its worth then move immediately leftwards for two metres via a complex traverse. From the wide pinch grip, blast straight up the wall above via an assortment of rubbish crimps and poor undercuts to eventually join *Bat Route* again at a vague rest before the final vertical wall. Finish on the ledge, lower off, and douse your fingers in the stream.

F.A. Steve McClure, 2013.

Settling into seat 27A on Jet2 flight LS680 to East Midlands I felt a little rise of excitement. Ten days earlier, in a different state of mind, I'd sat in exactly the same seat on my way out to the Verdon with mixed emotions haunting me as I tried to push them aside. Leaving Amelie, and now also Harry, as well as Vic, was never easy and a hurdle I knew I'd have to face from the moment a travelling plan came together. I'd hesitate in pressing the 'buy' tab in the flight booking process, I'd be committing to more than just a monetary outgoing. Missing my family was painful but it was easier these days, easier in that I knew the greyness would pass. I knew the process; in a few days' time I'd have found my feet, and then the trip would speed up out of control leaving me wanting more, just a day or two extra in climbing paradise. Nine or ten days was acceptable, on both sides of the parental equation, with Vic knowing fine well I'd whinge without a break and, for myself and my own state of mind, such a period being the perfect compromise between being worth going and feeling too long. It also just about fitted into a self-created reasonable 'away-from-home' time, with Vic having to bear all the work while I jollied around in the sun. Two weeks felt a weekend too far and a month was ruled out without question – though maybe reserved for something really special sometime in the future, with my level of 'acceptable' open for personal debate that I'd later pitch to Vic once I'd decided what was best, for me of course. Most people would consider it selfish, leaving your other half to do double the work. It is, no doubt about it, but the travel, exploration and moving over stone is part of who I am, I need it to be me. Take all of it away and I'm not sure where I'd end up, not good for much I'm sure.

> 'At the end of the day, climbing probably is irresponsible …
> But we're better parents because we're doing things that fulfil us.'
> Chris Bonington

Securing the aeroplane seatbelt a smile spread across my face, unusual for most people on the return leg of an outstanding holiday as they head back into the real world. I remembered 'real world' all too well, there'd be a pit of the stomach feeling churned by the inevitable Monday to Friday grind, early mornings and a winter's desk view with no natural light for months. Things had changed and the return home was now as exciting as the departure, if not more. It's all relative to what's waiting upon arrival. In a few hours I'd walk up the garden path and push open the front door. There'd be chatter and laughter, maybe some crying or the sound of some plastic junk being dragged around or knocked over. Whatever it was it would be alive and vibrant. In an earlier life there would have been silence, everything exactly as I'd left it. There would be some food, a beer and a few hours of TV; a quiet night in, just like the thousands stretching out for the rest of my life. Now there would be no sinking into the sofa, it would be straight into piggyback rides, building Lego, stories and games. There'd be tidying and sorting and bathtimes and bedtimes. It would be crazy and hectic, and sometimes frustrating and often exhausting, but with purpose and meaning that faded a past life almost into irrelevancy. I'd be needed and loved without boundary and through my kids I'd glimpse back into a world of fun and simplicity uncluttered by the trappings of age.

As I'd close the front door behind me with a click the noise would stop, whatever it was, and then they'd come running, leaping all over me like some kind of play park attraction, their faces full of joy and lit up with smiles, so, so happy to see me back.

The image made me chuckle and the lady next to me on the plane threw me a glance, so I stifled the laugh and switched thoughts, happy to leave them, like closing a book after finishing a satisfying chapter. It was an easy transition: I wanted to dwell on this past week in the Verdon, as good a trip as any I could ever remember, but this time there'd been even more than climbing and scenery and friendship. I felt I'd made some kind of discovery of self. Taking a pencil from my daypack I opened the climbing diary – I was only a few days behind but had a lot to catch up on. Yesterday's climbing had been amazing. I needed to write about it first so left a few blank pages for the preceding days:

Friday 12th July – Tom et Je Ris. 8b+ flash.
What a day, up and off by 8 a.m., hiking by 8.30, and what a hike, totally messed up and ended up marching solid with massive packs for two and half hours to arrive exhausted. Neil announced he wasn't keen, but we'd made the effort and I was going in. Dropping down the 60-metre abseil I glanced at the holds, hard not to, but didn't dwell. Jesus, it went on forever, and I gave up looking. On route I flash pumped and had to employ all my recovery skills including usual toe hook stuff, and put in a mega scrap, only just fluking one section snatching non-holds whilst toppling

off backwards. The last third felt easy, like a dream, topping out incredible.
What a buzz! Then I literally floated back to camp. What a day!

On the first day of this trip Neil Mawson and I stared over at the incredible *Tom et Je Ris*, the two parallel tufas scoring a line straight down the massive cliff opposite the tourist viewpoint. Originally un-apparent in my youth on impossible bulging walls, the route slid onto my radar a few years ago, the line a stand-out feature as I became fluent in tufa style. The name sticks too. 'Tom and Jerry', spoken correctly in French '*Tom et Je Ris*', 'Tom and I laugh'. A beautiful title from the first ascensionist, Bruno Clement, and named after his son. Somehow, after having my own kids it had gained a greater meaning.

Even for this recent trip I hadn't considered an attempt. The route was simply too big in status, having gained a worldwide reputation for quality and become the gold symbol of hard climbing in the Verdon. It summed up all of the Verdon in a single pitch: exposure, quality, line, commitment and position. It wasn't like I didn't want to try it because I didn't want to fail, I just wanted to treat it with respect, I wanted to try when I was ready. But when Marmot pro photographer Tim Glasby expressed an interest in joining us and said that he'd 'always wanted to take pictures of the route', well then I began to wonder …

But we still left it till the last full day, putting it off with storms rolling in most afternoons, lightning battering the rim. Unprepared, having watched no films and with no real idea of the approach we finally peered over the immaculate line into the void below. Neil announced he wasn't keen, something had drained his psyche, perhaps the ridiculous 'packhorse' walk-in, laden with multiple ropes, static ab lines, various cameras and a complete set of kit to cope with just about any scenario thrown at us. Originally he'd been well up for this route and, over the week as my interest gathered momentum, he'd apparently maintained his desire. Now I wasn't so sure and thinking back I'd noticed an out of character passiveness for the last few days. No doubt he'd already realised an attempt could wait for a different time. To have your partner suddenly announce they are not interested would normally kill any kind of motivation, especially when it was supposed to be the pair of us in it together, but the way he worded his feelings was so considered that this didn't happen. Neil's that kind of guy, the solid kind of character you want as a friend and as a climber. He's a real climber, getting out there for all the right reasons; cutting edge but not pushing his name, just loving the sport and now, on the rim of the Verdon Gorge, without any hint of apathy, he was right behind me. This involved a 60-metre abseil, a long hanging belay and a massive rope climb afterwards. He was probably undecided before we'd even set off this morning, yet still came along, offering a day of his life and accepting a knackering hike and frustration as I attempted one of the best routes in the world and he didn't. He showed no negativity whatsoever, only a genuine desire for me to do well, a selfless offering of friendship and partnership. Moved by this, as well as by Tim's enthusiasm, I suddenly felt incredibly energised. I really was about to try this monster, the route that had shouted out to me from across the gorge for years, constantly in view from just about every position. I wasn't alone, this was a team effort. I'd be giving it my all for the three of us.

Abseiling in I placed the 'draws, mainly to keep myself in to the rock – a straight abseil would leave you miles from the middle-of-nowhere belay – and that gave me a chance to glance at the holds too. Not that perfect on-sight style, and a pretty poor grade 'flash'. More of an 'abseil inspection flash', or simply a no-falls first-go effort. Someone will do better, maybe dropping in faster, or with a blindfold, but style seemed somehow irrelevant on such a masterpiece of nature. I scanned briefly, impossible to commit to memory the thousands of holds. I kept my distance and didn't touch or feel, this feeling the right level of respect to pay to such beauty while at the same time forming the threads of a relationship I'd build on later.

Clipped into the belay I crafted a makeshift warm-up, hanging from the few holds in front of my face. There was no other way. Then, with Neil behind me, I was off, like leaving the blocks in a sprint race, the difficulty hitting immediately and forcing sudden focus. I almost blew it, getting really tired really quickly and snatching my way through holds that should have felt better. A rest on two decent edges came in the nick of time. There I could take stock and consider; with Neil clearly in view, I obviously had a very long way to go. Aware of the tourists watching me from across the gorge there were sudden screams, their pitch not compatible with watching some tiny red speck inching upwards, more like they'd just seen something really impressive like … a second later a massive clap of thunder told me what they'd seen for sure. Lightning. The thought of a storm unsettled me, but at the same time brought focus. I wouldn't be going down again. This was my shot, this was my window of opportunity, hanging open for perhaps the only moment in my life. Pumped within thirty seconds of the start, the forty-five-minute journey was a recovery epic; just enough holds along the way, but with the clock ticking in both energy and increasing blackness. It felt like climbing at its very best, all memory of coming holds long forgotten but with a knowledge that there would be enough. I just needed to keep it together. At each break

I'd scan all the options, processing the data to come up with the most efficient solution whilst carefully monitoring the energy reserves, calculating exactly the moment to commit. With each grasp of a hold the pathway would be recalculated and recalculated again to account for subtle differences in size and shape. Feet remained pinpoint, pushing the incredible 5.10 Blancos to the limit of their edging capacity. For forty-five minutes I was in the zone; forty-five minutes of just me and the route. Only in the last metres did I realise the end was within reach. Topping out was incredible. The grade was irrelevant, as was the style of my effort; to have simply climbed such a route with such beauty was humbling.

The experience brought together pretty much everything I look for in climbing, scoring a perfect 10 in every category – but it was obvious that the overwhelmingly positive emotions were hugely dependent on success. I'd like to think I'd have been just as happy with a rest point on the rope, but let's face it, I wouldn't. In fact, I'd probably have been gutted and pissed off for a very long time. In relative terms a quick pull on a quickdraw or few seconds' hang on the rope is a miniscule difference in the ascent of a piece of rock, but registers massively on a personal scale of satisfaction. Such is the sport of rock climbing and the rules we impose. This is the game we play.

Filling in earlier days from the trip every page could stand alone as a great climbing experience, and each day slotted together to make up the perfect trip. There'd been easy days and hard days, multi-pitch 8as and short burly 8bs. There'd been 6b wanderings and rest days by the lake and, on the last day, there had been *Tom et Je Ris*. And even after all of that I'd managed to sneak in a final route on our final morning with just a few hours before the flight. The pull of flawless walls had enticed me back above an incredible cloud inversion. I didn't need a final fix of something hard or a battle to the limit, but instead was drawn by strong memories of good times and an attitude pure and uncluttered by performance. I just wanted to climb, to move and to flow and this last route had left a deep impression that would stay with me for many months, way deeper than any large number could ever score.

We'd abseiled in to *Boulevard des Stars*, pulled our ropes and committed. We organised ourselves, coiled ropes, equalised anchors and shared sips of water and food as we inched higher, towards the final pitch. And what a pitch – fiercely technical, absolutely old skool, desperate from belay to top, UK 6b moves coming at me over and over, with enough time to piece them together, but only just.

A pair of pockets below the final bulge allow few moments to soak up the exposure and plan for the crux, the grey rock washed chalkless by the rain and giving nothing away. Launching in, I battle with the difficulty, scanning the featured wall for all my options, arms fading fast and calling on years of fitness training. Only the most efficient sequence will do, I can't just pull my way up this one. Three points are fixed, my two handholds and the next hold I'm eyeing for my right hand. Use of feet determines success, a good spike out right is a stretch, an edge positive but high, a rubbish smear in the right place but, well, rubbish. The slap with my hand brings a disappointing hold, foothold choice was correct, accounting for this possibility, and then more and more, move after move, until at last, fingers uncurling, a classic Verdon finger jug arrives, its incredible positivity so unlikely but more than welcome, a joy to feel the sharpness and security of the jagged edge. Settling in on easy ground I float up the final few metres, almost in tears, overwhelmed by the intensity of the experience, the purity of the flow of movement so euphoric.

Sat atop *Boulevard des Stars* in the sun, I belayed Neil out, the vast expanse of the gorge spreading out before me, the gentle breeze cooling my face. Huge condors drift effortlessly by, floating above cotton wool clouds wafting upwards from the cool depths below. Neil appears into view, picking his way across the holdless walls, the cord between us forming a bond much stronger than if divided by a lower-off. Sitting on the rim I was knackered, the tiredness in my arms and body in no way reflected in the grade of the route, 7b. Challenged physically and mentally, with the flush of success and soaking up the delights of a multi-pitch adventure, I revel in satisfaction. I've just taken the best from the Verdon, perhaps the best cliff in Europe.

And I'd taken the best from climbing. I thought back to the previous day and my flash of the world famous *Tom et Je Ris*. Was this 7b better? Different. The ascent of *Boulevard des Stars* stood out as climbing in its purest form, my perfect style. This is what I've been looking for all of my life and yet it's been there all along. It's a matter of seeing it; for a while I'd been blinkered. Back when I was seventeen we climbed all day, every day, feeding off the total immersion in the movement combined with all the other ingredients of climbing. I didn't need to climb hard stuff, didn't need to rest up to perform, I didn't need that kind of workout to get my fix. I didn't need the numbers; or maybe my ego didn't. I played in a world without pressure, without expectations, without disappointment. Sure I pushed at my ability, but failure lasted but a moment, washed aside by the beauty of the experience, a game beyond limits. Over the years I'd become sidetracked by performance and caught up and frustrated by styles I didn't suit. I'd lost sight of the breadth of climbing. Now as I came full circle I found myself back where I started, with a simple desire to climb, but I'd added to the package with the exploration of my limits, pushing as far as I could go and thriving on the pressure. At last I'd learned how to play that game, I'd made it through the Performance Tunnel. Now I choose when to go back in and when to stay outside and enjoy the view. The two sides of climbing sitting together, both equally as valid.

I closed the book, running out of space. There seemed a lot to say, more than I could fit on the pages of a green-lined scrap book. I found my thoughts drifting despite the chatter of nearby aeroplane travellers. It was easy to do these days, drift aside and lose myself in climbing. There was a lot of stuff going on to ponder over.

Climbing just keeps on evolving, gifting me with more and more. It moves in new directions, revealing more of myself and letting me discover new life along unforeseen routes. I'm stronger for this, more complete. I'm one of the lucky ones, there are few of us, those that by good fortune, accident or determined design find themselves balancing all the ingredients of life.

It struck me that my moment is now. I have my health and my kids and my partner: a family. My parents still hike 10 miles a day and are good friends who still enjoy wild parties and camping holidays in the mountains. I'm climbing at my best, still getting stronger, and with a drive and desire as strong as ever. Really, I've got it all.

Right now I'm richer than I've ever been, richer than I ever will be. I need to see it, to see what I've got, and to understand that I'll never really find the perfect balance. I'll always be looking for something, pushing at the balance, gently rocking it, testing the limits. There is no eternal perfect balance, that's the point, it shifts because that's our design as we follow a constantly changing path through life. The key is to look inwardly and seize the day, see it for all that it is.

Blink, and you'll miss it.

INDEX